Practicing the Piano
The Russian Tradition Revisited

Marguerite Abatelli

Practicing the Piano: The Russian Tradition Revisited
By Marguerite Abatelli
Copyright@ 2020 Marguerite Abatelli
All Rights Reserved

No part of this work covered by the copyright thereon may be reproduced or used in any form or by any means, graphic, electronic or mechanical, including photocopying, recording, taping, Web distribution or information storage retrieval systems, without the written permission of Marguerite Abatelli. For permission to use material from this text, submit your request to margueriteaabatelli@gmail.com.

ISBN-13:978-1981517909;
ISBN-10:1981517901

To my fellow musicians

Contents

Introduction	1
Preliminary Notes for Practicing	4
Posture	5
Uniform Sound	11
Finger Exercises	13
Wrist	19
Tone	26
Grammar	28
Nazaroff	31
Further Study	35
Acknowledgments	36
About the Author	37

Practicing the Piano: The Russian Tradition Revisited

Introduction

Every so often, a historical person appears in the artistic world. Such a figure was Kyriena Siloti (1895 - 1989). Having great talent and knowledge, she had the rare ability to impart this erudition to others. Kyriena Siloti began her piano studies with her mother, Vera Tretyakova Siloti (1866-1940), herself an accomplished pianist. She was the daughter of Pavel Tretyakov (1832-1898), who in 1892 donated his art collection to the city of Moscow. This Tretyakov Gallery contains some of the finest Russian art in the world today. Kyriena Siloti's father was Alexander Siloti, the famous pianist, conductor, teacher and composer (1863-1945). His piano teachers included Nikolai Zverev (1832-1893), Nikolai Rubenstein (1835-1881), his brother Anton Rubenstein (1829-1894) and Franz Liszt (1811-1886). Although it is beyond the scope of these pages to adequately detail the historical significance of this family, the reader is encouraged to read Dr. Charles Barber's book, *Lost in the Stars*, a beautiful work on the extraordinary life of Alexander Siloti.

Although Kyriena Siloti's country of birth was Belgium, her family, education and artistic lineage were Russian. She attended the Imperial Conservatory of St. Petersburg and continued piano studies with her father. After the Bolshevik Revolution, she left Russia, traveled to China and arrived in the United States in the late 1920s. Although an accomplished pianist, Kyriena Siloti devoted her life to teaching piano in New York and in Massachusetts. She taught the Russian tradition as she herself had been instructed. Piano was a way of life, to be exercised with great dedication. This was the

1

Practicing the Piano: The Russian Tradition Revisited

path that her students were to follow. Many facets of this Russian tradition are being discarded, and eventually could be lost. This was my main impetus to write this text. Work from my notebooks, manuscripts and reflections on my long conversations with my teacher highlight the difference between how music was studied and many of today's practices.

Most pianists approach a new work by simply playing the music and rehearsing the sections that prove to be troublesome. There is no method to "drill" the fingers for uniformity of sound or controlled lift of the fingers. In direct contradistinction, the Russian school drew a sharp line of demarcation between practicing and playing music. Students were instructed to separate these sessions at the piano. During practice, one was taught to watch the fingers for the correct lift and position on the keyboard, as well as to listen carefully for a uniformity of tone and volume. The ensuing result would be a beautiful sound full of color and a secure technical control. Approximately four measures at a time were to be practiced (8 to 10 times) before one proceeded to the next four measures. With these repetitions, one watched the lift of the fingers and listened for uniformity of sound. Any difficulty was corrected by more drill and/or creating an exercise highlighting that section. This new exercise could be practiced using both hands and throughout all the major and minor keys if needed. Everything was loud and everything was slow. We all have heard the familiar quote attributed to Saint-Saens many times: "Slow practice is not a virtue. It is a necessity."

Creating music was a different experience altogether. Unlike practicing, if the lift of the fingers or the hand position fell short of perfection, one paid little if any attention. The creation of music was the only focus of attention. Inhibition is always the antithesis of performance. Studying the music away from the keyboard was greatly encouraged, and it was understood that the inner vision was your guide for the performance.

If students were to practice a piano work for twenty minutes, the playing time of that music would be ten minutes. The ratio of practice time to playing music was 2/3 to 1/3. In this manner the playing was the residue of the excellence of the practice session. It was also a commonplace practice to wait at least one year before performing a piano piece. Although the great virtuosi could master a work in a very short time, this one-year minimum allowed for the music to enter and live in the subconscious mind and bear fruit.

Kyriena Siloti said many times, that if a person had real talent, he/she would arrive at the same place as one who practiced in this tradition; however, the end result would consume much more time. She also preferred the Russian school of playing to the other great traditions as it enables the pianist to have more "colors" to express the music.

This is not a book about artistic performance. It is a blueprint of the foundation of practicing in the Russian tradition which is painstaking and arduous with no shortcuts. This work is well worth the effort.

Practicing the Piano: The Russian Tradition Revisited

Preliminary Notes for Practicing

All of the following exercises must be practiced without bodily tension of any sort. The fingers and wrists must be trained to lift lightly and strike with energy and vitality while always playing to the "bottom" of the keys. This is essential for the successful execution of these techniques.

As with all practice, there should never be a sense of strain or pain at any time.

The practice sessions should be no longer than twenty minutes in length. After a great deal of experience, one may gradually increase the time to forty minutes, but no more.

Posture

Before a note sounds, your posture at the keyboard should be precise. Your body centers with the "middle C" and both feet are on the pedals (damper and *una corda*). All ten fingers rest on the keyboard and your body leans slightly forward. Your shoulders are down and the elbows relaxed and away from your body with the hand and forearm level. **Relaxation is a prerequisite.** The Russian hand position has flat knuckles (the metacarpophalangeal joints) with the weight of the hand leaning slightly towards the 5th (little) finger. (This is different from the Germanic school's high knuckle position with the hand weight leaning slightly toward the thumb.) The flat knuckle position may be compared to a "kitten's paw." The distal phalanges (the bone segments of the finger which contain the nail) of fingers 2, 3, 4 and 5 are straight. The distal phalanges of the 4th and 5th fingers lean slightly to the side away from the thumb.

"Kitten's paw"

It is advantageous to practice this flat knuckle position on a table and do knuckle "push–ups." The knuckles which move upward and downward are the MCP (metacarpophalangeal) joints where the finger bones meet the hand bones. The distal phalanges are straight as described previously and then they move "on their toes" and then downward to the starting position. Repeat this exercise slowly 8 to 10 times daily to master the hand position of the "kitten's paw."

The fingers lift in one piece from the MCP (metacarpophalangeal) joints. They have the same position on the keys as well as for the lift. It is important to lift lightly as high as your hand allows without strain. (You can lift each finger gently with your free hand to observe what lift can be achieved and then work to that end.) Lifting the fingers lightly has the sensation of watching with detachment. The release is quick with an energetic forward thrust. Kyriena Siloti compared this motion to a "spitting" action."

8

Lift of index finger

6

Ink mark denoting the **thumb's** approximate landing point on the key

The thumb, which has only two phalanges, lifts lightly, no higher than the bridge of the hand. Like the other fingers, its position is the same on the keys as in the lift.

Practicing the Piano: The Russian Tradition Revisited

Beginners can use a table to practice lifting each finger (hands separately) as well as the exercising of the knuckles moving upward and downward.

More advanced players can translate these two exercises to the piano. In this case, all ten fingers will rest on the keys except for the finger that is being exercised which should always strike the key with "tip consciousness" (see p.11) to the "bottom" of the key. The lifting and the lowering of the knuckles are practiced with all the fingers depressing the keys.

Uniform Sound

Uniformity of sound is a very important part of piano practice. Utilizing this technique affords the pianist tremendous technical control. Our ten fingers may be very different in size and strength, so to achieve this consistency of sound and volume, we must train our fingers. The fingers are the "soldiers," and the pianist is the "drill sergeant." The finger stroke is the same as described in **Posture**, pp.5-10 (the hand position of the kitten's paw," the lifting of each finger lightly from the MCP joints keeping the "shape" of the finger and the quick energetic release to strike the key). This will maintain the consistency of sound.

The "light" lifting of the fingers is one of the critical components to execute this practice correctly. Raising a finger should feel "weightless;" however, the release to strike the key is fast and full of energy.

"Tip consciousness" is a sense of energy or tingling in the tips of each finger. Students can pinch their fingertips to be aware of that energy. This imparts a quality that does change the sound of your playing.

Practicing the Piano: The Russian Tradition Revisited

Imagine each finger carrying a package of a certain weight. Before proceeding to play the next note, one "transfers" the weight from the initial finger to the next. This transfer of the weight of the "package" is mentally executed **between** the sounding of the notes. The volume from each finger should be the same at the successful conclusion of this practice. The hand position, the lift, the release, "tip consciousness," and the weight transfer from one finger to the next are regulated by the ear. With practice, the uniformity of sound is achieved with concentrated listening.

The ear is the conscience of the fingers.

Practicing the Piano: The Russian Tradition Revisited

Finger Exercises

The following exercise is used to achieve finger strength and independence. Each finger may be played more than the two repetitions written in the following illustration. The hand position, lift and striking action mentioned previously are to be used throughout these pages. (This may be adapted for the more advanced pianist by holding down the adjacent fingers while the exercise is being practiced. Fingers 1 and 3 are held down while the 2nd finger plays; fingers 2 and 4 are held down while the 3rd finger is playing and finally fingers 3 and 5 are held down for the 4th finger strokes.)

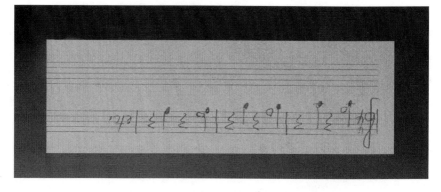

This exercise is used for all finger exercises if the uniformity or finger stroke needs some correction. For example, it is used during lessons for all digital work (scales, arpeggios, double notes, tremolos, etc.). This is also to be executed in "the air," as a gymnastic exercise.

13

In this case, only one finger is moving upward and downward while the other fingers remain in position. (It is easier to watch the fingers if it is executed at eye level.)

All scales (major, harmonic and melodic minor) are practiced in parallel and contrary motion. This includes chromatic scales and all 3rds, 6ths and 10ths. The parallel and contrary motion of scales can be rhythmically accented or played in uniform sound (without an accentuated beat). In practice, the fingers must **always** strike the key from their highest lift position. The practicing of the thumb must include the movement of the wrist to the side so that the thumb strikes the key from its highest position (no higher than the bridge of the hand). The wrist must then move to its original position **before** the striking of the next finger at its highest lift position. This insures that all the fingers lift and strike properly.

Scale practice includes playing one particular scale, beginning and ending on all the eight degrees. The C major scale is played from C to C; D to D; E to E; etc. The scale fingerings remain constant. For example, in the right hand, D to D starts and ends with the 2nd finger (left hand starts and ends with the 4th finger); E to E begins and ends with the 3rd finger (left hand starts and ends with the 3rd finger); F to F begins and ends with the thumb (left hand starts and ends with the 2nd finger); etc. Scale exercises are also used frequently during lessons. Portions of scales are played with different fingers. These are 123; 234; 345; 1234 and 2345. For the C Major scale, the right hand execution of the fingering 123 is cde; def; efg; etc., for the entire scale (with the left hand using 321 fingering).

Practicing the Piano: The Russian Tradition Revisited

The same notes are used for 234 (the left hand is 432) and the 345 fingering pattern (the left hand fingering is 543). The 1234 fingering is cdef; defg; efga; etc., for the entire scale (with the left hand using 4321 fingering). The 2345 scale fragment uses the same notes as the previous sentence (with the left hand using 5432).

The diminished 7th chords are practiced using all ten fingers to depress the chord tones. One should have a straight line between the distal phalanges of the 1st and 5th fingers (thumb and little finger). While the fingers remain on their depressed chord tones, each finger in turn lifts and plays its note 8 to 10 times. This is a great help for achieving independence and strength of each finger.

Arpeggios are very important as they stretch the hand and include all major, minor, diminished as well the dominant 7th of the next key (usually proceeding chromatically). Parallel motion and contrary motion are practiced. The passage of the thumb is controlled by the sideways movement of the wrist for the most optimal practice. For example, in the right hand's playing of a C Major arpeggio, in the ascent from the 3rd finger on 'G' to the thumb's placement on 'C,' the wrist should move sideways to give the thumb its full stoke from its highest position. The 3rd finger lifts completely **before** the wrist moves back to its original position, enabling the index finger to be placed above 'E' in its full lift position continuing the arpeggio's ascent.

15

Carl Tausig (1841-1871) was one of Liszt's most brilliant students. The Tausig exercises for the 3rd, 4th and 5th fingers and arpeggios (ascending and descending) are practiced daily. These exercises in Book 1, #s 22 and 17, may be found online (IMSLP/Petrucci). Double notes are to be practiced daily. The Tausig exercises in Book 2, #s 90 and 91 are important (IMSLP/Petrucci). Some students find using a slight "grasping" motion of the fingertips helpful. The *Daily Studies* of Carl Tausig may be purchased (see Further Study). This performer's reprint has the exercises that were given to me from Kyriena Siloti including #22 (Book 1). In this same volume, #17 for arpeggios is very important for increasing the stretch and independence of the fingers. Tremolo practice uses a "quiet" hand with two strokes per note. (See the manuscript example which holds down the previously played note on p.13.) C. L. Hanon, *The Virtuoso Pianist*, probably the most widely-used book on piano technique, is a wonderful source for fingerings (scales and arpeggios using parallel motion) and is used very often during lessons. Exercise #49 is to be executed with two strokes per note following the directions of the illustration on p.13. Also, the entire C. L. Hanon, *The Virtuoso Pianist* is played in all major and harmonic minor keys.

The following contrary motion was given to me during lessons. Using the "Cs" on the piano, the lowest sounding "C" is named C1 and the highest sounding "C" is C8.

Practicing the Piano: The Russian Tradition Revisited

With the C Major scale as an example, both hands (L.H. on C2 and R.H. on C3) play two octaves in parallel motion and then separate in contrary motion for two octaves. The hands play (two octaves) in contrary motion towards each other and then proceed (L.H. on C4 and R.H. on C5) in ascending parallel motion (two octaves). The hands descend in parallel motion for two octaves, separate in contrary motion (two octaves), and then come together again in contrary motion. At this point (L.H. on C4 and R.H. on C5), the hands descend in parallel motion to the final notes (L.H. on C2 and R.H. on C3). Major and minor arpeggios in contrary motion follow the same schema as the scales (in contrary motion). The diminished 7th and dominant 7th arpeggios in contrary motion follow the same procedure; however, they begin with four octaves parallel motion ascending and then descending. Without any interruption, these arpeggios **then** follow the same procedure as the scales in contrary motion. During scale and arpeggio practice, it is not uncommon to have your right elbow "pulled" to the right with the forearm, wrist and hand following while ascending the keyboard. Likewise, the left elbow is "pulled" in a similar fashion during the scale's descent.

Of course, the only execution possible is a slow one. We were always told that a practice session "was not music." Listening to a practice session, the non-musician frequently complains that everything is so slow and it is so loud. **Exactly!**

17

Practicing the Piano: The Russian Tradition Revisited

Beginners start with scales, one octave with hands separate and progress to hands together using two octaves. The scales used are C, G, D, A, E, F Major.

Intermediate players begin with the first book of Hanon, *The Virtuoso Pianist*, in the key of C Major and progress to transpose these 20 exercises in different Major keys (G, D, A and F Major). The easier Carl Czerny exercises (Opus 599) can be introduced with scales progressing to 3 and 4 octaves parallel motion including all major and harmonic minor scales. Arpeggios are to be played separately with the hands together only when the finger lift and stroke are well executed. Muzio Clementi's *Gradus ad Parnassum* can be introduced, gradually.

Advanced students use the more advanced Czerny exercises (including opuses 299 and 337), *Liszt Technical Exercises*, the Carl Tausig exercises and Muzio Clementi's *Gradus ad Parnassum* (Books 1 and 2). All scales (major, harmonic minor, melodic minor) and arpeggios (major, minor, diminished 7th and dominant 7th of the next key) should be practiced in parallel as well as contrary motion. All arpeggios are to be played in root position as well as all its inversions. All combinations should be practiced (left hand plays the arpeggio in root position while the right hand plays its first inversion; left hand plays the first inversion while the right hand plays the second inversion; etc.). Tausig's *Daily Studies* Book 2 has important double note exercises (#s 23-26). Trills, double notes, tremolos, stretch exercises, etc., can be found readily in the aforementioned texts.

18

Practicing the Piano: The Russian Tradition Revisited

Wrist

Wrist technique is a very important part of every practice session. There are four components to this basic exercise.

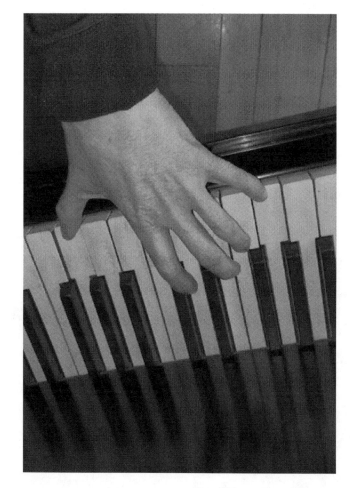

Step 1: The distal phalanges (1 and 5) are in a straight line.

Step 2: Using the hand and finger positions as described in earlier chapters (flat knuckles and fingers "in shape"), the wrist is sloped upwards maintaining the straight distal phalanges of the fingers. The point of contact with the keys is slightly closer to the fingernails as a result of the raised wrist position.

Step 3: The hand is now raised keeping the wrist's exact position in the air and the fingers stay "in shape." The wrist acts as a hinge to raise (and lower) the hand.

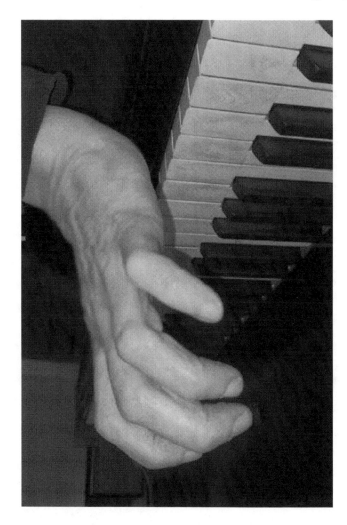

Practicing the Piano: The Russian Tradition Revisited

Practicing the Piano: The Russian Tradition Revisited

Step 4

The imaginary string "breaks" and the hand falls in one piece sounding the octave. It is important that the wrist maintains its position in the air and is not lowered.

As the hand lifts lightly, it is as though an invisible string around the proximal (bone segment of the finger which is closest to the hand) phalanx of the 3rd finger pulls the entire hand upward in one piece. It is important to watch the fingers so they do not "fall" and lose shape.

Practicing the Piano: The Russian Tradition Revisited

Octaves are practiced with fingers 1 and 5, 1 and 4 and 1 and 3. The distal phalanges of these fingers sounding the octaves should be in a straight line as shown in Step 1.

At first, the fingers may strike notes that were not intended to sound. This is only temporary. Using fingers 2 and 4 with the C Major scale in thirds is a good way to begin. This progresses to fingers 1 and 3 and then 3 and 5. Hands should begin separately to make sure the fingers do not "drop" and the wrist maintains its raised position in the air. The same scale in 6ths is practiced beginning with fingers 1 and 5 and then progresses to 1 and 4 and 2 and 5.

Octaves are practiced with a special exercise attributed to another Liszt student, Bernard Stavenhagen (1862–1914). Octave exercises are played with fingers 1 and 5; 1 and 4 and 1 and 3. The fingers playing the octaves have the distal phalanges in a straight line on the piano as discussed previously.

The octave using fingers 1 and 5 is played, and these two keys remain depressed while the hand moves inward towards the piano lid (the inside of the piano) as far as possible. At this point, the fingers within the octave 2, 3, and 4, depress keys so that now all 5 fingers are holding down keys. The hand now moves to the edge of the piano keys while holding down all 5 fingers. The wrist moves downward and upward lightly three times (this should feel "weightless") and then remains in its raised position. Lifting the 2nd, 3rd and 4th fingers, the wrist exercise previously described is executed: the hand is raised

23

(perpendicular to the wrist) and falls to the keys playing the octave with fingers 1 and 5. The octaves to be practiced are A, G and D, and each octave is repeated 8 to 10 times for this Stavenhagen study.

This exercise is also practiced with fingers 1 and 4, keeping fingers 2 and 3 depressed while moving outward from the inner part of the keys. The 5th finger is lifted throughout this exercise. Using fingers 1 and 3 to play the octave, the 2nd finger is depressed as the hand moves outward toward the edge of the keys and fingers 4 and 5 are lifted throughout this particular octave study. As stated before, it is important that the wrist as well as the non-playing fingers maintain their position in the air and are not lowered.

While practicing scales and arpeggios using octaves, it is important to lift upward in a straight direction **before** moving into position to play the next octave. It is customary to use two or more strokes per octave, especially for difficult skips. Two wrist exercises written by Tausig are to be practiced every day. These exercises may be found in the text, *Daily Studies* #33 (chord triads) and #s 41-46 (for skips), and both are to be practiced slowly. The Tausig exercises for skips, #s 78–83, can also be found in the Petrucci Edition, Book 2 and all the 16th notes are practiced with the wrist. Kyriena Siloti told me that her father practiced octaves using the J. S. Bach's *2-Part Inventions*.

Beginners start wrist exercises on a table using fingers 2 and 4 and gradually move to using fingers 1 and 3 and 3 and 5. This is to be done hands separately.

Intermediate students play the above exercise in thirds on the piano. The octaves are practiced on a table, and then moved to the piano when the student is ready. Hands are not played together until proficiency is accomplished playing each hand separately.

Advanced students learn the Stavenhagen octave exercise and the Tausig triads and skips #33 and #s 41-46 (*Daily Studies*, Book 2, Performer's Reprints). C. L. Hanon, *The Virtuoso Pianist* and the *Liszt Technical Exercises* method books also have excellent materials

Tone

The singing tone, which characterizes the Russian school so well, is produced by rolling the fingertip downward on the keys with the help of the wrist. The hand and fingers are shaped as discussed earlier (**Posture**, p.5); however, the wrist raises and the key is depressed as the wrist is lowered. In this way, the fleshier part of the fingertip sounds the note. As the wrist is raised to enable the finger(s) to play the next key(s), it moves in a slightly circular motion. Touch the key first and then press using "tip consciousness".

Another "color" is created by using the elbow, forearm, wrist and hand as one piece (lifting and lowering) as the fingertip depresses the key. *Portamento* (**Grammar**, p.28) may be exercised with this stroke as well. In this case, the notes are detached with close attention given again to the "tip consciousness" of each finger.

The digital finger stroke described in **Posture** (pp.5-10), the "singing" tone and practicing the arm as "one piece" are preparation for music playing.

Addenda:

Glissandi are to be practiced with a relaxed arm, wrist and hand. For the right hand, one uses the third fingernail (ascending) and the thumbnail (descending). The left hand uses the thumbnail for an ascent and the nail of the third finger for a descending passage.

Practicing the Piano: The Russian Tradition Revisited

With the required relaxation and the almost complete supination of the wrist (right and left hand's use of the third finger), it is possible that no sound at all will be heard for a short time. If this exercise is practiced diligently, the beauty of the tone that ensues will repay all the effort.

The wrist technique (**Wrist**, pp. 19-25), is to be used for all practice involving chords, octaves and skips.

Intermediate students begin by "rolling" the tips of the fingers on a table. This can then be transferred to the piano in simple 5-finger exercises (hands separately). When a level of proficiency is achieved, hands are played together using scales, arpeggios and single-voiced melodies. Chopin's *Preludes* in E and B minor are used specifically to practice this "rolling" technique. Scales, arpeggios and simple 5-finger exercises may also be used to practice using the arm as "one piece" (*legato* and *portamento*).

Advanced students may use any exercise employing the techniques described above. Repertoire is practiced with these "colors" to prepare the fingers for the actual music playing.

27

Grammar

Students are always encouraged to use an *urtext* edition of the piano repertoire. The markings of the composer, or the grammar, are to be followed to the best of his/her ability. This includes the dynamics, phrase markings, tempi, etc. These elements of music help create the unique style of each composer which is critical to the music's interpretation.

If a phrase line is extended over a bar line and ends on the first beat of a measure, there is not the natural accent on this beat. That first beat can be the same volume or less in relation to the preceding note, not more unless specifically notated by the composer. If a phrase line encompasses many measures in length, the drop of the wrist, which signals the first note, may not be "dropped" again until the next phrase line begins. There was an occasion of a student whose practicing included too many "drops" of the wrist where the composer had written very long phrases. Kyriena Siloti instructed this pianist to practice these phrases correctly, with the initial drop of the wrist only at the beginning of the phrase line, 240 times a day for two weeks. Anticipating a public performance, this was the formula that was used to ingrain corrections into the subconscious for a proper execution, thus respecting the wishes of the composer.

The staccato markings need to be consistent within the piece of music. The *staccatissimo* is the shortest sound (approximately 1/4 of the value of the note), the *staccato* (approximately 1/2 of the note's value) and finally the *portamento* (approximately 3/4 of the value of the note).

These lengths are only a point of reference to distinguish the values of the notes within the music score. It may seem very pedantic to be so detail oriented; however, all of these small details add up to a very fine result. They make a very big difference.

Dynamic markings must be understood in context. One may play at a *forte*; however, it is only *forte* in relationship to what was played beforehand and afterwards. The *sforzando* is not necessarily played loudly. It is meant to startle. Its dynamic level depends on your interpretation of the clues that are given by the composer. An accent, a *tenuto*, a *martellato* and a *marcato* all need to be distinguished from one another in a given piece of music.

Repeats in a composition were generally not observed unless one had something different to "say." As the notes, rhythm, dynamics, tempo, phrasing, etc., usually are not altered by the composer, it is your inner interpretation that changes. For example, the first time a phrase is played, it could be a straightforward presentation of the musical idea. The repeat could be more emotionally emphatic or more introspective depending on your interpretation and concept of the work as a whole.

Lessons also included discussions of the art, literature, music and history of the time in which the composer lived. This knowledge holds great value for the interpretation as well as discerning stylistic *moves* of the music.

Students should remember that they are only "the intermediary" standing between the genius and the listener. We are always advised to follow the path illuminated by the composer. Adhering to the wishes in the music score, we tread in those footsteps, albeit imperfectly.

In today's world of the internet, videos of performances are numerous. Many "musicians" are learning their craft from someone else's web concert.

In the years preceding the 21st Century, one heard music from a recording or a concert, fell in love with the music and purchased the score. Once the process of studying the music commenced, there was no listening to any performances of that work until a completion of that task was achieved. The journey of learning the music was a solitary one. There was a great personal effort expended to interpret the wishes of the composer. This artistic individuality constitutes one of the most prized attributes of a musician. We must present a vision, a new perception, otherwise we have nothing special to offer.

My teacher used to say that if five artists played the same music and followed faithfully the wishes of the composer, all five performances would be different.

We cannot borrow someone's soul; we must find our own.

Intermediate/Advanced students learn at least seven of Chopin's *Mazurkas* because of the grammatical details in the music.

Nazaroff

Pavel Nazaroff (1890?-1942) was a Russian archeologist, geologist and writer. He met Kyriena Siloti after the Bolshevik Revolution and gave her a series of gymnastic exercises that he had invented. Although Pavel Nazaroff was not a pianist, he had studied the physiology of the hands. These twelve exercises were to be practiced daily with 8–10 repetitions per example. At first, the hands should be practiced separately and then gradually exercised together. All motions should feel "weightless" with a sense of detachment.

This first example is an addendum as it was an additional exercise to be used only if needed for the thumbs. Fingers 2, 3, 4 and 5 are straight and held together and the thumb is held at a 90 degree angle to the hand. The thumb rotates in a large circle counterclockwise. The two phalanges of the thumb are straight (like a pencil) while executing these rotations and then repeat going in a clockwise direction.

1. While looking at your palm with all fingers straight, move each finger away from the others towards you in a straight line. The finger then moves back to its original position. This is practiced for fingers 2, 3, 4 and 5. The thumb moves slightly downward in an arch-like motion arriving and touching the base of the 5th finger bending its distal phalanx slightly. The thumb now straightens the distal phalanx and returns to its starting position.

This exercise is now repeated with fingers 2, 3, 4 and 5 each separately moving forward in its straight line and at its forward limitation bends at the proximal interphalangeal joint (knuckle between the proximal and middle phalanges). The finger in motion straightens that joint before returning to its original position.

2. Fingers 2, 3, 4 and 5 are bent so that the tips of these fingers are touching the palm of the hand. The thumb bends backward away from the palm and then moves forward quickly, bending its distal phalanx to strike the 2nd finger at the proximal interphalangeal (PIP) joint.

3. Fingers 2, 3, 4 and 5 are bent and curled so that now the fingernails are touching the palm of the hand. The thumb moves backwards away from the palm and then strikes the PIP joint of the 2nd finger with its distal phalanx as in the previous exercise (#2).

4. Fingers 2, 3, 4 and 5 are straight and then bend so that the tips of these four fingers are touching the palm and then return to their original straight position. The first or proximal phalanges (bone segments of the fingers closest to the hand), are straight throughout this exercise. The next part of this exercise is to curl the fingers from their original straight position so that the nails of these fingers are now touching the palm of the hand and then the fingers "unfurl" and return to their starting straight position.

Practicing the Piano: The Russian Tradition Revisited

5. "Zeros." This is to be practiced with fingers 1 and 2, 1 and 3, 1 and 4 and 1 and 5. The thumb separates from each finger in turn and the fingertips meet with a vigorous stroke. The fingers involved in this exercise are bent in the same shape when separating from each other as when striking.

6. "The Fan." There are four parts to this exercise. The first part has fingers 2, 3, 4 and 5 in a straight line. The 2nd finger bends towards the palm of the hand followed by the 3rd finger, the 4th finger and finally the 5th finger. All fingertips are now touching the palm of the hand. Each finger follows the other and gives the appearance of a fan. The second part of "the fan" uses the 5th finger moving upward to its original position followed by the 4th, 3rd and 2nd fingers. The third part of this exercise begins the "fan" motion with the 5th finger followed by the 4th, 3rd and 2nd fingers until all four fingertips are touching the palm of the hand. The final position begins with the straightening of the 2nd finger followed by the 3rd, 4th and 5th fingers.

7. "Pinch of Salt." The fingertips of fingers 1, 2, and 3 are joined together as if to pick up a pinch of salt. With the palms of the hands facing the floor, the hand moves upward and downward with the wrist acting as a hinge. The wrist does not move, only the hand.

8. Circular "Pinch of Salt." With the palm facing downward, the tips of fingers 1, 2 and 3 are touching as the hand moves in a circle counterclockwise and then clockwise. The wrist should not move.

33

9. The palm of the hand is on an invisible table with all five fingers together. The hand is flat and moves from side to side.

10. The hand makes a fist and then proceeds to circle in a counterclockwise direction and then circles in a clockwise motion. The top of the hand should face upwards and not "tilt" to the sides during the rotations.

11. Both arms are stretched out at shoulder level. The backs of the hands touch at this height. Fingers 1, 2 and 3 join fingertips and then separate the hands, approximately 8 to 10 inches from each other. The height of the arms, wrist and hands is not lowered while the hands execute the "pinch of salt" exercise (#7), only performing the motions sideways.

12. "Ballerina." In a standing position, raise both arms and touch fingers together in a circular pose above your head (ballet arm position #5 at the *barre*). Separate your fingers approximately 8 to 10 inches and mentally "feel" your ten fingers and drop them keeping your hands in their original positions in the air. Only the fingers move. Then drop your hands without moving the wrist. The wrist and forearms drop next with the elbows in their original positions. Finally, the elbows and the upper arms drop in a "rag doll" fashion finishing with your arms at your sides.

Further Study

Barber, Charles. *Lost in the Stars*. The Scarecrow Press, Lanham, MD, 2002.

Clementi, Muzio. *Gradus ad Parnassum* Books 1 and 2. G. Schirmer, New York, 1986.

Czerny, Carl. *Practical Method for Beginners on the Pianoforte*, Op 599. G. Schirmer, New York, 1986.

Hanon, C. L. *The Virtuoso Pianist*, Vol. 925. G. Schirmer, New York, 1928.

Lhevinne, Josef. *Basic Principles in Pianoforte Playing*. Dover Publications, New York, 1972.

Liszt, Franz. *Technical Exercises for the Piano*, Editor, Julio Esteban. Alfred Music, Van Nuys, 1971

Tausig, Carl. *Daily Studies* Schirmer Edition. Performer's Reprints, New York, 1880. IMSLP-240080.

Tausig, Carl. *Daily Studies*. IMSLP/Petrucci Music Library, Public Domain.

Acknowledgments

As with any publication, there are numerous people to thank. A debt of gratitude is owed to Mary Pat Gannon, who edited this text with such care. Thank you to Christopher J. Miller and Edward P. Walsh for their photographic talents. Again, I would like to express my gratitude to Christopher J. Miller for his assistance with computer technicalities involving this text. Deep appreciation is owed to Dr. Melvin J. Breite, MD, who helped me with the anatomical terms for the fingers and hand. Thank you to Anthony Gilroy who kindly granted me permission to use images of a "Steinway and Sons" piano (Model A) for this text. I would also like to express my appreciation to Thomas G. Southard for his professional expertise and to the late Carmen Mannion Southard, whose pianistic talent inspired me to play the piano. My heartfelt thanks are given to Fabiola Leon for sharing her memories of studying with Kyriena Siloti. Finally, I would like to thank my family and friends for their support and encouragement.

Practicing the Piano: The Russian Tradition Revisited

About the Author

For over three decades, Marguerite Abatelli was actively involved with teaching music in the school system. This included the elementary through university levels. Her performances include solo, operatic accompaniment and chamber music recitals. Ms. Abatelli studied piano with Constance Keene, Wanda Maximilien and Kyriena Siloti. She graduated from Manhattan School of Music with a BM in piano. Her graduate work was completed at the Aaron Copland School of Music, Queens College, with a MS in music.

Made in the USA
Las Vegas, NV
04 May 2024

BOOK 1 - SUCCESS

WHY YOU FAIL WHERE OTHERS SUCCEED - 5 LIFE-CHANGING PERSONAL DEVELOPMENT TIPS YOU WISH YOU KNEW

INTRODUCTION

I would like to thank you for downloading this e-book. I hope it will become a valuable tool for your personal growth.

In this e-book, rather than giving you simple tips to improve your life I will provide you with several key concepts that I believe you absolutely need to understand and master in order to fully reach your potential and attain the level of fulfillment you truly deserve in life. These principles are the foundation on which you should base your personal development work. They will require that you work on yourself before you master them but I assure you that the investment of time and effort is well worth it. As Jim Rohn said "Learn to work harder on yourself than you do on your job. If you work hard on your job you will make a living, if you work hard on yourself you can make a fortune." The time to work hard on yourself is NOW!

Master Your Life With The Mastery Series

If you're interested in further improving your life, you can check the **"Mastery Series"** at the URL below:

mybook.to/mastery_series

YOUR FREE ACTION GUIDE

To help you take action on what you'll learn in this *"Success Principle Series"* I've create free action guides. Make sure you grab them at the URL below:

https://whatispersonaldevelopment.org/success-series

1
YOUR CURRENT «REALITY» IS NEVER REALITY AND CAN ALWAYS BE CHANGE

> *A human being always acts and feels and performs in accordance with that he imagines to be true about himself and his environment.*
>
> — MAXWELL MALTZ, PSYCHO-CYBERNETICS

Our vision of life is nothing more than a constructed reality. We weren't born with limitations on what we can or cannot do. Those limitations were artificially created afterwards. What your current mindset and way of thinking identifies as impossible could very well sound perfectly achievable for someone else with more empowering thoughts.

Have you ever noticed how babies have almost an unlimited potential to grow and learn? It is simply because they intuitively trust their brain which allows them to make full use of their potential. They don't place artificial limitations of what they can and can't do. The human brain is an extraordinarily powerful machine but, unfortunately, most people don't know how to use it properly. The reason why our subconscious mind is so powerful is because it is a mechanical goal-seeking device. It works through trial and error and will make all the adjustments needed over time until it reaches the goal it was programmed to achieve. The truth is that our mind needs failure! No great inventions would have come into existence without failure. Remember Thomas Edison's "failures." He didn't define them as failures but rather he said "I have not failed. I've just found 10,000 ways that won't work."

One reason why many people fail to use the full power of their mind is simply because they forget to apply this trial and error process in order to move forward with their life. In other words, they are afraid to fail and because of that they never make the mistakes that our brain desperately needs in order to achieve our goals. Another critical reason is that they have limiting beliefs - artificial limitations existing only in their mind and created through their interpretation of past events. Phobias and fear of abandonment are both strong examples of limiting beliefs.

We all have different perceptions of the world that resulted from our past experiences and the way we chose to react consciously or unconsciously to those past events. For that reason, what I think is possible might be different from what you think is possible. Have you ever heard someone tell you to be realistic? Or have you ever told someone to be realistic? If you analyze this expression closely you realize that it is entirely subjective. What people are telling you is simply "What you are trying to accomplish is not aligned with 'my reality' based on what I conceive as possible through the belief system I'm currently operating upon." However their reality is not your reality!

Our reality is in fact based on our personal interpretation of the world and what we choose to focus on constantly. Our current reality is not the result of our past experience. It is the result of our personal interpretation of past experiences in addition to specific parts of reality that we choose to focus our attention on.

Your reality is not the true reality because:

- You are operating under a belief system that is the result of

your personal interpretation of past events. Your beliefs determine your actions and prevent you from realizing your potential.
- You can only grasp a tiny part of reality and it's the part you choose to focus your attention on.

Now let's see how you can create a more empowering reality by:

- Becoming more optimistic
- Identifying your limiting beliefs and deconstructing them

How to become more optimistic

Do you know what the difference between pessimistic and optimistic people is? It's simply their focus. In your daily life, you can always identify an infinite number of negative things, but you can also identify an unlimited number of positive things. Being pessimistic or being optimistic is a choice. Every day we are creating our reality by choosing what to focus on.

In reality, pessimism is of very little use. How does it help you improve your life? It is absolutely critical that you work on being more optimistic and have a positive outlook on life. Negative thoughts are harming your mental health and limiting your potential. They don't help you get the life you deserve. Now, being optimistic doesn't mean denying reality! It just means making a conscious choice to focus on the positive side of life and, while acknowledging the reality of unpleasant facts, choosing not to spend time or energy focusing on them. It is a perfectly rational behavior! Actually, any time spent worrying is irrational. It is important for you to understand this and do what you can to worry less.

Actually, we have a strong bias towards negativity. We are more sensitive to unpleasant events than we are to pleasant events. In the past, it was critical for our survival that our brain notice every possible kind of danger that could threaten our life. That's why we are so sensitive to negative events. However nowadays it's useless

99.9% of the time. Why should you worry about a future that doesn't exist? Why should you worry about a past that is no more? Why complain about what is happening to you right now. Reality is. That's it!

Studies show that the ratio between the amount of positive and negative interactions between a married couple can predict their likeliness of divorce. To ensure a healthy relationship, this ratio must be at least 5:1. The bottom line is that we already have a strong negative bias. Thus, it is important that we make an effort to focus on positive things in our life to offset that bias and maintain our inner peace.

What about you? Do you see the glass as half full or half empty? Why not retrain yourself to become more optimistic? That is exactly what I did.

Here is what you can do to become more optimistic:

1. Stop watching TV

Jim Rohn once wisely observed that "Poor people have a big TV. Rich people have a big library." TV can certainly be entertaining but it won't help you grow. The real wealth of knowledge is accessible in books and in your real life - not on TV! Be aware of this, it's important. Why not challenge yourself to stop watching TV for a week or a month and see how you like it?

Still not convinced? Here are some good reasons to stop watching TV:

a. It manipulates your emotions

Kelly McGonigal in her book "The Willpower Instinct" wrote: "Studies show that being reminded of our mortality makes us more susceptible to all sorts of temptations, as we look for hope and security in the things that promise reward and relief." Another study demonstrated that we react more positively to advertisements for status products like luxury cars and watches when exposed to reports of death on the news. We unconsciously try to find comfort and safety by buying things. Were you aware of how advertisers manipulate your emotions?

b. It steals your time

It is easier to watch TV than to do many other activities but does watching TV leave you with a sense of fulfillment at the end of the day? Could you use your time for something else that is more important or productive?

c. It dictates to you what to think

TV and other forms of media subtly form opinions for you - what color of clothes you should wear this spring, how to behave, how much income to earn and even your definition of success and happiness. It is an impediment to personal growth. It robs you of your ability to think clearly and independently.

d. It distorts reality

For obvious reasons, there are more negative than positive things on TV. We generally don't talk about positive things because they don't scare well which means they don't sell well. The vast majority of folks are getting just fine? BORING! Let's create fear by talking about the latest terrorist threat, robbery or tragedy. TV gives you the illusion that the world is headed for disaster. I have a friend who is constantly complaining about politics and economics, he's always going off about how the experts on TV are all idiots. Recently he was warning me that the ebola virus was going to kill all of us. He is, perhaps as you may have guessed, also struggling in his personal and professional life – he's unhappy. I advise him to stop focusing on things he has no control over and focus on changing himself instead, by working on his attitude, his mindset and his skills. The truth is that you are not responsible for changing the world, you are only responsible for changing yourself. The more you work on yourself, the more you will be able to influence the world.

e. It prevents you from enjoying quality time with your family or friends

Are you watching TV during lunch or dinner at home? Watching TV with your family can be enjoyable but it can also rob you of more meaningful conversations with people you care about. When I came to Japan, I was surprised to see that many restaurants had TVs. You see customers watching TV rather than talking to each other.

2. Spend less time reading/watching the news

The news is way too negative and gives you a distorted view of reality. One tip: check the news weekly instead of daily in order to reduce your daily intake of negativity or read inspirational material/watch inspirational videos after reading/watching the news.

3. Spend less time with negative relatives or remove yourself from them

Do you have negative people around that criticize everything you do? Negative people can consume a lot of your energy and make it hard for you to maintain a positive outlook on life. According to Jim Rohn "You are the average of the five people you spend the most time with." You'd better choose them wisely!

4. Start your day by reading inspirational material or watching inspirational videos

Chicken Soup For The Soul by Jack Canfield is a good start. It is a collection of very short uplifting stories divided into several categories such as "on love," "learning to love yourself" or "live your dream." Many inspirational videos can be found on YouTube – check them out! Inspirational videos aren't everything, but if you listen to them daily they will help you stay motivated. Remember Zig Ziglar's words: "People often say that motivation doesn't last. Well, neither does bathing – that's why we recommend it daily."

5. Use positive affirmations/visualization daily

Affirmations are words you repeat to yourself every day until they reach your subconscious mind. As you start to believe in those words, the way you feel and behave will change. Here is what you should consider when using positive affirmations:

- Use the present tense and not the future tense ("I am" not "I will")
- Avoid negative forms: don't say « I'm not shy » but "I'm confident"
- Repeat the sentence for 5 minutes (use a timer for convenience)
- Do it every single day without exception for at least a month, and preferably 2 months.

Note that when there is too much discrepancy between the positive affirmation you're saying to yourself and what you really believe about yourself, at the subconscious level, the affirmation might not work or it will take several months more before it works.

Here is how you can use positive affirmations efficiently:

1. Support your affirmations with real life experiences.

For instance, just saying to yourself « I'm confident » won't work if deep down you don't believe it. However, if you ask yourself Am I really not confident all the time and in every area of my life without exception? - you will come up with things you feel confident doing. You will start realizing that your belief « I'm not confident » is not entirely true. Questioning yourself is a powerful tool because you are no longer fighting against your subconscious mind by affirming things that it doesn't believe; you simply question your subconscious mind to see whether it misinterpreted reality. You start working hand in hand with your subconscious rather than fighting it. (See below "Deconstruct your limiting beliefs" for more information). Include things you are already confident about, regardless of how small they

may be, and say to yourself I'm confident because of ____ and ____.
You will find that it works better than simple affirmations.

2. While saying positive affirmations, visualize yourself embodying what you want to be.

Your mind cannot tell the difference between something you simply imagined and an actual experience. If you want to be more confident visualize yourself being confident in the desired situation. You can imagine yourself being confident at a party or during a presentation for instance. By doing this you create new experiences. Because those experiences are interpreted as real, your subconscious mind won't stand in your way anymore. Build a reservoir of empowering "experiences" to bolster your confidence.

3. Add movements and emotions

Your words, your body and your thoughts are interconnected and influence each other. Using all three together is more powerful than simply using words.

4. Learn to reframe any situation by focusing on the positive

You can always find the positive in any situation and you should train yourself to do so. The more you practice this the more it will come naturally. Why waste your energy trying to deny reality wishing things were different? Yet this is exactly what most people do all the time and it's absurd!

Always accept reality. What is is so don't fight it! Why deny it? In fact, reality in and of itself is neutral. It is your interpretation of it that creates your problems. You are empowering your worst enemy, stop it! Eckhart Tolle wisely advised: "Whatever the present moment contains, accept it as if you had chosen it." Once you have accepted your situation focus on all the positive aspects you can think of. Ask yourself:

- What can I do about it?
- How can I reframe the situation?

- What can I learn from this situation? How can it help me become a better person?
- Will I remember this in 20 years?

When I went to Philippines in 2012, I was stuck on a small island unable to reach my final destination, Boracay, because of a flood. We were stuck in a hotel and didn't know when we would be able to finally reach Boracay. We planned to spend only 3 nights there and we had already missed one and it was looking like we may miss the remaining 2 nights. Let's try to apply the above framework:

What can I do about it?

Nothing. Just wait for now.

How can I reframe the situation?

It will make a great story to tell to my friends and it's the first time I've experienced a real flood. I can meet new people – that I otherwise wouldn't have been able to meet – here at the hotel and if we can reach Boracay tomorrow we will better enjoy our time there (knowing how precious the opportunity is).

What can I learn from this situation?

How can it help me become a better person? I can feel proud of myself for staying calm and not wasting energy by needlessly panicking or complaining about a situation I can do nothing about.

Will I remember it in 20 years?

Probably, but it won't be a bad memory at all!

Now we were able to reach the island the next morning and I actually enjoyed the short time I had there far more. Have you ever hiked a mountain? Have you noticed how good your simple meal tasted after a day of hiking? Nearly losing my trip and my positive reframing engineered gratitude that made the trip that much better. Start small by reframing mundane events that irritate you in your daily life. Soon you will become a master!

Remember that no situation has the power to make you miserable without your consent

It is not the situation that matters, it is how you choose to react to it. Tip: Instead of seeing problems start seeing "challenges" or "opportunities." I try to never use the word "problem" because I believe it is not an empowering term. Reframe problems as challenges and failures as learning opportunities and big failure as massive learning opportunities! Lastly, ask yourself "What can I learn from this situation that will help me to grow?"

Our reality can only exist through our thoughts and what we choose to focus on. Our problems in life are only as big as we desire them to be. A problem, no matter how big it is for you right now, was created through the thoughts you are having about it and it will continue to exist as long as you commit time to thinking about it. If you were to never think again about that particular problem again, it would disappear. Why? Because your reality is always created by your own mind. If you don't think about something, for your mind it simply ceases to exist. Conversely, focusing on a problem, reinforces the connection in your brain between the problem and the emotional attached to it.

Now, I understand that in reality it is difficult to completely stop thinking about a problem that bothers you. Especially, because we have a strong tendency to compare ourselves to others which is s-t-u-p-i-d. However, you can make your problems smaller by spending less and less time thinking about them. If it is something you cannot change, you should definitely stop thinking about it right now. If you were born with no arms and no legs, there is no point wishing you had arms and legs as said by the motivational speaker Nick Vujicic who were born with no arms and no legs. Your problems are only as big as you want them to be. That's it! Now do you want larger or smaller problems?

Some of us have great difficulty getting rid of our problems because they've slowly become part of our identity, sometimes this occurs without us being consciously aware of it. If you are stuck where you are, it might be because you are buying into your current struggles or problems without necessarily being aware of it. I remembered how I use to take pleasure in having the problems I had a few months ago. Maybe you are proud of struggling with money or having low self-esteem? Are you getting addicted to your struggles and playing the role of the victim, or are you taking full responsibility for your life? You might enjoy the role of a victim without even being aware of it. You may enjoy the temporary attention that your "problems" generate from friends or family but it's an illusion that is keeping you mired in mediocrity. Try to catch yourself playing the victim. We all play this role at times and of course some more than others. It is time to stop playing the victim and re-empower yourself. You are the victim only in your own mind.

Now, let's have a look at how your reality was actually created.

Your reality is defined by your belief system

Your belief system consist of all the beliefs that make up your subjective reality.

What is a belief? A belief is simply something that you accept as true, regardless of whether or not it actually is.

Where do your beliefs come from?

Your beliefs come from the way you interpreted past events and are the result of:

- What you have heard (from your parents, your friends, your teachers, the media…)
- What you have experienced

Positively: love from your parents, good results at school…

Negatively: trauma (abuse, humiliation, failure…)

There are two ways your beliefs were created:

1. Strong emotions
2. Repetition

1. Strong emotions

A shocking event in your childhood sends a strong signal to your subconscious mind that it should protect you from experiencing similar events in the future. That's how phobias or fear of failure is created in the mind.

2. Repetition

Repetition is the key to create new beliefs and it is also how most of your current beliefs were created and often it's done unconsciously. Have you heard of religious cults where gurus have total control over the members? After repeating the same message again and again our subconscious mind actually starts to accept the message as true. People who join such cults are usually vulnerable and in search of a better reality than their current one. As a result, they are more likely to accept new beliefs as the truth. Propaganda is based on the same principle. We are weaker than we often think and can be easily influenced, whether we admit it to ourselves or not.

The bottom line is that, when we were young we accepted some limiting beliefs as reality without being consciously aware of it. It is not uncommon that a limiting belief you have came from your parents who possibility inherited it from their parents who inherited from their parents. Not only are some of your beliefs not yours but they are generations old! How many people suffer from a scarcity complex derived from the generation that survived the Great Depression? Let me share with you one example given to me by my friend: "I used to use the same pot of coffee for days if not an entire week, to save what – 30 cents? One day a friend of mine pointed this out as strange. I had no idea it was odd, because my father does that as well so I asked him why and he said his father did the same thing. During the 1930's nothing was wasted in order to survive, yet even though my father and myself are both perfectly capable of affording an extra coffee pot we are behaving as if we are in the midst of another great depression!" Examine your own beliefs and behaviors and consider if they are still relevant to this age in history and to your own life.

Your subconscious mind is like big brother

Some limiting beliefs might prevent you from living the life you want. However, the first step is to understand that your subconscious mind means to do no harm to you. Your subconscious is always doing its best to protect you. Let's use phobia as an example. Phobias are the result of traumatic past experiences. Our subconscious mind associated a strong negative emotion to a particular situation. In order for that situation to never happen again, your subconscious mind creates a mechanism that keeps you away from similar situations that could endanger you.

So don't get angry at your subconscious mind but give the little guy some credit – he's trying to protect you! Collaborate with him and work at uncovering the root causes of your disempowering beliefs or phobias.

Your subconscious mind is in reality way more powerful than you can even begin to imagine. It regulates all of your bodily functions without you needing to be conscious of it. In addition to that, it acts in accordance with the beliefs you consciously or unconsciously accept as true. Ultimately, it controls most your life.

Why does it control your life? Because your belief system creates your thoughts, those thoughts create emotions and those emotions create behaviors. That's why profound changes are impossible without working with your subconscious mind.

Big brother is quite dumb

Your subconscious mind has no critical thinking skills and has no way to tell whether what you are telling him is in your interest or not. If you repeat something to your subconscious mind enough times, it will eventually believe it. That's why you have to be extremely careful about the way you talk to yourself. That's also why positive affirmations work. Be aware that your mind is constantly eavesdropping on your thoughts.

How to get rid of limiting beliefs

As mentioned previously, limiting beliefs are beliefs that you've accepted as true and don't help progress your life. They come from what your parents, your friends, your teachers or society has been telling you repeatedly. During your childhood, you accepted those beliefs as true either consciously or unconsciously. To overcome your limiting beliefs the first thing to do is to identify them.

Tips: Look at all the major areas of your life and ask yourself honestly how you have been doing. How is your financial situation? How are you relationships? What about your career? Your health? Take the areas where you are not completely satisfied and ask yourself why are you not getting the results you want? What is preventing you from achieving your goals in these areas? You are likely to have some limiting beliefs in these areas.

Identify your limiting beliefs

I would like to...but

If you are not satisfied with your current job for instance try the following:

I would like to change my job but...

What are all the reasons that popped into your mind?

I would like to have a better job but

- I'm not smart enough
- I don't deserve to have a better job
- I don't have the right qualifications

Or

I would like to find an amazing girlfriend but

- I don't have money
- That girl is too good/smart/beautiful for me
- Girls are always dating jerks

In certain cases it is necessary to dig deeper to uncover the real reason for that belief.

In order to do that, you can use the following technique: Ask yourself "If that's true, what will that mean to me?"

Here is an example extracted from "Life Coaching: A Cognitive Behavioral Approach" by Michael Neenan and Windy Dryden:

Jane was anxious about attending a party because she thought:

- I won't get off with anyone
- If that's true, what will that mean to me?
- That I'll go home alone
- If that's true, what will that mean to me?
- No one fancies me
- If that's true, what will that mean to me?
- If no one fancies me, then I'll be all alone
- If that's true, what will that mean about me?
- That I'm undesirable (limiting belief)
- What limiting beliefs are holding you back? Can you uncover them?

Deconstruct your beliefs

The next step you want to take is to deconstruct those beliefs little by little by realizing that they are not true. Start by checking whether your beliefs are really true all the time and in all situations.

Often, without being aware of it, we heavily distort reality. We look at our weaknesses and compare them to someone we know that has a lot of strengths in that specific area. Have you noticed how we tend to compare our weakest points directly to our friends' strongest points? It is totally biased and doesn't make any sense so stop comparing apples to oranges. Because of this pattern of thinking we start to believe that people around us are better off than we are. Jim is smarter than me, John is way more confident than me, Jerry is definitely better-looking than me... So what? Is it a fair comparison? It misses the most important point: you have no way to tell how happy they really are. And if they are happier than you, so what? What does it have to do with you? The way we constantly compare ourselves with others diminishes our self-esteem and clouds our judgment regarding our own great abilities and strengths.

In reality, we have far more to be proud of than we think we do. This is also why a great friend or parent is critical, they often remind us of our own unique strengths. You might think that you are not good enough for X, Y or Z but are you really not good enough all the time in absolutely all areas of your life? Maybe you think that you stink at math, how about science or history or baseball? Maybe you don't know much about politics but a lot about the technology or fashion industry. Ok so you're not the fastest runner, perhaps you make a killer lasagna. The cheetah doesn't look at the elephant and think "wow I'm so small." You can always come up with thousands of things you are good enough to do, stop focusing on the few that you find difficult. Your subconscious acquires new beliefs through repetition so here is one exercise you should do to leverage the power of your subconscious mind and change your beliefs.

- When you feel like you are not good enough, come up with all the reasons why you are good enough.
- Take a few minutes every day to remind yourself all the things you are good at (you might want to write them down).

Remember that whatever you choose to focus on in life, your subconscious mind will look for more of that. If you tell your subconscious mind all the things you are good at then it will start looking for more things that you are good at. It will progressively change your current perception of reality. Similarly, taking 5 minutes to focus on what you are grateful for in life will train your subconscious mind to focus on things to be grateful for.

Look for information that demonstrates your beliefs are False

Sometimes, a single piece of information can shake your beliefs and change your perception of reality. Maybe you believe that you are too old to realize some dream you have, then you meet someone who followed his passion and created a business in his sixties or seventies. Or maybe your relationship is not really fulfilling anymore and you say to yourself that, after 15 years of marriage, it is normal. But then, you see a documentary on TV showing couples married for 50 years and still completely in love. Suddenly you no longer accept your previous belief system entirely. You realize that it was not the true reality but only your self-constructed reality.

Be aware that even in today's world where access to information is easy - or maybe precisely because of the information overflow - many myths still endure.

To give you an example, when I experimented with vegetarianism for a month I read a few books and did some research online. I used to believe that if I were to become a vegetarian then I would lose weight but then I learned that some famous bodybuilders were actually vegans. It instantly shook my beliefs about vegetarianism or veganism.

One other example was when I came across a Ted Talk video by Dan Buettner « How To Live To Be 100+ » that shows footage of centenarian gardening or riding their bikes. It made me realize that it was possible to grow old while still remaining healthy and active and this realization gave me the motivation to eat healthier food.

Once you have identified a disempowering belief, look for any information you can find that will show you why you are wrong. Read all the books you can read, watch all the documentaries you can find and look for people who have what you want.

Surprisingly, most people don't take responsibility for their current situation and reject people who have what they want as outliers. They just lucky! Don't do that. Learn everything you can from them. Find what they are doing and emulate it.

The basic assumption upon which you should act in your life is: if other people can do it then I can as well!

2

YOUR THOUGHTS NEVER DEFINE WHO YOU ARE AND WHO YOU CAN BECOME

> *If there were nothing but thought in you, you wouldn't even know you are thinking. You would be like a dreamer who doesn't know he is dreaming. You would be as identified with every thought as the dreamer is with every image in the dream.*
>
> — ECKHART TOLLE, A NEW EARTH

Decartes wrote I think therefore I am but is this really accurate?

If you have tried meditation before, you probably noticed how your mind is constantly thinking. Buddhist call our mind the monkey mind. Our thoughts are like a monkey that is relentlessly swinging through the trees. Are you aware of this voice that is always commenting on your life, and often negatively?

As I explained in the previous section, our mind is constantly eavesdropping on our thoughts. For that reason, we should be careful of the way we talk to ourselves internally.

However, what shall we do about thoughts that are coming from our mind?

You are not your thoughts

The simple truth to realize and that most people aren't aware of is that we are not our thoughts. In reality, even today we still don't understand where our thoughts come from.

Intuitive readers claim that they can read their clients' minds or that thoughts are out there and that it is possible to tap into those thoughts.

David R. Hawkins in his book Power vs. Force wrote "It is the vanity of the ego that claims thoughts as "mine". Genius, on the other hand, commonly attributes the source of creative leaps of awareness to that basis of all consciousness, which has traditionally been called Divinity".

Even today, scientists are still trying to understand what thoughts really are.

One more thing you should also realize is that 90% or more of the thoughts you had today are the same ones you had yesterday. Your mind is running the same old thought patterns again and again. Needless to say that those thoughts are totally useless.

The bottom line is that we don't even know what thoughts are, so why should we accept every single one of our thoughts as the truth? We shouldn't let our thoughts determine who we are. If we constantly react to our negative self-talk sooner or later we will get depressed.

You are not your ego

You may have read some personal development books that tell you that you are the sum of your thoughts and from a certain perspective this is true. However, it only holds if you believe that you are your ego. If you have some understanding of enlightenment, you might know that reaching enlightenment requires letting go of your ego. What ego means here is not what we usually mean by ego. What we mean by ego here is basically your entire identity. Your ego is created by your thoughts - all those thoughts about the past or the future create your identity. They are what you call "your personal story." Your personal story is changing all the time though because you are constantly interpreting events that happen to you through your thinking process.

I'm not telling you that you should seek enlightenment today, but what I would like you to realize is simply that your ego is not the essence of who you really are. You don't have to identify yourself with any single thought or act on your thoughts as if they were the absolute truth. They are not!

Actually, all your problems come from your thoughts. Test this out right now: try to be depressed without thinking. It's going to be very difficult because your natural state, like other animals, is not in a state of depression but rather a state of joy.

It's so important that it's worth repeating: you don't need to listen to your negative thoughts. Don't engage them and don't give them your attention, with nothing to hold on to you'll find that they start to disappear.

We can only live in the present

We can only live in the present. Of course you know this but have you really taken the time to think about what it really means?

The only thing that exists is now. Every time we think of the past or the future, the thinking occurs in the present - now. Your past does not exist anymore and thus cannot define who you really are unless you think of it in the present. And when you think of the past in the present, what you do is only recreate a memory of your subjective interpretation of a limited fragment of your past reality. How real is that! What about your future? Your future is just created through expectations.

Be careful that you don't need to cling to your "personal story." Work on progressively detaching yourself from it by focusing more on the present. Practice observing your thoughts and your emotions without identifying with them.

If you are interested in learning more about enlightenment you might want to read:

- *The Power Of Now* by Eckhart Tolle
- *A New Earth* by Eckhart Tolle
- *Awareness* by Anthony De Mello
- *I Am That* by Sri Nisargadatta Maharaj (this book is more advanced so I recommend that you start with Eckhart Tolle books)

A simple exercise to realize what you are not

Try this simple exercise:

Stop thinking for a moment - even a few seconds is okay - now ask yourself: "Who am I?" Descartes said "I think therefore I am." If it is true, who am I when I don't think? Am I nothing? Stop thinking. Who do you think you are? You are that presence, that awareness you can sense.

For now just keep in mind that you don't have to let your thoughts define you. When you live in the present moment and stop thinking, the reality is that you still exist! Use this new perspective to lessen the power you give to the thoughts that are coming out of your mind.

How to better control your thoughts

If you want to start becoming the master of your mind rather than being enslaved by it, meditation and mindfulness are awesome tools. They will greatly help you become aware of your thoughts. Start bringing awareness into your daily life by observing yourself. Instead of being lost in your thoughts, try to be present when you wash dishes, take a shower or go for a walk. Here is what you can do to bring awareness in these moments:

- Become aware of the thoughts that pop up during the time you spend doing what you are doing. Don't get caught by your thoughts. Just observe them.
- Become the witness of what you do. Watch every movement you are doing.
- Focus your attention on your body. How do you feel in your body while doing your current activity? (It helps you become more aware of your body and prevent you from thinking. You cannot think and focus your attention on your body at the same time)

Meditation is a great way to boost mindfulness. When you meditate, you train yourself to acknowledge your thoughts and let go of them. After practicing meditation for a while, you will become better and better at spotting negative thoughts and will be able to better deal with them - and it is only one of the countless benefits of meditation. You will progressively become the master of your mind instead of being its slave.

Mindfulness has a lot of benefits and can even be more effective in reducing stress, unhappiness and procrastination than medicine or other popular treatments. Kelly McGonigal demonstrates in her book "The Willpower Instinct" how repeatedly being aware of any urge we have (smoking, drinking, checking email, etc.) and "surfing the urge" - that is to become aware of how we feel and how the urge is manifesting itself in our body - can effectively reduce non-productive cravings and desires. Generally speaking, staying in touch with our negative emotions and observing them as if we were external observers is more effective than trying to repress those emotions. This is a critical distinction, too often we try to repress such emotions only to find them rebounding ten times stronger.

How to deal with your thoughts

Do you know about the white bear experiment? When participants of an experiment were told not to think of a white bear, do you know what happened? Well of course they couldn't stop thinking about a white bear! In another experiment, participants who were told not to think about chocolate, ended up eating more chocolate than participants who were told to think about chocolate.

Instead of trying to suppress your thoughts or your emotions learn to accept them. The fact that you are having a thought is the reality, but this thought doesn't have to become your reality.

Every time you have a negative thought:

- Accept it
- Observe it as a scientist would (how does it manifest in our body? Which parts of your body are tensed? How does it make you feel?)
- Ask yourself if you can let go of that thought and consciously discard it

The more you accept your thoughts and stop trying to suppress them, the less power they will have over you.

Replace Negative Thoughts with Positive Thoughts

Another thing you can do is to replace your negative thoughts with positive thoughts. Each time you experience negative thoughts, ask yourself if it is entirely true and come up with reasons that prove it's not.

Ex: "I'm not good enough"

Is it entirely true? Does it hold up in all situations?

- I'm good enough to make my friends happy
- I'm good enough to cook
- I'm good enough at my job
- I'm good enough to travel by myself

The point of this exercise, as seen previously, is to gradually deconstruct the limiting belief behind those thoughts by realizing that it is not true, or that it is true only in a few cases.

3

YOUR DEFINITION OF SUCCESS IS ALL THAT MATTERS

> *Success is not something you pursue, success is something you become.*
>
> — JIM ROHN

We all want to be successful and success is a recurrent theme in the media. However, have you taken the time to define what success really means to you? What kind of person do you want to become? Here is my personal definition of success:

"Success is when you work on becoming the best you can become, do what you love and give your best contribution to the world.

What is your definition of success?

Success is...

Too often people seek fame, recognition and money just to realize after years of hard work that those goals don't bring them real fulfillment and often they are left feeling empty.

You need to take time to determine what success means for you. Don't let society, the media, your family or your friends define it for you. Only you know what success means to you. Ask yourself "How can I serve people while doing what I love?" Think about what you can give, not about what you want to get. As the Bible says "Give and it shall be given unto you."

What is the meaning of life?

Generally, there are two types of thinking regarding the meaning of life

- We were all born with a specific purpose (this is called the Dharma in India)
- We have to give meaning to our life

I like both ideas and I don't know which one is true but it doesn't really matter.

Main characteristics of a great life purpose

Below are some characteristics of a great life purpose that you might want to consider.

- **Timeless:** If you could use a time machine and go back in time or into the future, your life purpose would remain the same.
- **Universal:** If you were born in a different part of the world your purpose would still be the same.
- **Inspiring:** Your life purpose should be truly inspiring and allow you to unleash your full potential and experience a real sense of fulfillment. When your purpose really resonates within you, what you are doing doesn't really feel like work anymore.
- **Transcend your ego:** most of us work in order to make a living, to gain recognition or to feel accepted by society. A true life purpose should come from a place of love not fear. When you have a clear life purpose you don't act out of fear anymore (fear of not being good enough, not being worthy, not being smart enough...). Although we are unlikely to

completely get rid of our ego, we should try to base our actions from a place of love as much as we can which becomes possible when our ego is under control.

Powerful questions to ask yourself

Let me give you several ways that can help you identify your life purpose

How can I leverage my problems? Think about how you can give meaning to your problems and challenges. Rather than complaining about a problem, it is often possible to take advantage of it by seeing the meaning it brings to your life.

Take the Australian motivational speaker Nick Vucijic for instance. He was born with no arms or legs yet he found a way to be happy and give meaning to his life by sharing his story around the world and inspiring millions. Victor Frankl in his book "Man's Search For Meaning" observed the odd phenomenon during his time in a Nazi concentration camp where individuals that were physically very strong often died long before smaller, skinnier and weaker individuals simply because the smaller guy had found meaning to his suffering.

- How can I get paid to do what I love? What is it that you like to do? How can you find a way to make a living out of it? Did you know that the word "enthusiasm" means "god within." It is impossible to be very successful if you don't really love what you do. If you don't follow your passion, you won't be able to keep moving forward after multiple failures. Only a strong "why" will allow you to keep going despite the hardships. Having passion will lead to fulfillment, which is real success, not just money or fame.
- How can I better serve? How can you create more value for society? Stop thinking about what you can get from society. Think about what you want to give to society.
- If you had all the money and time in the world what would you do? What do you love so much that you'd pay to do it?

- Take a pen and a piece of paper and answer the following question: "What is my life purpose?" Don't overthink just write whatever comes into your mind. Keep doing it until the sentence you write makes you cry.

Don't lose sight of the only thing that matters in life: being happy!

4

YOU ARE RESPONSIBLE FOR EVERYTHING IN YOUR LIFE

> *If you don't design your own life plan, chances are you'll fall into someone else's plan. And guess what they have planned for you? Not much.*
>
> — JIM ROHN

You can be either the victim, or the creator of your life? Which one would you like to be? Many of us fail to realize one very important factor in life: everything is a matter of choice. You are responsible for all areas of your life.

Are you giving your power away?

Each time you fail to take responsibility in any area of your life, you give your power away to circumstances and people around you. Each time you play the victim you disempower yourself and limit your ability to change yourself and move forward. Not taking responsibility means that you refuse to acknowledge that you have at least some control over most of the things that happen to you. You refuse to look for possibilities to make your life better.

Taking responsibility is not easy

Taking responsibility is not always easy, because it requires that you tell yourself the truth, that you accept the fact that you may have done something wrong or that you could have done things differently. Emotionally speaking, blaming people or circumstances is much easier than looking within yourself for possible shortcomings and mistakes you might have made. For some reason it feels more natural to blame people or circumstances. Refusing to take responsibility and letting go of our control gives us a false sense of relief. It also protects our ego. It is always easier to blame others than to change.

However blaming others is a huge impediment to personal growth. You are unlikely to reach your goals in life if you cannot get rid of this habit and start acting as the creator of - rather than a player in - your life.

Commit to take responsibility for your life

Commit yourself to take full responsibility for your life even in situations where you don't really believe you are responsible. Taking extra responsibility ensures that you are not overlooking possibilities for growth and change in life and are fully empowering yourself.

Taking responsibility never means beating yourself up or blaming yourself. That kind of attitude is likely to be counterproductive and result in self-sabotage, leading you to give up and giving you further excuses not to change and move forward. Taking responsibility is accepting the reality and realizing you have at least some power to change it.

Am I responsible for absolutely everything?

I know you are thinking: what if something I have absolutely no control over happens to me? What if my husband or wife gets killed in a terrorist attack? I am responsible for that? While you are not responsible for this event you are responsible for the way you choose to react to it. You can find meaning from the tragedy and move forward with your life or you can live in the past, thinking all day long about ways to track the terrorist down and take your revenge. Revenge is a current theme of many movies and is appealing for a lot of people. However, revenge is an ego game and without a doubt one of the most destructive behaviors in the world. Revenge is the antithesis of peace of mind and cannot bring fulfillment.

Martin Luther King once said: "Darkness cannot drive out darkness; only light can do that. Hate cannot drive out hate; only love can do that."

Unfortunately, too often our focus is on taking revenge, getting even or being right rather than on being happy. However, you should realize that in the end, the reason why you forgive people and move on is not because you are an extremely nice and completely selfless person, it is because you understand that it is the only way to be at peace with yourself. Forgiveness is nothing more than a declaration of love to yourself. It is a critical part of the commitment you made to yourself to be happy no matter what.

Events that happened to you happened to you, the question is "what are you going to do about it?" Are you going to let them ruin your life or are you going to build strength and meaning out of them - only you can decide.

I invite you to take some time to identify areas of your life where you are giving power away by refusing, consciously or unconsciously, to take full responsibility. Your family or your friends may support you in life but in the end you are always alone. The reality is that nobody is coming to save you. Nobody can get married for you and die for you. Don't live your life by default, create your life!

Some areas where you should take responsibility

Here are some areas where you should take responsibility:

- Accepting reality

- Your attitude
- Your happiness
- Your relationships
- Your emotions
- Your career
- Your time
- Saying no

Accepting reality

You are responsible for accepting reality as it is. If your life sucks well then admit it to yourself. You have to be completely honest with yourself. No real change is possible before you accept reality. Now get real with yourself but don't make it worse than the situation actually is. The purpose isn't to depress yourself but rather to realize that awareness is the prerequisite for change.

Your attitude

 It is hard to convince people sometimes that the world experience is the reflection of their attitude. They take the attitude that if people would only be nice to them they'd be nice in return. They are like the person sitting in the front of a cold stove, waiting for the heat. Until they put in the fuel, there ain't gonna be any heat. It is up to them to act first. It has to start somewhere. Let it begin with us.

— Earl Nightingale, Lead The Field

Working on your attitude is one of the most important things you can do for your personal growth. Most people when they leave their house in the morning have a neutral attitude. They don't choose their attitude. By not being aware of your attitude you give power to your environment. For instance, if you happen to be surrounded by cheerful people you will react to that cheerfulness and everything will be great. However, if you are surrounded by pessimistic people, you will easily be influenced by their negative attitude. By refusing to deliberately choose your attitude you disempower yourself, you become a chameleon that simply reacts to your environment. You are being influenced rather than influencing. You might say to yourself "That person is not smiling at me. He is not friendly. Why should I be friendly with him?" The problem with this is that that person might be thinking the exact same thing about you! Don't give your power away, choose your attitude and be the scriptwriter of your life not a chameleon reacting to life.

If other people insult you, make fun of you or disrespect you it is their problem not yours. Don't take anything personally. Realize that most people haven't done enough personal development work to master their emotions and are still acting at a low level of consciousness. Understand that they probably have their personal issues which explain why they are behaving like they are. And anyway they might judge you but what do they know about you? Nothing! You have nothing to gain by reacting. Do you value your happiness and your peace of mind or some criticism from someone who knows nothing about you? Don't give your power away by reacting. You are better than that.

Decide to leave home every morning with a great attitude

Influence people by your positive attitude and don't let people influence you with their negative attitude. If people are angry, stressed or in a bad mood it is their problem not yours. Don't change your attitude. Do your best to react to people who are rude the same way you would react to people who are nice.

Remember:

"Your attitude not your aptitude, will determine your altitude."– Zig Ziglar

Your happiness

 It is only when we assume responsibility for our happiness that we will have a reasonable chance of gaining it.

— Irvine, A Guide to the Good Life

I often hear people saying that happiness is subjective. Although it is true that what makes me happy might not make you happy, I believe that the mechanism that leads to happiness is the same for every human being and should be known by everyone.

Happiness: Are we all equal?

Sonja Lyubomirsky's book "The How Of Happiness" shows that we all have a different baseline in terms of happiness. Some of us are born happier than others and, according to Sonja, roughly 50% of happiness is determined by genetics. The remaining 50% is divided as follows: 40% comes from what we do and how we think and 10% comes from life circumstances. The implication is that, what happens to us has very little impact on our happiness level. The only way we can significantly increase our happiness is by changing our thoughts and our actions. Happiness comes from within you not from outside of you.

Now we have all heard that happiness comes from within and that material things won't make us happy, but the question is: do you believe it? Have you ever thought about it seriously?

Let me ask you this: Can you think about something that you were sure would make you happy once and then you finally it? Did it really increase your happiness? How many minutes did the feeling of elation last? It didn't really transform your life as you had expected, right?

You probably believe that having more money or more recognition will bring you happiness. I'm also guilty of sharing the same flawed belief. I focus on my goals and tell myself that I need to achieve these goals in order to be fulfilled. I truly believe that the accomplishment of a particular goal will make me happy. However, when I take some time to think about my past accomplishments and how they contribute to my present happiness, I start becoming skeptical.

When I envision my future self having realized all of my goals I feel happy and excited, but at the same time, when I come back to earth and ask myself: If right now all of my goals were accomplished, given my current mindset, would I be significantly happier than I'm now?

Ask yourself that question too: If you could achieve all your goals today, would it make you happier knowing your current mindset? It might give you some comfort or satisfaction for a while, but is it going to transform your life and significantly contribute to your happiness? Probably not.

Does it mean that you shouldn't set goals at all? Of course not. But you should choose worthy goals to pursue. Goals should help you become the person you want to be rather than getting things you want to have. Setting ambitious goals is important because during the process that leads up to those goals you grow as a person. See the "Set Goals" part for more information.

Gratitude

Feeling grateful every day is a key way to increase our happiness. However it's not always easy to feel grateful. We know we should be grateful but we often don't feel it on a deeper level. The best way to feel more grateful is by practicing and getting into the habit of shifting your focus from what you don't have to what you have no matter how difficult your current situation may be.

What I personally do that works well for me is to make a list of 10 things I'm grateful for but here is the trick - while writing my list I listen to a great song I found on YouTube. It really helps stir the emotion of gratefulness and the simplicity of the lyrics are really powerful: "I'm so blessed, I'm grateful for all that I have"

Don't be grateful only for what you have in terms of material things, but also be grateful for your family, the freedom you have or the sense of security you experience every day (just to name a few). Remember that things that were given to you for free (your family, your friends, your brain, nature, freedom...) are far more valuable than any material things you can ever dream of acquiring. How much would you sell your freedom for? Your mother's love? Your arms? Take time to acknowledge how much you have to be grateful for.

Be grateful for who you are as a person. Focus on your qualities and look for more of those qualities every day. Look for new things to be grateful for daily. Walk around your place, look at everything you have, touch things and think of the benefits they provide you.

After a few weeks you will experience more happiness and will be able to progressively shift your thoughts from a sense of scarcity to a sense of abundance.

Remember, you are responsible for your happiness. No external success will bring you happiness or peace of mind no matter how successful you are.

Your relationships

There are two people in a relationship so when something goes wrong you always share of portion of the responsibility. Stop avoiding responsibility. Often, when you listen to a couple having an argument it always seems to be the fault of the other for some reason!

Example of things you are responsible for in a relationship:

Understanding women/men psychology

You should study the psychology of women and men. Many arguments can be avoided by understanding some fundamental differences between men and women.

Nurture the relationship

It is always shocking for me to see how in Japan many couples complain about their marriage while they are making no effort to nurture the relationship. Relationships are like everything else in life, they require effort!

Communicating clearly your needs and how you feel to your partner

You are responsible for letting your partner know what you want and how you feel. By failing to do that on a consistent basis you are likely to build resentment towards your partner over time.Resentment accumulated over a long period of time is a relationship killer. Communicating openly with your partner about things that bother you in the relationship, even small things, is crucial. It is something I'm really struggling with and I know I have to seriously work on this aspect of my life. I expect women to know how I feel and what I want without clearly communicating my feelings. I focus too much on my partner's needs and not enough on myself and fail to communicate clearly my needs. Then I secretly resent her for not responding to my needs!

Being clear on your values and expectations

It is your responsibility to know your values and to stand up for those values. Don't try to change your partner's values and don't try to change your values to adapt them to your partner's values. We are attracted to people who are similar to us and this is also true for values. If you practice meditation two hours every day and have no interest in material things you probably don't want to marry a very materialistic woman. A while ago, I was talking to a Japanese man who was very sad about the way is marriage was going. He told me he didn't communicate enough with his wife and he realized after a while that they didn't have the same values, they didn't want the same things in life. Don't let that happen to you! Be clear about your values and expectations and share them with your partner.

Your emotions

 An emotion has a very short life span. It is like a momentary ripple or wave on the surface of your Being.

— Eckhart Tolle, The Power Of Now, A Guide To Spiritual Enlightenment

Happiness, sadness, stress, hopelessness and any other possible kind of emotion that you feel doesn't actually exist out there. They are only created by your mind. You are responsible for your emotions so it's up to you to do something about your emotions. If you constantly think about bad events that happened to you in the past, you are responsible for that! If you constantly worry about the future, you are responsible for that too! If you react too emotionally to a present situation guess who's responsible? That's right, you are responsible! That's why many spiritual teachers stress the importance of:

- Living in the now (the only reality that exists)
- Acceptance (stop resisting and begin to fully accept reality)

Being responsible for your emotions doesn't mean that you are always full of joy and can completely get rid of your negative emotions, though it is a noble ideal that you should try to pursue. By accepting responsibility for your emotions you start improving your situation. If you realize that stress is not because of a specific situation but is the result of the way you yourself react to that situation you can start taking full responsibility for your stress and look for ways to reduce it. If a situation or a job is really too stressful for you to deal with, you can always choose to leave.

Similarly, getting angry doesn't have to be an automatic response to someone who insults you, disrespects you or makes fun of you. You always have a choice. Be aware that each time you react and get angry, or try to take revenge you're choosing to give your power away to the person who is offending you. You actually make that person more important than he or she is. You might feel a strong need to react. You might insult that person in return, be sarcastic, take revenge, badmouth him behind his back or even worse chose to fight him. However, you have absolutely nothing to gain by doing that. You are just wasting your time and your energy. Actually, those behaviors reveal how insecure you are inside no matter how confident you might pretend to be on the outside. A person with high self-esteem feels less need to be respected or approved of by others. What about you? How secure are you?

By the way, the Greek stoic philosopher Epictetus said "What is insulting is not the person who abuses you or hits you, but the judgment about them that they are insulting. Another person will not do you harm unless you wish it".

Having said that, it doesn't mean that you should never react. It is also important to speak up in a polite and non-aggressive way when needed. It is especially true if the person who is disrespecting you is someone you meet on a regular basis, at work for instance. You really don't want to feel any kind of resentment towards that person. So if you have something to say, please say it but don't spend any time being angry about what someone did to you when that person is not even around. While you are worrying he/she is probably enjoying life and likely does not even know that you are angry at them. Say what you have to say but always be a gentleman about it. Write an email or ask someone else to convey your feelings to that person if you need to.

We know when we are offended. We just feel it. We also know when we will feel some resentment if we don't speak up in a given situation. For that reason, if right now you are someone who feels offended rather easily it is necessary that you speak up. However you will find that the more you work on yourself, learn to reframe situations, understand that you are too important to react to most of the situations and develop self-esteem the less you will feel offended. Trust your feelings and speak up to tell people how you feel when necessary. Don't insult, make sarcastic comments or try to take revenge!

What I personally do to deal with my anger

I acknowledge that I have a feeling of anger and focus on how anger feels in my body. Focusing on my emotions allows me to dissociate from them. Then I analyze why I am feeling that emotion.

I reframe the situation: This person has probably some problems in his life (he lost his job, he just broke up with his girlfriend, someone died in his family or maybe he is just a jerk). I transform my anger into pity and see them as weak for lacking self-control. Often, when people get angry at you, it is not personal. You just happen to be there at the wrong moment when they needed to let off some steam. I see myself as too important to spend any time or energy reacting to people who don't deserve it. My peace of mind is too important.

If I feel somewhat offended I try to understand why? If someone criticizes you and you feel offended, generally it means that there is at least an ounce of truth in their message. Try to find it but be aware that it is not necessary an "objective truth." It could be something that your subconscious mind perceives as a truth. For instance, I tend to believe that no matter how hard I work it is never enough. So if someone I know were to come to me and criticize me by calling me lazy I would likely feel offended. Not because they are right because I am objectively working hard but because my subconscious mind ridiculously believes it to be true.

Your career

When you accept complete responsibility for your life, you begin to view yourself as self-employed, no matter who signs your paycheck. You see yourself as the president of your own personal service corporation. You see yourself as an entrepreneur heading a company with one employee: you.

— Brian Tracy

You are responsible for creating more value for your company and for the society as a whole. You are responsible for making yourself more valuable by reading material in your field of expertise, constantly increasing your productivity, learning new skills, participating in training sessions or working on your communication skills. Your company might be very supportive but ultimately it is always your responsibility to grow.

Your time

 Being busy is a form of laziness – lazy thinking and indiscriminate action.

— Tim Ferris

Are you controlling your time? Or are you letting situations and people steal your time?

Your life can be described as a very short period of time that you were given on earth. Your time is one of the most precious assets you have. Nevertheless, most people waste a lot of their time pursuing things just to realize that those things don't really matter.

You have to realize that you are always the one who decides how you should use your time. You should take full responsibility for it.

Saying no

Before accepting an invitation, or responding favorably to a request, you should always ask yourself, is it the best way for me to spend my time right now. Learn to say no especially when the request is not in line with your core values and things that really matter to you.

5

YOU CAN TURN YOUR DREAMS INTO GOALS WITH THE POWER OF GOAL SETTING

> *A goal is a dream with a deadline.*
>
> — Napoleon Hill

> *Nothing happens, no forward steps are taken until a goal is established. Without goals individuals just wander through life. They stumble along. Never knowing where they are going, so they never get anywhere.*
>
> — David J. Schwartz, The Magic Of Thinking Big

Have you defined clear goals in your life? Did you take the time to write down your goals? Setting goals and writing them down is probably one of the best gifts you can give yourself. It is the best way to tap into the power of your subconscious mind and let it support you. Setting goals provides you with a lot of other benefits and helps you clarify what you really want in life. However, surprisingly, few people go through the process of writing down their goals. That's exactly why I felt the need to write a book on goal setting. Goal setting is so powerful that I believe everyone should learn about it.

Here are 5 great reasons why you should set goals in your life:

1. **It gives direction to your subconscious mind** that Maxwell Maltz calls a mechanical goal-seeking device.

Here is a quote from his book Psycho-cybernetics "Your automatic creative mechanism is teleological. That is, it operates in terms of goals and end results. Once you give it a definite goal to achieve, you can depend upon its automatic guidance system to take you to that goal much better than "you" ever could by conscious thought. "You" supply the goal by thinking in terms of end results. Your automatic mechanism them supplies the means whereby."

2. **It empowers you:** when you set goals in all the areas of your life, you act as the creator of your life not the victim. You realize that you have the power within you to achieve goals that truly excite you and get you the life you deserve.

3. **It contributes to building a healthy amount of self-esteem:**

High self-esteem seeks the challenge and stimulation of worthwhile and demanding goals. Reaching such goals nurtures good self-esteem. Low self-esteem seeks the safety of the familiar and undemanding. Confining oneself to the familiar and undemanding serves to weaken self-esteem. – Nathaniel Branden

Achieving goals you set for yourself is a powerful way to build self-esteem. Start with small goals. The more goals that you achieve the more you will believe in your ability to achieve even greater goals and build an even healthier level of self-esteem.

4. **It changes your present reality:**

"The value of goals is not in the future they describe, but the change in perception of reality they foster." - David Allen, Getting Things Done

It opens you up to new opportunity and makes you realize that you can overcome your limiting beliefs. You progressively become aware of the fact that your present reality can be changed.

5. **It improves your health:**

"Use goals to live longer. No medicine in the world – and your physician will bear this out – is as powerful in bringing about life as is the desire to do something." – David J. Schwartz, The Magic Of Thinking Big

People who have truly exciting goals that give meaning to their life are healthier and can live longer. One of the 9 common characteristics of people who live to be one hundred years old, according to Dan Buettner the author of "Blue zone," is that they have a life purpose. Here is a powerful example: a mother who contracted cancer when her son was 2, decided that she would live to see her son graduate college. She went through many surgical operations, her cancer was never fully cured but she lived for 20 more years and saw her son graduate college before passing away six weeks afterward.

How to set personal goals you will achieve

> *The key to goal setting is for you to think on paper. Successful men and women think with a pen in their hands; unsuccessful people do not.*
>
> — BRIAN TRACY

The very first thing to do when you want to set some goals for yourself is to put them on paper. The mere act of writing down your goals will instantly make them more concrete in your mind. Putting goals on paper moves those goals that you enjoy daydreaming about from the abstract world to the physical world. Daydreaming is a trick that you might use to feel good right now but it is an illusion that rarely produces results. Once you take the time to write down your goals you'll find that they start becoming part of your reality.

Are you ready to set your goals? Take a piece of paper and pen and write down all the goals you would like to achieve if you were guaranteed to succeed no matter what.

Go for goals that really excite you even if they sound totally crazy to others. What is it that you really want? What would your dream life look like? What is your way to contribute to the world? Unleash your imagination!

Take the goal that excites you the most and ask you "how?" "How can I achieve it?" Questions that start with "How" are very powerful. They foster your imagination and are based on the assumption that whatever it is that you want to accomplish is possible. By brainstorming about your goal, you will progressively make it part of your reality and by chunking it down and choosing a realistic deadline and working at it daily you will start realizing that it is possible. Not easy but possible!

Be specific

 Know what you want. Clarity is power. And vague goals promote vague results.

— ROBIN SHARMA

The biggest mistake is to set goals that are vague like "I'm going study English" or "I want to become rich." Your goal should be very clear. Clarity is the key!

Rather than simply deciding to study English you should choose what you want to be able to say in English by the end of the month/semester or year.

For instance: I will meet my American friend John during the last weekend of June and I will have 1-hour conversation with him about my experience traveling in Asia.

Rather than saying you want to make more money, decide the exact amount of money you want to earn and commit to a specific deadline. Ex: I will earn $10,000 per month by December 31st of next year.

Decide on the specific day you will achieve your goal. The clearer the better. Find a way to measure your goals because otherwise you cannot be held accountable and cannot track your results. When you find a way to measure your goals it will become suddenly more real, more tangible.

Choose a challenging goal

You want a goal that will push you out of your comfort zone and make you feel better once you achieve it. If the goal is too far beyond your reach then you will lose motivation and your self-esteem will suffer. Don't compare yourself to others. No matter how small the achievement, if you had to push yourself a little bit to achieve your goal it is a big success that you should celebrate. It might not be a big deal for others but it is for you. And you matter!

I'm a big supporter of ambitious goals, but they should be backed up with massive action in order to be achievable.

Write all the reasons why your goal is so important

 When the why get stronger the how get easier.

— JIM ROHN

Having a goal is like being on a cruise. You don't care that much about the destination but you definitely want to enjoy the journey!

Why is that goal so important for you? Make sure your goal truly matters to you and is not something you are doing just for your family, your friends or your colleagues. Intrinsic motivation is always better than extrinsic motivation. Make sure you don't spend years pursuing a goal that is not going to make you happy. Don't expect that once you achieve your goal you will be happy. Your goal should inspire you and the journey toward your goal be enjoyable.

Make the necessary preparations before starting your goal

 If you would like to be thinner, spend all your time with skinny people. Have all your meals with skinny people.

— Vasant Lad

You have limited willpower so save it as much as possible. Try to create a friendly and supportive environment that will help you achieve your goal. If you want to become a vegetarian then have a list of vegetarian recipes ready, fill you fridge with vegetables and fruits or join a vegetarian association before getting started. Research shows that the easier it is for you to grab a certain type of food, the more you will eat of it. I noticed that I often eat food that is on my desk without even being aware of it. Fortunately (and not by accident), the only food on my desk is a box containing nuts which are great for health ;-)

Share your goals

If you want to lose 10 kilos it might be a good idea to make a public announcement at work in front of your colleagues and to tell all of your family members about your goal. You might also want to tell people you encounter that you are on a diet and you will lose 10 kilos by March 31st. If you don't feel confident enough to do that, it means that your goal might be too ambitious for you right now and or you don't really want to accomplish it. In that case, you might want to check whether your goal is achievable or not and modify it if necessary.

However, be aware that your goals may change over time as you acquire new knowledge and new perspectives. If you believe your goal is likely to change, make sure that telling everyone about your actual goal won't put too much pressure on you. If that goal is not relevant to you anymore, you should be able to drop it. Remember that goals are here to improve your present reality and help you get the life you want. A goal that doesn't meet that criterion should be dumped.

When talking about your goals, avoid using - I will try, I think, maybe or if it goes well.

Instead use - I will, when I achieve, I know I will or I definitely will. The words you use contribute to your reality so use words that support your motivation to take action.

Anticipate all possible ways it can go wrong and create a strategy

 The fastest way to succeed is to double your failure rate.

— Thomas Watson

We tend to be overoptimistic regarding our ability to achieve a goal and underestimate the amount of work and time necessary to perform the required tasks. Ask yourself what things can happen that will prevent you from achieving your goals? If your goals are long-term goals, chances are that you will face multiple setbacks before you succeed.

In the past I had many goals but I didn't achieve most of them. One of the reasons was my lack of confidence. Other major issues were that I was overly optimistic and was not prepared mentally to face major setbacks. I would try to create a blog about Japan but would give up due to some technical difficulties I encountered or I would wait for everything to be perfect before launching the blog. Needless to say that this blog never got anywhere! I planned to make videos of my trips abroad and publish them and it never happened.

Once I understood that failure was actually part of the process and not an anomaly it helped me significantly to achieve my goals. Here is how I see setbacks or failures: setbacks are here to test you, to see how bad you want it. When you set a goal, you have to be clear not only about your goal but about what you are ready to go through to in order to achieve that goal. If you already made up your mind up that huge setbacks are likely to occur, you will be prepared to face them and be able to keep moving forward. You should already know how you're going to react to potential setbacks before they occur.

Avoid putting yourself in difficult situations

If your objective is to lose weight or to stop smoking for instance, you should avoid temptation. Identify all those situations where you are at risk, think of what caused you to fail in your previous attempts and see how you can avoid repeating such situations. Maybe you like to have a cigarette when you are drinking coffee, when you eat outside or when you are under stress. Identify those kinds of situations and come up with an effective strategy.

How to create a list of goals

When you create list of goals you want to make sure that you cover all the areas in your life. It should include your career, your health, your wealth, your relationships, your hobbies and other areas you can think of.

Here are the characteristics of a good list of goals:

- Covers all areas of your life
- Goals are all measurable and have a deadline
- The wording is positive. Don't use "not" or other negative words but use "I am" or "I will"
- Check your list every day to keep your goals fresh in your mind and to give a signal to your subconscious mind to focus on these specific goals

Should you achieve all your goals?

You might want to achieve all your goals, especially if you share them with everyone like I do but in reality you don't have to and you won't. I felt a lot of pressure when I first updated my goals on my website. I thought I should accomplish all of them no matter what and prove to my readers and to myself that I could do it. However, after a while, I realized that some of those goals weren't really exciting me or that they weren't my first priority. I also realized that marketing my blog required a lot of time. As a result, I decided to drop some of my goals in order to focus on things that matter the most for me: working on my blog, studying, and writing articles and e-books. Things cannot always go as planned, so you should be flexible enough to adapt your goals and to trust your feelings to decide which goals you should drop when necessary. Goals are here for one purpose and that is to help you!

To start setting exciting goals you can refer to my book *Goal Setting: The Ultimate Guide to Achieving Goals that Truly Excites You*

Additionally, if you want to become an unstoppable goal achiever and set in achiever one of your most exciting goals in 90 days, you can refer to my goal setting planner, *The Ultimate Goal Setting Planner: Become an Unstoppable Goal Achiever in 90 Days or Less.*

CONCLUSION

Thank you very much for downloading this e-book, I hope that it helps you in your quest for a happy and fulfilling life. I'm looking forward to seeing you soon on my website. Don't hesitate to leave a comment or question as I do my best to respond quickly and thoroughly.

I wish you the very best in your life.

Thibaut Meurisse

Founder of whatispersonaldevelopment.org

BOOK 2 - CRUSH YOUR LIMITS

BREAK FREE FROM LIMITATIONS AND ACHIEVE YOUR TRUE POTENTIAL

Who is This Book For?

You'll greatly benefit from this book if you want to:

- Stop feeling stuck where you are now and turn your life around
- Transform your vision of yourself and the world by adopting powerful beliefs that will earn you remarkable results
- Discover how much more potential you have and start tapping into your greatness
- Program your subconscious to reach higher levels of success, and
- Overcome mental blocks such as feelings of worthlessness and money-related fears and move freely towards your goals.

What You'll Discover in This Book

In this book, you will:

- Learn how much you've been limiting yourself, and be challenged to expand your thinking to grow more than you thought possible
- Uncover disempowering assumptions that have been sabotaging your success and undermining your happiness and peace of mind for years
- Learn how to replace limiting beliefs with more empowering ones to help you move freely towards your goals and dreams, and
- Be challenged to redefine your relationships with key concepts such as time, money, work and success, which will leave you with a whole new perspective and will inspire you to take massive action.

How to Use This Book

I encourage you to read all the way through this book at least once. After that, I invite you to revisit the book and focus on the section(s) you want to explore in more depth. As you'll learn here, repetition is key. Don't hesitate to read this book multiple times.

You'll find many exercises in this book. Most of them are simple and don't require much time, so make sure you do them.

Also, I highly encourage you to join the 30-Day Challenge, which will help you start reprogramming your mind and create a powerful mindset that will serve you for the rest of your life.

If you feel this book could be of any use to your family members or friends, make sure to share it with them.

FOREWORD BY MIKE PETTIGREW

Limiting beliefs are one of the biggest reasons people fail to achieve their goals and fail to attain a better quality of life.

Everyone has limiting beliefs, and they sabotage your chances of success. Sadly, most people are blissfully unaware of their own limiting beliefs, even though they enact a powerful influence over their lives.

Many years ago, I became acutely aware of my own limiting beliefs surrounding money, at a time when I was experiencing a financial rollercoaster.

Three years earlier, I started my first real business, which was going quite well except for the fact that I was constantly experiencing financial difficulties. It was literally, feast or famine. One month there was plenty of money, while the next there was barely enough cash for me to eat properly. At that point, I had no idea the root source of my money problems lay in my low self-worth.

As a child, I suffered from asthma, and I couldn't run very far. My classmates soon discovered I was useless at sports and that I was the worst player to be on their sports team. They used to argue over not having me on their team. They would say things like, "We don't want Pettigrew, we had him last week and he's useless."

Most of our beliefs are formed through repetition and emotion, and when you hear you are useless again and again, you can start to believe it, just like I did.

As Henry Ford, creator of the first automobiles used to say, "Whether you think you can, or you think you can't – you're right." What we believe becomes our reality. If we think we can't achieve something, no matter how hard we may try, our beliefs will sabotage that goal.

Right through my teens and into my early twenties I thought I was useless at all sorts of things and, because I thought I was useless, I *was* incompetent and clumsy.

This became a vicious circle and, no matter how hard I tried to improve my finances, I still continued to experience money problems. Then I hit a brick wall—a problem so big I thought I was going to have to fold up the business.

I discovered that I owed our suppliers more money that month than was coming in during the following two months. I was deeply shocked, and I had no idea what to do. I considered all sorts of strategies but could not envisage any of them working.

I almost decided to close the business and work for someone else when it dawned on me, if I ceased trading, I would have wasted four years of very hard work—and all for nothing.

Around the same time, I experienced other events that showed me I had low self-worth. I started thinking about those experiences and wondered whether my money problems could also be related to my poor self-value.

As a last-ditch attempt to rescue my business and livelihood and to boost my self-worth, I doubled my prices. Even if half my clients stop doing business with me, my business would have still been in a far better position financially.

So, I wrote to each of my clients, explaining that if they wished to continue receiving the same level of service they had come to expect from my business, we would have to increase our prices dramatically.

Amazingly, every single one of them agreed to the 100% price increase, and one of them even told me that he had always thought that I was charging far too little anyway!

From that point forward my business start to thrive and become seriously profitable. So much so that a few years later, I sold the first business to a multinational, and by that point, I was a millionaire with lots of self-value!

Everything changed as soon as I started rooting out and overcoming my limiting beliefs.

Your limiting beliefs are among the biggest obstacles you face in your life. They hold you back enormously and stop you from achieving success, happiness, freedom and wealth. You may think you have no limiting beliefs, or that limiting beliefs don't hold you back from achieving your dreams, but you are mistaken.

From the moment you were born, you have been conditioned to believe certain things that are simply not true. You have been "told" by your parents, siblings, friends, and teachers how you should think, feel, react and behave. You have also been conditioned to believe you can only achieve certain things, and that certain aspirations are too unrealistic and impossible for you.

Then, as you move through life, you experience difficulties and setbacks that compound the problem. By the time most people reach the age of thirty, they have experienced so much conditioning and so many painful experiences their realm of possibility has been dramatically reduced.

How many people give up on the dreams they had as a child, a teenager or while in their early twenties? It is a sad reality, but most adults end up settling for a dissatisfying mediocrity—for the rest of their lives!

But what if there were a different way? What if it were possible to dramatically reduce the stream of negative thoughts and limiting beliefs that go through our minds continuously?

Imagine what it would be like if you were able to switch off those limiting beliefs. What might start happening in your life? Many people have found the secret that allows them to do this, and their lives have changed in miraculous ways as a result.

When you overcome your limiting beliefs, what once seemed impossible suddenly becomes possible. You wipe the slate clean and you can start again. It does not matter how many failures and setbacks you have experienced in the past. The fact is, you can recreate yourself every single day of your life—providing you choose to do so.

Then again, you can continue to live your present and future life based on your past failures, thereby locking yourself into a restrictive and disempowering future. The choice is yours.

I have discovered from abundant personal experience over many years that the greatest secret to success lies in the ability to root out and overcome our limiting beliefs. This may seem difficult, or even impossible to do, but it is a lot easier than you may currently believe.

Thibaut Meurisse has created a vitally important book on overcoming your limiting beliefs, and I applaud him for creating this masterpiece. In the pages of this groundbreaking book you will learn the easy way to overcome all your limiting beliefs, so you can finally create the life you truly yearn for.

I absolutely love this book, and I am so excited that Thibaut has written it. This is because I know it will help millions of people around the world to transform their lives and become happy and deeply fulfilled.

You really *can* wipe the slate clean. You absolutely *can* start again. You definitely *can* create the life you were born to live! And you can do all this more quickly than you may have ever dreamed possible.

Read this book through once, so you get a good understanding of how it works and what you can gain by using it. Then go back to the sections that apply most to you. Pick out the limiting beliefs holding you back in any area of your life and follow the simple steps Thibaut shares with you.

This book is one-of-a-kind, and it can totally change your life. You are holding in your hands the key to achieving the life that you yearn for. Expect massive transformations from this point forwards!

Very best wishes,

Mike Pettigrew

Serial entrepreneur and author of the bestseller, *The Most Powerful Goal Achievement System in the World*.

INTRODUCTION

If you put a chain around the leg of an elephant when it is still young, initially, it will try to escape. However, unable to do so, it will eventually give up and stop resisting. As it grows bigger and stronger, it could easily break free, but it never will. Instead, it will remain under the control of its trainer for the rest of its life. Why? Because it has been conditioned to believe it can't escape.

What if the only thing preventing you from living the life you want is the illusion that you can't? What if the reasons you're not where you want to be is the result of similar conditioning to that of the elephant? What if this conditioning is the result of the many assumptions you hold in various areas of your life?

Now, imagine if you could transform your life simply by changing these assumptions. Could you be a few *new* assumptions away from success and happiness?

The truth is you're operating far below your maximum capabilities. In fact, we all are. Your current assumptions lead you to think, feel and act in a way that is incongruent with the results you want to obtain and the person you want to become.

I believe it is possible for you to experience more happiness, success and fulfillment than you can ever imagine. How? By reframing your life, by questioning the way you think, feel and act, and by replacing your current limiting assumptions with more empowering ones.

This book will help you reframe your life to unlock the whole of your potential. With this book, I want you to expand your horizons and fully realize the field of possibilities ahead of you. Throughout this book, we will work on loosening and reforming your assumptions, and we will remove unsupportive assumptions. On many occasions, I will challenge the beliefs you hold in various areas of your life. You may not agree with everything I say. Occasionally, you may even become defensive or angry, and that's fine. What matters most is that you start questioning all your limiting assumptions.

As you read this book, I will ask you to be proactive. Nothing works until you do. And only you can do the work. This is *your* life. Work it. Improve it. Win!

Here is a more detailed summary of what you'll learn in this book:

In **Part I**, we will define assumptions and discuss how they limit you. You'll learn how your assumptions have been affecting your life more than you probably think.

In **Part II**, we will review fifty common assumptions that may be preventing you from reaching your full potential. We'll discuss the assumptions you hold about yourself, life, success, emotions, work and time.

Finally, in **Part III**, we will learn how you can replace your disempowering assumptions with more empowering ones, so you can make positive changes in your life and achieve your goals and dreams.

YOUR FREE ACTION GUIDE

To help you take action on what you'll learn in this "*Success Principle Series*" I've create free action guides. If you haven't yet, you can grab them at the URL below:

https://whatispersonaldevelopment.org/success-series

PART I
UNDERSTANDING ASSUMPTIONS

1
EACH ASSUMPTION YOU HOLD LIMITS YOU

Right now, you hold thousands of assumptions that limit your field of possibilities. While some assumptions bear little to no significant consequences, others impact your entire life. Some examples of major assumptions include: "I can't be happy because of X, Y or Z," or "I can't ask for what I want." These two assumptions alone can limit you dramatically and prevent you from designing and living the life you want. And these are just the tip of the iceberg.

A minor assumption could be something as simple as, "I should always answer the phone," or "I should avoid blanks in the conversation."

Your assumptions—minor or major—determine the choices available to you in any situation. They are the rules you add to the game of life which often make it more challenging than it needs to be.

My hope is that, while reading and working through this book, you'll realize how much you've been limiting yourself, and you'll be able to start unlocking the unlimited potential within you.

Are you really stuck?

Perhaps you feel stuck right now. You may have been in a dead-end job or in an unfulfilling relationship for years. Perhaps you have not been making enough progress in your career or your business. Perhaps, you've been struggling to lose weight for as long as you can remember.

If you're feeling stuck, it's mostly the result of the way your mind works. Your mind operates within a certain set of rules. These rules are what I call "assumptions." These same assumptions determine the way you interpret your thoughts and the events around you and, as a result, the actions you take. Therefore, to obtain different (and better) results, you must challenge your assumptions. The first step is to assess whether they are true and whether they are limiting or empowering you.

Are you really stuck? Or is your situation determined by one of these assumptions? If so, ask yourself, if I knew what to do, would I do it? What can I do to improve my situation?

Sadly, many people believe they have no power to transform their lives. I firmly believe this couldn't be further from the truth. In fact, the way you currently think, feel and act is only a tiny fraction of the almost infinite possibilities available to you. It probably doesn't even represent 0.1% of the thoughts you could have, the feelings you could experience or the actions you could take.

In what way are you limiting yourself right now? What disempowering story are you telling yourself? What options haven't you reflected on yet?

Consider the following: every single day we have thousands of thoughts—some research suggests fifty thousand or more—and make over thirty-five thousand decisions. How much power do you think you can harness once you start changing some of your thoughts for the better? How fast do you think you can change your life once you start making a few different (and better) decisions each day? The same way an airplane can land in a totally different place if it slightly deviates from its course, a human being will end up in a totally different position if he or she changes a few dominant thoughts or habits.

In my experience, simply adopting a few new, and positive, daily habits can lead to dramatic improvements in the long term. Changing two to three daily habits is usually all it takes to achieve almost any goal, be it becoming an author, losing weight, changing career or earning a promotion. Even simple habits like avoiding hitting the snooze button or taking a few minutes to set goals every day can dramatically impact your life long-term. You certainly don't lack opportunities to change, you merely lack perspective.

2

HOW YOUR ASSUMPTIONS AFFECT YOUR LIFE

For years, I've been fascinated by the effect assumptions can have on people's lives. Simply assuming you can't do something means you'll probably never be able to do it. Or, as Henry Ford once said, "*Whether you think you can or think you can't—you're right.*"

In reality, you *can* do most of the things you believe you can't—even if you're convinced of the opposite.

In his book, *The Success Principles,* Jack Canfield relates the story of Victor Serebriakoff, the son of a Russian émigré who grew up in a London slum. His story illustrates well how an individual's assumptions can affect their whole life. Victor's teachers labeled him a dunce and encouraged him to drop out of school. Victor believed his teachers and became an itinerant worker. He was often forced to live on the streets and had lost any hope to ever live a "normal" life.

At age thirty-two, he joined the British army. The intelligence test he took revealed he had an IQ of 161. He was a genius! This single number alone changed his destiny. Because he started believing he was smart—as the test said—he acted in a whole different way. After training recruits in the army, he joined a timber company and became a major player in the industry. By inventing a machine for grading timber and through holding several patents, he even transformed the timber industry. Later, he was elected chairman of Mensa International, the largest and oldest high IQ society in the world.

Victor's story shows how one false assumption can have major consequences on our lives. We could even argue that if Victor had been lied to—and was in fact of average intelligence—his life would still have changed almost as dramatically.

What about you? What single assumption you currently hold prevents you from living the life you want? What are you convinced you can't do? What if you could actually do that very thing?

Tip:

A great way to shift your perspective is to identify something you believe is impossible and do it. By learning to complete apparently impossible tasks, you'll start shattering your assumptions about what is and isn't feasible and, as a result, open yourself up to a whole new world of opportunity.

What assumptions are

Your assumptions act like filters, coloring your experiences and preventing the light within you from shining. The more filters you add to your lens, the less your light shines and the narrower your field of possibility becomes. In the same way the things in your room don't cease to exist when you turn off the light—you just can't see them in the dark—your potential doesn't suddenly vanish when obstructed by your filters. Your potential has been there all the time, but your self-imposed filters made you blind to it.

Removing your filters means letting go of your assumptions. This doesn't necessarily mean you believe *everything* is possible, but rather that you don't believe or disbelieve anything. For instance, once you have removed your limiting assumptions, when you look at what extraordinary people are doing, you will be able to assume that if they can do it, you can do it as well. You will hold the space for that possibility. In short, you will allow light to penetrate your room rather than obstructing it by holding onto disempowering assumptions.

On the other hand, whenever you add filters, you artificially limit yourself. You start closing the blinds and end up making your room darker than it needs to be. In these circumstances, you believe:

- You're too old (or too young)
- You're not smart or good enough
- You don't know the right people
- You don't have the right education
- You're too shy, or
- You can't do X, Y, Z because it's not "who you are."

In addition, society keeps adding new filters to block even more light. Social pressures define what you're supposed to eat, how you should behave, what you're allowed and not allowed to do.

By the time you're seven, you already operate within a narrow band of possibilities defined by the assumptions you've already adopted unconsciously. As a result, your room is dark and will stay that way. Worse still, it might even become darker as you grow older.

Isn't it time for you to remove these filters and reclaim your power?

Are your assumptions serving you?

Your assumptions can prevent you from unlocking your potential and achieving the life you want. However, some assumptions are better than others and can actually serve you well. In this book, I'll introduce you to powerful assumptions that will greatly expand your field of possibilities and enhance what you can accomplish.

Please note, an assumption doesn't need to be true. In fact, most of your assumptions are false or, at best, only partially true. What matters most is for you to select the assumptions that empower you and allow you to live a more fulfilling life.

A key question to ask yourself is, "Is this particular assumption serving me or working against me? Is it moving me toward my ultimate vision, or is it preventing me from achieving it?" Whenever you come across an assumption that doesn't serve you, replace it with a more empowering one.

What are your specific assumptions?

The way you live your life is ultimately based on major assumptions you hold in various areas of your life. Assumptions are nothing more than ways you relate to different key concepts such as: love, time, money, work, success and emotions.

In short, your entire vision of the world is based on your relationship with concepts and the emotions you attached to them. Just one 'false' assumption—a disempowering way to relate to a key concept—can make your life challenging and create a great deal of suffering.

For example, let's look at the concept of time. Each of us attaches a certain meaning or story to time, which leads us to feel a certain way. You may think you don't have enough time or that time is money and, as a result, you become frustrated when you waste your time. Or perhaps you believe there is no such thing as wasting your time and you savor each moment. Money is another concept to which you may attach all sorts of assumptions, such as money is bad, rich people are greedy or money doesn't grow on trees. Or maybe you think money is great and you want to make as much of it as you possibly can.

The assumptions we hold for all the concepts stored in our minds determines how we think, feel and act, as well as how we perceive the world. While we tend to assume that other people see the world more or less the same way we do, that is certainly not the case. There are as many worldviews as there are people living on this planet.

In this section, we'll look at empowering assumptions about key concepts such as life in general, work, money and time. But before we delve into that, I would like you to reflect on your own relationship with these major assumptions. Bear in mind that how you currently see yourself, money, time and any other concept, is based on the assumptions you hold, and this is just one possible interpretation.

To make the most of this book, keep an open mind and be ready to challenge your deepest beliefs whenever necessary.

Take a few minutes to do the following exercise before you read further. This is the foundation for the work we'll do together throughout this book, and it will allow you to pinpoint areas in which you can adopt more empowering assumptions to make a positive difference in your life.

Exercise:

Complete the following sentences with whatever comes to your mind. Write as many answers as you like.

- Life is ...
- Success is ...
- Emotions are ...
- I am ...
- Money is ...
- Time is ...
- Work is ...

Now you have uncovered some of your assumptions, let's have a look at some major assumptions that may be limiting your success.

PART II
UNCOVERING COMMON ASSUMPTIONS

In this section, we'll investigate fifty common assumptions. We'll cover the following topics: life in general, success, money, emotions, work and time. For each assumption there will be a simple exercise. I encourage you to spend a little time to go through it.

In addition, once you finish reading about one assumption, spend a few seconds imagining how that assumption will impact your life if you adopted it.

3

ASSUMPTIONS REGARDING YOUR ASSUMPTIONS

Did you know you have assumptions about your assumptions, or, if you prefer, beliefs about your beliefs? Below are two common assumptions you may have.

Negative assumption #1—I'm convinced of something therefore it must be true

Are you convinced your religious or political beliefs are the correct ones? Guess what? Terrorists are just as convinced as you they're right—if not more so. Your level of certainty regarding your current beliefs is *not* an indicator of their validity. In fact, it's often the opposite.

To start reframing your life and replace disempowering assumptions with more empowering ones, you must realize that your emotional attachment to your current assumptions doesn't make them right.

I encourage you to start challenging your biggest assumptions—the ones that impact your life the most—before moving on to minor ones. Note that your biggest assumptions are often the ones you're the most emotionally attached to.

Here is a new assumption you can adopt instead:

My emotional attachment to a belief doesn't mean it is valid.

Exercise:

Write down your major assumptions. These are the core beliefs you're most strongly attached to. Start opening yourself up to the possibility they may not be true.

Negative assumption #2—My beliefs need to be accurate

You probably want your beliefs to be accurate. If you thought you were wrong, you would choose better ones, wouldn't you?

While striving to hold the most accurate vision possible is great, in truth there are many things you'll never be able to prove. If so, why even have beliefs in the first place?

My answer is: to help you live a better life! That's what this book is all about: adopting empowering assumptions that will allow you to live the best life possible—whether or not these assumptions are true.

For instance:

- Believing God put you on earth to accomplish a specific mission may give you a strong sense of purpose and help you live a better life.
- Believing in life after death may alleviate your fear of death and help you live a more productive, peaceful and joyful life.
- Believing you have the power to achieve any goal may help you achieve more than you otherwise would.

Therefore, rather than holding the assumption that your beliefs must be accurate, why not adopt the following assumption:

I consciously choose to adopt empowering beliefs that transform my life for the better.

Exercise:

Select two or three empowering beliefs that would make the biggest difference in your life, if you were to adopt them.

4

LIFE ASSUMPTIONS

In this section, we'll introduce general assumptions about life.

In the first part, we'll discuss the assumptions you hold about the outside world. That is, the beliefs that the world prevents you from doing what you want to do (e.g. "I'm a victim of my environment.")

In the second part, we'll talk about assumptions you hold about yourself. These are self-imposed limitations, e.g. something is wrong with me, I'm not good enough, etc.

I'm a victim of my environment

Negative assumption #3—Life is hard

Life is hard, isn't it? But what if it isn't? What if life is easy, and you're simply making it harder than it needs to be? Could this be a possibility?

Have you ever thought of the consequences of holding such a negative assumption? Do you think it helps you live a better life?

Once your mind believes something, it looks for evidence to prove it. Your mind likes to come up with answers to your questions, and it accepts your assumptions whether they are empowering you or not. Tell your mind "life is hard," and it will come up with reasons to support this assumption. Tell your mind "life is easy," and it will find evidence to support this as well.

Try it now. Ask yourself, why is life so easy?

Start shifting your assumption toward "life is easy." Whenever you find life hard, ask yourself, "How could I be making my life harder than it is? What beliefs do I hold that lead me to struggle more than I need to?"

Perhaps you believe you need something to make you happy and, because you don't have it right now, you are miserable. Maybe all your friends are successful while you see yourself as a "failure." But how do you know they are any happier than you are? What if they have severe issues you don't know about?

Here is a new assumption you can adopt:

Life is easy. And I do whatever I can to keep it this way.

Exercise:

Write down all the reasons why your life is easy. Come up with at least twenty reasons. For instance, life is easy because:

- There is food on the table every day
- I have access to water and electricity
- I have great friends I can meet regularly
- I have access to many incredible services such as the postal service or public transportation
- I have access to great information online for free or at an affordable price.

Negative assumption #4—Others are happier than me

Nowadays, the need to compare ourselves with others is everywhere. Our friends look so happy, especially on Facebook (or so we think). In addition, our email box is full of messages telling us we aren't good enough the way we are. We should make more money, lose weight or be happier.

Believing your friends are happier than you are is a dangerous assumption to hold. How can you know what's going on in their lives? People you envy could be depressed or severely ill and you wouldn't necessarily know it. Even smiles can hide pain. Sometimes a little pain, sometimes tremendous agony. So why assume others have it easier? What you do you have to gain by doing that?

Here is a more empowering assumption:

I'm as happy as anybody else.

Exercise:

Answer the question, "why am I probably as happy as anybody else?" Write down as many answers as you can think of.

Negative assumption #5—I'm the product of my environment

Do you see yourself as a victim? Do you believe you have no power to change your life? If so, you probably assume your social environment determines what you can and cannot do. What if this is not the case? What if your environment isn't the issue here? What if your environment is the product of *you* and, as you change, your environment will change also?

Sadly, most people tend to dismiss their power of creation. They perceive themselves as insignificant and powerless, failing to realize that the visible is always a manifestation of the invisible. The real power is nonphysical and is within you; it comes from your mind, not from the external world.

The truth is, your environment is largely a reflection of yourself. It tends to give you what you give yourself first. The more you respect yourself, the more people respect you. When you don't respect yourself, people are more likely to treat you as a doormat. The more you love yourself, the more you allow people to love you. The more you can keep your promise to yourself, the more others trust you.

More generally, as you change your thoughts and expand your vision, your environment will change, too. People will start behaving differently and you will meet new people that support your growth. You may be promoted at work or come across new opportunities. In short, when you become a different person, your environment reflects those changes.

Consider your thoughts as seeds that need to be watered regularly if they are to flourish. Or, if you prefer, think of them as sunrays that become exponentially more powerful with the use of a magnifying glass—your focus. When you focus on a specific thought consistently and for long enough—from a few months to a few years—you will eventually turn it into a tangible thing in this world. This is how every man-made thing was created.

If you've been in the same environment for years, unable to get out of it, ask yourself why this is the case. What needs to change in you for things to improve for you? What do you need to focus on?

I recommend you adopt the following assumption:

As I change, my environment also changes.

Exercise:

What could you do to change yourself (and change your environment)? Come up with a couple of simple things you could do to start changing your life.

Negative assumption #6—I need to be realistic

Have you ever been told to be realistic?

Everybody has a different sense of what is possible in this world. Most people operate on the assumption that most of the things they want are not realistic. Meanwhile, other people are making it happen. Your assumptions determine what you can accomplish. If you listen to everybody around you and adjust your mindset to their (small) thinking, guess what? You won't accomplish much.

If I had listened to people around me, I wouldn't have quit my job to create my own business. Even today, family members and friends tell me some of my goals are impossible. They try to limit me in many ways. They want to reduce my field of possibility, my potential, to match theirs. This often happens unconsciously. The truth is you're already underestimating what you're capable of achieving. Why limit yourself even more by allowing other people to define what you can and cannot do?

I believe your number one priority should be to surround yourself with people who lift you up and encourage you to be the best person you can possibly be. You want to be with people who see more in yourself than you do. When people demand more, you'll raise your standards to match their expectations. The two most important things you must upgrade to change your life are your own psychology—your belief system, emotional well-being, attitude etc.—and your environment. The good news is that your psychology will change almost automatically as you find yourself with the right people in the right environment.

Remember, whatever you think you can do now, you are capable of achieving more. Whatever fear you have, you can overcome it. Whatever limiting belief binds you, you can break through. And whatever you need to know, you can learn. There is no need to be "realistic" here. Be as unrealistic as you want to be!

I recommend you adopt the following assumption:

I create my own reality. What other people believe I can or cannot do is irrelevant.

Exercise:

Answer the following question: in what way are you holding back your potential due to the limitations imposed on you by others?

Negative assumption #7—If I received more, I would give more

Have you ever thought you would work harder if you were paid more? Have you ever said you would invest more in yourself if you had more money?

Now, what if you're never paid more? Are you going to do the bare minimum for the rest of your life? You can, but you'll likely be paid the same ten years from now.

Are you going to wait until you get a pay rise to hire a coach, purchase an improvement program or educate yourself in ways needed to achieve your future goals?

The idea that you'll give more of something once you receive more of it is limiting. It ties in to the belief that one day you'll be ready. One day you'll finally have enough money to invest in yourself. One day you'll finally get paid enough to give your very best. This way of thinking is backward.

Now, what if you held the assumption that by giving more, you'll receive more. By investing more in yourself, you'll receive more joy, money, confidence or all three. By doing your best at work, you'll be promoted, move on to a better job or create your own business. By helping people and giving more, you'll end up receiving more in the long term.

I encourage you to start giving more and see what happens. Consider adopting the following assumption:

By giving more, I open myself to receiving more.

Exercise:

Answer the following question: What is one thing you could give more of?

Negative assumption #8—Having (too many) problems is a problem

People often assume that problems shouldn't exist and believe they will be happy once they overcome all their challenges. However, in reality, problems are life itself. It doesn't matter how smart, handsome, wealthy and famous you become, you will still go through tough times. For instance, you may have health, relationships or money issues, or you may be shy and insecure.

Trying to escape your problems and believing that one day, once you remove all of them, you'll finally be happy is a poor strategy. Even if you could, other complications would appear.

Now, it is important to realize that problems are subjective. They arise from expectations and false assumptions, not from the way reality is. That's why you can put two people in the same situation, one will be fine, the other will seem to experience a lot of troubles.

For instance:

- If you believe you need to be married before the age of thirty and you aren't, you might perceive that as a problem.
- If you believe you need to make a certain amount of money to feel secure, when you make less, you'll constantly worry about it.
- If you believe you need to be more handsome and aren't, you'll see that as an issue.
- If you believe you should be a certain body weight and aren't, you'll probably feel bad about yourself and have self-esteem issues.

In short, many problems exist only in the human mind, and they depend on the way we interpret what happens to us. For instance, rain can be seen as a problem if you plan to go on a picnic, but it can be seen as a blessing if you are a farmer during a drought.

A great question to ask yourself when you face a problem is, "What do I need to believe to perceive this particular situation as a problem?" As you do this, you'll start realizing that your interpretation of the event causes the suffering, not the event itself. Change the way you interpret the event, and the issue will disappear —or at the very least, it will become more manageable.

As such, having too many problems is not an issue in itself. It's usually a sign that you need to look deeper at the assumptions behind each of your problems. You're probably trying too hard to fight reality. And, there is no doubt, reality wins every time.

Here is a new assumption you can adopt:

Having problems is normal. The less attached I am to my problems, the more irrelevant they become.

Another way to reframe problems or challenges is to perceive them as opportunities. I believe that within every problem lies an opportunity. A problem might offer you an opportunity to make changes in your life. For instance, it might help you learn something about yourself, allowing you to become more peaceful and happier. Or it might make you wiser. Even if you can't see any opportunity, consider these two assumptions:

With any problem comes a new opportunity

Problems are problems and must be avoided

Which one of those assumption is the more empowering? Which one will help you design your ideal life and allow you to live at peace with yourself? Again, the role of your assumptions is to empower you. Whether they are actually true or not is mostly irrelevant.

In fact, seemingly false assumptions, when believed enough, often become self-fulfilling prophecies. Think of visionaries. By setting a clear vision and committing to making it happen, these individuals create a new reality that wasn't there initially. They didn't wait to see it to believe it, they believed it and therefore ended up seeing it. For instance, Elon Musk, whose mission is to colonize Mars, believed he could create a reusable space shuttle that would take off and land. Despite all the critics and multiple setback along the way, he eventually reached this goal.

You can adopt the following assumption:

In any problem lies an opportunity.

Exercise:

Make a list of all your problems. How could you reframe them so they become less of a problem, or even have them open doors to new opportunities?

Negative assumption #9—Things "should" be a certain way

Most people hold the assumption that things should be a certain way. This happens each time you use the world "should."

- There should be no war.
- There should be no famine.
- Corruption shouldn't exist.
- People should be nice to me.
- People should keep their promises.
- I shouldn't have to do X, Y, Z.
- My friends should encourage me instead of putting me down.
- My colleagues should cooperate with me.

These things seem to make sense and would be ideal. Unfortunately, reality is what is, not what you think it should be.

People's desire to argue with reality is understandable but creates more challenges than it fixes. There is no need to argue with reality, nor is there any benefit. Whenever you argue with reality, you lose.

Whenever you refuse to see things as they are but as you want them to be, you suffer. As long as you try to deny reality, you'll struggle. Reality just *is* and can't be any other way. It's never wrong, and it's never a problem.

Consider the following examples:

I work so hard. I should be making twice as much money.

Reality: you don't.

What does believing you should make twice as much money do to your happiness and peace of mind? How does it serve you?

There should be no war.

Reality: wars are happening right now.

What does believing there should be no war do to your happiness and peace of mind? Does it even encourage you do something about it?

People should keep their promises.

Reality: most people don't.

What does such a belief do for your happiness and peace of mind? Does it help you?

Believing things should be different is as ridiculous as believing a $1 bill should be a $100 bill. A $1 bill *is* a $1 bill, and it is that way, whether you like it or not. Why? Simply because it is!

Accepting things as they are doesn't mean you need to like them. I don't like wars, but they're happening regardless. I don't want people to die from starvation, but people still do. Reality doesn't give a damn about my opinion on how things should be. It doesn't report to me.

The bottom line is this: whatever is happening is supposed to be happening. Every bit of it. Why? Because it's happening. If it shouldn't, it wouldn't.

I understand this concept may be difficult to grasp but can you see how important it is? It means you can start releasing and redirecting all the energy you're currently using trying to change the present reality.

Now, does that mean you have no power to change the world whatsoever? Absolutely not. While you have no power to change what is, you can change what *will be* through your actions.

There is a big misconception that if you accept reality as it is, you're not doing anything about it. This is false. Ironically, the opposite is true: the more you accept reality as it is, the more power you have to change it. Conversely, the more you assume things should be a certain way, the less power you have.

Thus, *the first step to changing anything in your life is to accept it as part of your reality right now*. Accept it exactly as it is. For instance, rather than thinking you should lose twenty pounds, accept that you weigh exactly what you're supposed to weigh right now. Why? Because that's what the scale indicates! Once you've accepted that reality, you can reformulate your statement as follows: I *could* lose twenty pounds. And from that place, you can start taking action to create a new reality. Again, it might seem contradictory, but you don't change reality by believing things should be different. Instead, you change reality by accepting it exactly as it is, while envisioning how things could be in the future.

Could vs. should

As we've seen, an effective way to change our thinking is by replacing the world "should" with the word "could". Below are some examples:

There *should* be no war (denial of reality). —> There *could* be no war (openness to a future possibilities).

I work so hard, I *should* be making twice as much money (denial of reality). —> I work so hard, I *could* be making twice as much money (openness to future possibilities). You could probably make twice as much money but for that, you have to design a plan to achieve that goal.

People *should* keep their promises (denial of reality). —> People *could* keep their promises (openness to future possibilities). Yes, they could. Will they? Perhaps. Maybe they would if you asked them in a different way. Or they may become reliable one day and start keeping their promises. Who knows?

My friends *should* encourage me instead of putting me down (denial of reality). —> My friends *could* encourage me instead of putting me down (openness to future possibilities). Maybe you could make it clear that you want them to support you. You could even tell them exactly how you would like them to give you their support. They may end up encouraging you—or not.

As you can see, "should" is not an empowering word. I hope by now you realize that wanting reality to be different doesn't empower you to change it. If anything, it makes you resentful, powerless or angry, and it can disturb your peace of mind. Wouldn't you feel more at peace if you accepted reality is exactly as it should be?

On the other hand, "could" creates options and possibilities. It opens you up to new actions and encourages you to make changes. When you use the word "could", you assume things are as they are now, but they may change in the future.

- Yes, people could do X, Y, Z under different circumstances—but they don't right now.
- Yes, there could be no war or famine in the future—but people are fighting wars right now.
- Yes, your friends could encourage you—but they don't right now.

I would like you to start taking notice whenever you use the word "should." Perhaps you tell yourself the story that you should work harder or that you should be smarter or better in some way. Realize this is a false assumption. You are exactly as you're supposed to be now and there is nothing wrong with that. Yes, you could work harder, become smarter or improve yourself in countless ways, and if you're determined to do so, you will.

The new assumption you can adopt is:

I fully accept what is, and I can create what will be.

Exercise:

Make a list of five things you believe should be a certainty but aren't right now. Then, replace "should" with "could". How does it make you feel?

Negative assumption #10—My past equals my future

Do you live in the past? That is, do you still carry with you the same assumptions that created your past?

Your past in no way predicts your future. It only seems that way because you keep operating with the same system (i.e., you keep holding the same assumptions). As the saying goes, if you keep doing what you've always done, you'll keep getting the same results. To change your life, you must change your assumptions, which means changing your beliefs, and changing your actions.

Let's say you're currently overweight. If I were to implant the belief system of a personal trainer in your brain, what do you think would happen? You would lose your weight quickly. It would be inevitable. If you're struggling financially and were to wake up tomorrow with the exact same mindset as a multi-millionaire, you would quickly start earning more money. This would also be inevitable. This is because, with a different set of beliefs, you cannot help but take different actions and thus obtain different results.

In the end, what you do every day—starting from today—will determine your future. Armed with your new empowering assumptions, you have the power to think, feel and act differently. As you do so, you'll be able to alter the course of your life and obtain better outcome as a result. You're largely the product of what you think every day. As the Buddha supposedly said, *"what you think, you become."* Replace old assumptions with more empowering ones, and your future will change.

Another way to look at your past is to think of it as a "sunk cost"—a cost that can't be recovered. This is a common term used in business. What if you could see your past as a sunk cost? How much lighter would you feel? This approach is what the success expert Brian Tracy calls "zero-based thinking."

To apply zero-based thinking in your life ask yourself:

"Knowing what I know now, what are some of the things I'm currently doing that I wouldn't continue?"

Below are some more specific questions:

- Knowing what I know now, would I still launch that new product? If your answer is no, you'd need to discontinue the product launch.
- Knowing what I know now, would I be in this relationship? If your answer is no, you'd need to muster up the courage to end it.
- Knowing what I know now, would I take my current job? If your answer is no, you'd need to find a new job.
- Knowing what I know now, should I stay the same? If the answer is no, you'd need to start making changes in your life.

What about you? Knowing what you know now, what are you going to start doing differently today? Knowing your current disempowering assumptions, what new assumptions will you adopt?

The bottom line is you can make changes at any time. The belief that your past determines your future is just that, a belief—and an erroneous one. Your past by no mean equals your future. You have the power to reframe your life and start anew from today. What you start doing from today will create your future. So, forget past mistakes. Instead, start thinking as the person you want to become and act that way—from today.

Your new assumption:

Every day I start anew, free of all past burdens.

Exercise:

Close your eyes and imagine you could start your day free of any burden from the past. How would it make you feel?

Something is wrong with me/I'm not good enough

Negative assumption #11—I'm not good enough

Do you feel unworthy? Do you believe something is wrong with you and nothing you can do will ever fix it?

For some reason, many people believe something is inherently wrong with them. They feel as though they are a fraud. No matter what they do or how hard they try, they always fall short. As a result, they keep seeking external validation, hoping something outside of them will finally make them "good enough."

What if this is nothing more than an erroneous assumption? When you were born, did the doctor tell your parents, "I'm sorry but your son/daughter won't be good enough."?

What does not being good enough even mean? This is probably the first question you want to answer. In the end, it's all a matter of perspective and boils down to the way you choose to interpret what happens to you. Edison "failed" thousands of times when trying to invent the light bulb. Imagine if each time he "failed" he told himself how stupid he was? Do you think he would have been able to persevere?

The truth is most successful people have failed hundreds, if not thousands of times in their lives. However, they perceive failure in a different way than most people. For them, they just tried something, and it didn't work out as planned. Unsuccessful people might add, "therefore I failed" or even worse, "therefore I'm a failure" to the statement and build a whole story around it.

Failure is never personal. Whether you fail one time, or thousands of times has nothing to do with who you are as a person. At the core, you're still the same individual. No amount of failure can ever make you a failure. The only reason you feel like a failure is because you hold false assumptions. The only real failure is not learning from your mistakes. As long as you constantly seek to learn and improve, failure does not exist. Period.

The bottom line is you don't need to do something to be good enough, and "failures" can't make you a lesser person. The only thing you need to do is to change your perspective and adopt different assumptions. Below are some empowering assumptions to adopt:

I'm good enough for now.

This presupposes that, 1) I'm good enough and, 2) I can always improve whenever is needed.

I like this one. I used to have unrealistic expectations and beat myself up each time I wasn't living up to them. Now, I just assume everything I do is good enough *for now*. I don't think my work should be better. In fact, it is exactly as it should be now. Why? Because it is how it is. Sure, it might not be as good as I would like it to be in the ideal world but, over time, I can always improve.

I'm perfect in my imperfections.

No matter what you think, you're not broken, and you don't need to be fixed. The same way failure is not something separated from success, your imperfections aren't preventing you from being perfect and whole. They are part of your perfection.

My intent is pure.

Whatever the external results, we usually have good intentions, and this alone is a wonderful reason to celebrate ourselves. I believe the size of your bank account or your status is irrelevant. Your intention is what matters most. During challenging times, I remind myself that my intentions are pure, and I acknowledge myself for that. What about you? Could you take a few seconds now to give yourself a pat on the back and acknowledge your intention to better yourself and do good in the world?

I matter.

In case nobody told you that before, you matter! With that and the pat you just give yourself on the back, you must feel wonderful now! It's okay to be proud of yourself and celebrate your life. As time passes, I've learned to celebrate my accomplishments—both small and big—because, if I don't celebrate myself and my life, in most cases, nobody else will.

In fact, for people to value you and respect you, it is important you value yourself first. If you don't set boundaries and standards in your life, people will end up disrespecting you. You matter, so celebrate every one of your accomplishments and give yourself motivational rewards each time you achieve your goals. The more you focus on your accomplishments and all the things you're doing well, the better you'll feel about yourself. And the better you feel about yourself, the more likely you are to feel good about others, too.

You also need to understand it is possible to be a high achiever and still feel as though something is wrong with you. That is very common. It shows that self-worth is not linked to what you do—although it does play a role—but to what you choose to focus on, acknowledge and celebrate.

People with a healthy self-esteem constantly focus on the things they're doing well. They celebrate their successes and shrug it off when things don't go as planned. In other words, they have a biased (but positive) way to look at their life and a selective memory. They give little importance to negative things and focus their attention on all the positive aspects of their lives.

Conversely, people who don't feel good enough, focus on all the things they're doing wrong and dwell on negative events. Even when good things happen, they dismiss them as being no big deal and, instead, focus only on the things they could have done better—because, from their perspective, they aren't good enough.

For more on how to overcome feelings of unworthiness, refer to my book, *Master Your Emotions: A Practical Guide to Overcome Negativity and Better Manage Your Feelings*.

Exercise:

Look at one area in which you tend to blame yourself for not being good enough. Now, say to yourself, "I'm good enough for now." Then, take a step back and put things in perspective. Realize how much room you have to improve and how much time you have to do so. You're good enough *for now*. You can always improve yourself in the future if needed.

Negative assumption #12—I will believe it when I see it

Many people fail to realize how much power they have to create their future. They don't understand that, by believing enough in something, they can create it. If they were to decide today how they want their future to look in five or ten years—and resolve to make it a reality—they would likely end up where they intended to be.

What if instead of thinking you'll believe it when you see it, you decide you'll see it when you believe it?

What do you want to believe hard enough to be able to see in the future?

Consider adopting the following assumption:

I believe it therefore I'll see it.

Exercise:

Think of one thing you really want to make happen in the future. Hold the space for it. Make it part of your field of possibilities. Ask yourself:

What if I could create it?

What if it is possible?

Negative assumption #13—I'm not ready yet

Have you ever postponed something because you didn't feel ready? Perhaps you believed you needed more training or the timing wasn't right.

In my experience, there is no such thing as being one hundred percent ready for anything. There will never be a "right time" to quit your job, start a business or enter a new relationship. You can always find excuses to put off things you're scared to do, and that's what most people end up doing. However, in reality, the best time is often now. As the proverb says, the best time to plant a tree was twenty years ago, the second-best time is now.

Muscles only grow when they are under pressure, and the same is true of human beings. When we move beyond our comfort zones and do something a little scary, we start growing. This doesn't happen when we're perfectly ready. When we start stepping out of our comfort zones we can grow more in one year than we normally would in ten years. In fact, there is no other way. Working hard on ourselves and facing our fears little by little is the only way we can discover our true capabilities. Remember the best time is now!

Look at some of your goals or dreams and ask yourself, "What if I could start now?" Here is the thing: you can always start right away. There is always one simple step you can take to start moving toward your goals.

Adopt the following assumption:

Because I start before I'm ready, I can achieve anything I want faster than I ever thought possible.

Exercise:

Identify one thing you haven't done (yet) because it makes you feel a little uncomfortable. Hold the space for it to happen in the near future.

Could you do it?

Will you?

Negative assumption #14—If I believe it, I can achieve it

This assumption ties in to the previous one. When you feel unprepared, you assume you don't believe enough in yourself or in your goals to achieve the results you're after. Therefore, you must do more visualization, recite more affirmations, gain more experience or get more training. In short, you must be confident of success before you can achieve your goal. Or so you think.

But what if this is pure BS? What if you don't need to believe in something to achieve it? In fact, that may be one of the biggest lies you've been told in your life. This lie could prevent you achieving everything you want in life.

This type of thinking is a cognitive distortion called "emotional reasoning", which means believing your emotions are telling the truth. In this case, because of fear and self-doubt, you assume you're not ready to raise your price, ask for a raise, ask someone out or ask for whatever else you want to receive.

Fortunately, you are *not* your emotions or your beliefs. You don't need to believe something to actually achieve it. For instance, you can ask for a raise and get it regardless of your level of confidence. Sure, the more confident you are, the better, but there is no rule that says you need to believe in something before you can receive it. As the founder of Virgin Group, Richard Branson, said, "*If somebody offers you an amazing opportunity but you are not sure you can do it, say yes—then learn how to do it later!*"

The bottom line is you can ask for things you want even if you don't believe you can receive them. You'll be surprised by what you can receive and achieve by doing so. Remember, it's normal to feel nervous when you try something new. This doesn't mean you should study more or wait until you have an unshakable belief in yourself before doing it. If anything, by doing it, you'll gain confidence in yourself. Confidence is built through action.

Here is a new assumption I encourage you to adopt:

I go after what I want, regardless of how confident I feel.

Here's a bonus assumption:

Action cures fear.

Exercise:

Think of one thing you believe is impossible. It could be something you want to ask for or something you want to do. Could you challenge yourself to do it? Will you?

Negative assumption #15—It's just who I am

"I'm shy, it is just who I am."

"I'm stupid, it is just who I am."

How often have you used such statements in the past? Have you noticed that you rarely use either expression to express positive sides of your personality? You seldom say:

- "I'm awesome, it is just who am."
- "I'm smart, it is just who I am."
- "I'm kind and generous, it is just who I am."

"It's just who I am" is more than an assumption you hold. It's a convenient excuse you use to avoid making changes. It's another way you narrow down your field of possibilities. If you believe shyness is part of your identity, how likely are you to overcome it? If you perceive yourself as being stupid, what are the chances you'll keep persevering and learn from your mistakes?

Your self-perception influences your decisions and ultimately creates your own reality but, often, this self-perception is nothing more than a story you use to avoid making painful changes in your life.

I'd like to suggest a better assumption:

I'm the scriptwriter of my life and can rewrite any story I wish.

Exercise:

What disempowering story have you been telling yourself for years? What if the opposite is true? Come up with twenty reasons why this story may not be true.

Negative assumption #16—I lack motivation/I'm lazy

People often struggle with motivation. They see themselves as lazy and beat themselves up as a result. But is it true? Are they lazy? I don't believe in laziness. While it is true some people are less motivated than others, people who struggle with motivation usually lack a *motive for action*. They lack a larger purpose behind what they do. If you look at people who are passionate, they seldom lack motivation. They are naturally motivated and pulled toward their vision. This is because they have a *motive for action*.

If you lack motivation it may be because you're doing the wrong things or you're doing them for the wrong reasons (e.g., reasons that don't inspire you). Therefore, the first step to motivate yourself is to find out the "why" behind your goal. Why are you pursuing a particular goal? What values do you attach to it and what benefit will you receive from achieving it?

For instance:

If you want to lose weight, why does that matter? Why is that new identity of "being a fit, slim and healthy person" important to you?

If you lack motivation at your current job, ask yourself why is this job important? What is your bigger vision behind it? If you don't enjoy your job, what could you do to feel more motivated?

- Could you change the way you do things?
- Could you work on different projects?
- Could you see your current job as a stepping stone toward your dream career? If so, how?

The second step is to start taking small actions consistently every day. The more progress you make, the more confident and disciplined you become.

Here is a new assumption you can adopt:

I'm motivated because I have a motive for action.

To learn how to find what you love and make a living out of it, refer to my book, *The Passion Manifesto: Escape the Rat Race, Uncover Your Passion and Design a Career and Life You Love*.

Exercise:

Look at one area of your life in which you lack motivation. Now, try to identify why that's the case. Is it because you have no interest? Is it because it isn't aligned with your deepest values?

Negative assumption #17—Self-discipline sucks

Do you hate self-discipline? Do you want to live your life on your own terms without having to follow a rigid schedule?

Have you ever examined what a lack of self-discipline costs you? Do you realize that with enough self-discipline you could achieve almost anything you want in life?

Often, people crave more freedom and perceive self-discipline as something that robs them of their freedom. But is that so? How much freedom do you have if you can't discipline yourself to do what you need do to create the life you want? Is being overweight because you lack the self-discipline to eat healthily a sign of great personal freedom? Is procrastinating on important tasks what you would call freedom? And I'm not even talking about the emotional cost of a lack of self-discipline, which often includes low self-esteem, lack of motivation and the absence of a clear purpose in life.

If you have little control over your body, your mind and your emotional state, can you really be free? I believe freedom is the ability to have absolute control over our mind, body and emotional state, and this all starts with self-discipline.

As the motivational speaker Les Brown said, "*Do what is easy and your life will be hard. Do what is hard and your life becomes easy.*"

When you can discipline yourself to do what is necessary when you need to do it—whether you feel like it or not—you'll experience freedom and will achieve incredible things. As a result, your life will become easier.

You can adopt the following assumptions:

Self-discipline equals freedom. With enough self-discipline, I can achieve anything I want.

For more on how to develop self-discipline, refer to my book, *Upgrade Yourself: Simple Strategies to Transform Your Mindset, Improve Your Habits, and Change Your Life.*

Exercise:

Imagine if you could do all the things you know you should be doing. How would you feel? What difference would it make to your life? What single habit could help you build self-discipline?

To help you implement a powerful morning ritual you'll keep for many years, feel free to refer to my book, *Wake Up Call: How to Take Control of Your Morning and Transform Your Life.*

Negative assumption #18—It's selfish to focus on myself

Do you believe focusing on yourself is selfish? What if the opposite is actually true?

If you've taken an airplane before, you've probably listened to the procedure to follow in case of an emergency. Do you remember what you're supposed to do to ensure the safety of your children in a case of an emergency? You're supposed to take care of yourself first by putting on your oxygen mask. Then, and only then, can you take care of your children and ensure their safety. The same can be said for life in general.

If you don't focus on yourself, learn more about yourself and cater to your own needs, how can you support other people and bring out the best in them? Jim Rohn, the motivational speaker said, *"I'll take care of me for you, if you will please take care of you for me."* What a wonderful statement. How can you take care of other people if you don't take care of yourself first?

- Do you make other people suffer because of your inability to deal with negative emotions?
- Does your lack of self-understanding prevent you from being your best?
- Does your poor health and lack of energy negatively impact your family?

Imagine how much better off your family and friends would be if you were happy, healthy, energetic and living your life on purpose? In fact, one of the best gifts you can give people you love is your personal development.

As you focus on becoming a better person, everybody around you will benefit. Thus, focusing on yourself is not selfish. If anything, it is selfless. What if you replace the assumption, *I'll take care of you* with, *I'll take care of me for you*? What difference would this make to your life and to your family, friends or colleagues' lives?

You can adopt the following assumption:

I take care of me for *my family and friends.*

Exercise:

Identify one quality that, if you were to develop it, would have a positive impact on people around you. It could be keeping better control over your anger, keeping your promises, becoming a better listener, stopping criticizing people, etc.

Negative assumption #19—I'm too old

I wish I received a $100 bill each time someone told me they're too old to learn a foreign language, travel, change their career or learn whatever it is they want to learn. I hate when people tell me they're too old to do something. Why? Because it is usually not true.

The assumption "I'm too old" is a defense mechanism people use to avoid facing the truth. In fact, what most people really mean when they say, "I'm too old," is one or several of the following things:

- I don't believe in myself (anymore).
- I'd rather buy into the story I'm too old than to admit I just gave up on myself.
- I'm not willing to put a lot of effort into something that may not work out.
- I'm actually not that interested in doing the thing I say I want to do. I just pretend I am to strengthen my victim mentality and keep feeling sorry for myself.

In short, "I'm too old" is another story you're telling yourself. I understand you may be too old to become an NBA player or an Olympic athlete, but you're not too old to achieve most of your goals and dreams. The issue here is a lack of commitment. Do you really want it? If so, what price are you willing to pay?

If you don't want to pay the price, that's fine—but don't moan about it. Your time and resources are limited, and you must use them wisely. Just be honest with yourself.

You can adopt the following assumption:

I'm never too old to do what I want to do.

Exercise:

Have you ever told yourself you're too old to pursue your goals? If so, identify one goal you talked yourself out of because you considered yourself too old. Go to your favorite search engine and search for "old" people who have accomplished that same goal. For instance, search "oldest people" + your goal.

Negative assumption #20—Telling the truth hurts people and should be avoided

Are you afraid to tell the truth because it could hurt or upset people? Now, is the fear of hurting people the real problem here? Often, it isn't. In fact, not telling the truth is often what ends up hurting people the most.

The main reasons we don't tell the truth is not to avoid hurting people, but:

- to avoid facing rejection, and
- because it's uncomfortable for us.

In short, lying or omitting the truth is an easy way out. Now, you might think, "okay, I admit, I don't always tell the truth, but it's not a big deal, right?" Wrong. Very wrong.

I would argue that not telling the truth is an act of selfishness disguised as an act of courtesy. When you refuse to tell the truth and fail to give people honest feedback, you rob them of a valuable opportunity to grow and correct erroneous behaviors they may not even be aware of. You don't provide them with the external perspective they need to improve.

But that's not all. Not being honest with people also prevents you from building more meaningful relationships. Sadly, most of our relationships are superficial. The typical relationship goes as follows: I rub your back, you rub my back, and everybody is happy. That's great because nobody needs to:

- Be vulnerable
- Uncover deeply rooted fears and work on overcoming them
- Take the risk of offending the other person, or

- Be disapproved of or even rejected.

Telling the truth is necessary to grow and overcome your problems. Most people pretend everything is okay when they know deep down it isn't. By failing to tell the truth, they build resentment and are unable to have healthy relationships. In romantic relationships, we're often scared to say what we really think. By shutting ourselves off and failing to share how we feel, we build resentment which, over time, can negatively impact the relationship and may even destroy it. Doing this, we selfishly rob the other person—who is often unaware of the situation—of the opportunity to change his or her behavior. We may also interpret things incorrectly, not even realizing our partner has good intentions. It might just be a misunderstanding. Unless we share our feelings and concerns, we can't clear the misunderstanding, which may fester over time.

To me, there is nothing more annoying than not being told the truth. I want to improve whenever I can. If I'm not told the truth, if I'm unaware of my shortcomings, changing them is difficult, if not impossible. Even if the truth can be painful, it always serves well me long term. Think about it. If you've been doing something wrong, would you prefer someone telling you right away or learning it years later?

The bottom line is, omitting the truth is often not about protecting other people's feelings; it's about avoiding making ourselves vulnerable and/or avoiding being rejected. We don't omit the truth in the interest of the other person, but in our own selfish interest.

When we tell the truth, we put other's interests before ours, which requires tremendous courage and concern for the other person. Yes, telling the truth and hearing it can be scary, but it can also be extremely powerful. Telling the truth creates meaningful relationships, develops trust and gives others the opportunity to grow and improve so they can reach their full potential.

Also, the beauty of truth is that it destroys everything we are not, such as our delusions and limiting beliefs—sometimes via a painful process—and reveals to us what we really are.

You can adopt the following assumption:

I help others and myself grow by telling the truth whenever possible.

Exercise:

Answer the following question: If you could tell only one truth you haven't told before, who would be the person you would tell it to and what would that be?

5

ASSUMPTIONS ABOUT SUCCESS

Do you want to be successful? Do you want to design a life you don't need to escape from? Unfortunately, you may have many assumptions that prevent you from attaining the level of success you want. In this section, we'll look at some of the most disempowering assumptions about success and see how you can shift your perspective and adopt more empowering ones.

Let's get started.

Negative assumption #21—Success is possible

Do you believe that success is possible? If so, you're more likely to succeed than people who believe success is out of reach. However, what if this assumption is actually limiting you? Is it possible to replace it with a more empowering one?

After reading over a hundred books on personal development, I came to the initial conclusion that success is highly predictable and luck only plays a small part. While we may fail repeatedly in the short term, as long as we keep moving toward our goals, learning from our mistakes and making the necessary adjustments along the journey, we're "very likely" to achieve our long-term goals. "Success is very likely" is how I felt until I came across Christian Mickelsen, a coach who says the following:

 I really believe that results are inevitable if people are willing to do the work. If you keep taking action and you keep working on your inner game stuff and you never give up, you will achieve your results. It's just a matter of time.

Immediately, I thought, *"What a great assumption!"*

What if you replace the assumption, "success is very likely" with, "success is inevitable?" How do you think it would impact your level of confidence and the actions you take? What if by working hard on your goal—and most importantly working hard on yourself—success was just a matter of time? After all, you can always learn from your failures and improve as a result. You can always adapt your strategy and make adjustments as you proceed. And what prevents you from receiving help from people who have already achieved your goals?

As Tony Robbins says, *"Resourcefulness is the ultimate resource,"* and with enough passion, motivation, determination, love, creativity and desire to contribute, you can attract all the resources you need to help you achieve your goal. You have another great assumption here.

Perhaps you feel this is far-fetched. Now, the question is, would adopting such an assumption increase the chances of achieving your goals? If so, would you rather believe that success is possible or inevitable?

Here is the assumption you can adopt:

With perseverance, success is inevitable.

Exercise:

Look at your biggest goal or dream. Now, imagine you were absolutely convinced success was inevitable. How would this make you feel? What action(s) would you take? Spend a couple of minutes playing that scenario in your mind.

Negative assumption #22—Success is having more

A widely spread definition of success is having more material things, such as a bigger house, a better car, more expensive clothes. While all these things are nice, it's a very limited view of success.

Success is not about what you have, it's about who you become.

Striving to become more by removing your fears and limitations so you can express the essence of who you are in all its magnificence is a better definition of success, isn't it?

What if you could become fearless, remove self-doubt and procrastination and help more people than you could ever imagine? What if you could feel great about yourself every day? What would this mindset do for you? Perhaps success is not even about becoming anything, but more about removing what you are *not*, to let who you *are* shine through.

This is why having stretching goals that inspire you is so invaluable. To achieve difficult goals, you need to become a better person.

You can adopt the following assumption:

Success is not about what I have, it's about who I become.

Exercise:

Look at the bigger vision you have for yourself. Now, write down all the qualities and skills the future you would embody.

Negative assumption #23—Success is an outcome

If you believe that success is an outcome, you'll constantly chase it and will never catch it. You'll be seeking more but failing to appreciate all the things you already have.

Success is not an outcome. There is no end to it. Success is who you are every day. It's a way of being. It is a constant work in progress. If you do your best every day and implement solid habits that move you closer to your ideal life, you're already successful. As the motivational speaker, Earl Nightingale, said, *"Success is the progressive realization of a worthy goal or ideal."* Please note, he didn't say success is the achievement of your goal, but he said it is the progressive realization of the goal.

I suggest you adopt the following assumption:

I'm moving toward my goal, therefore I'm successful.

Exercise:

Based on your current goals, write down your ideal successful day—what you would need to do to feel like a success every day. Select a few simple habits that move you toward this goal. Start with tiny daily goals and achieve them for thirty days. This will help you build more confidence and increase your self-esteem.

Negative assumption #24—Failure is the opposite of success

What if you fail? Most people are afraid of trying something new in case they fail. They identify with their past failure and declare, *"I am a failure."* But what really happens when you fail? *You tried something, and it didn't work out as expected.* That's it. Is that such a terrible thing?

You've probably been taught there is success on one side and failure on the other. This couldn't be further from the truth. In reality, success and failure work hand in hand. Success is a process and this process includes so-called failures. You don't succeed by avoiding failure, you actually "fail your way to success." This is the only way to succeed. Therefore, failure is nothing more than *a built-in feedback mechanism that is part of the process leading to success.* Failing is merely receiving feedback that what you're trying to do doesn't work and you need to change something. That's all there is to it. Anything else is a story in your mind. If you can change the way you perceive failure, you can achieve almost anything you want.

Unsurprisingly, successful people have a different relationship with failure. They don't seek to avoid mistakes. On the contrary, they expect to fail many times before reaching their goals. If anything, they try to fail more and earlier, when making mistakes isn't as costly. As a result, by the time they achieve their goals, they have probably "failed" hundreds of times more than the average person. Their secret? They don't label their setbacks as "failures" but as stepping stones towards their goals.

I kept falling short of my goals again and again for several years, but I've avoided focusing my attention on those so-called "failures." Instead, I focused on improving my skills while sticking to my vision. I did what I had to do every day to get where I wanted to be. During this journey, I (not so) happily failed my way to success.

The bottom line is that failure and success are two sides of the same coin. You can't have one without the other, and neither of them is good or bad.

Whenever you "fail" say to yourself:

- I just tried something, and it didn't work out as planned. Next!
- I just tried something, and it didn't work out as planned. Let me learn from it and try again.

Here is a new assumption for you:

I happily fail my way to success. I fail faster and better each time.

Exercise:

Clear your mind and connect with your deepest sense of self. Now, realize that none of the "failures" from your past have ever done anything to you. And no failure will ever. This is a very powerful realization.

Negative assumption #25—I'm either a success or a failure

Often people adopt a black and white vision of things. They set a goal and when they don't reach it, they declare themselves a failure. Perhaps they wanted to lose twenty pounds but only lose five. Or they only make one quarter of the amount of money they wanted to generate with their side business. In reality, anyone who makes progress can't be a failure. A better reaction would be to celebrate their success and look back at how far they've already gone. The truth is you can't always achieve every goal as fast as you would like to. That's why it is so important to focus on the process—what you do every day—and be less attached to the outcome, especially if you don't have one hundred percent control over it.

Adopt the following assumption:

I'm successful because I'm making progress toward my goal.

Exercise:

Select one goal you have failed to achieve. It can be a current goal or a past goal. Focus on what you did well. What progress did you make? What did you learn? What could you acknowledge about yourself? Was your intent pure?

Negative assumption #26 - I need to be lucky to be successful

Do you play the lottery hoping to become rich one day? That's extremely unlikely. Not because the odds are against you (they are) but because you believe in luck to begin with.

In fact, I believe self-made millionaires (before becoming wealthy) are significantly less likely to play the lottery than the overall population. Why? Because to get where they are, they had to ignore luck. Ironically, people who choose to play the lottery, because they tend to see success as an "event," have almost no chance of ever becoming rich (except by the exceedingly rare possibility of winning the lottery).

Success is not an "event," it's a process. You don't become wealthy, create an amazing relationship or lose weight by purchasing a $49.99 program online. Otherwise, everybody would have everything they ever wanted. Anything of value takes time and effort. It is the result of a specific process that must be followed diligently over an extensive period of time. (I know. Nothing very sexy here).

Unfortunately, most people have adopted what I call a "lottery mentality." They constantly look for the magic pill that will allow them to achieve results instantly and effortlessly. Let me tell you a secret: *There is no such pill!*

In reality, you don't get what you want by believing in luck and hoping for the best. You must provoke luck by carefully planning what you want and keep pushing until you "get lucky."

To sum up, luck is not an effective strategy on which you can design your life. Don't rely on it. Instead, focus on the process—what you do every day. The process is what allows you to grow and become the person you need to become in order to achieve your goals. Remember, success is not what you have, it is who you become. It's not an event, it's a process.

Here is an empowering assumption to adopt:

I choose to create my own success, regardless of external circumstances.

To learn in more detail how to achieve your most challenging goals, refer to my book, *The One Goal: Master the Art of Goal Setting, Win Your Inner Battles, and Achieve Exceptional Results.*

Exercise:

Imagine there is no such thing as luck and you are guaranteed to achieve anything you want. What would you do?

Negative assumption #27—I'm not there yet

Have you ever felt frustrated knowing you could do so much more? Does this mean you're not there yet? Do you have to beat yourself up every day for not being good enough? What if you change the assumption, "*I'm not there yet*" to, "*I'm already there.*"? Is it possible you've already reached your destination and everything else you'll accomplish is icing on the cake?

You can choose to see success as a journey to be enjoyed. Thus, by taking the first step toward your most important goals, you're already successful. People often say they "made it," but nobody really does. You can't make it and just relax for the rest of your life. Because life is always changing, the only way to feel happy and successful is to keep moving. For instance:

- You don't stop meditating one day because you realize you've done enough of it.
- You can't stop exercising one day and expect to keep the same body and energy levels forever.
- You can't maintain a healthy body by dumping your healthy diet and eating junk food every day.
- You can't stop making an effort in your relationships just because you're now married to the perfect wife/husband.
- You can't stop innovating and improving your services/products and processes just because your business is successful now.

The point is, success is an ongoing process. It's something you do every day, not something you'll reach in five or ten years. How would you feel if you adopted the assumption that by doing your best today to build a better tomorrow, you're already successful?

To be honest, for many months (if not years), I've been frustrated because I "failed" to obtain the results I wanted with my business. While not making enough money has been part of it, the most frustrating aspect was not being able to reach out to more people. As a result, I felt jealous of other peoples' success, believing I deserved it as well. I was angry at myself for not being good enough. However, over time, I made peace with it—at least to a certain extent. To do so, I started questioning my assumptions about success. I realized that perhaps all I had to do was enjoy the journey. Was it possible that I was already successful by doing my best each day?

Your new assumption:

I'm already there, and I'm more than enough for now.

Exercise:

What if you've already arrived? Imagine there was nowhere else to go, nothing more to do to make you happy and complete. You could just release all the tension for one moment. How would it make you feel?

Negative assumption #28—I need to achieve big things to feel like I'm a success

Do you want to make a huge impact on the world and leave a legacy? What if you fail to achieve even ten percent of this goal? Will you spend your entire life feeling as though you aren't good enough?

Many high achievers spend their lives trying to prove to themselves and to the world they are good enough. They fail to appreciate all the things they've already accomplished, focusing only on what they need to accomplish in the future. What if I told you that you don't need to achieve big things to feel like a success?

Let me ask you one question: Would you sell your eyes for one billion dollars? What about your legs? What does that say about the intrinsic value of a human being's life?

What if you change your assumption. Consider the following more powerful assumption:

If I can change the life of one person, even in a minor way, I'm a huge success

Think about it. If all you did in your entire life was to help just one person make some changes in his or her life, couldn't you see yourself as successful?

As I mentioned previously, I used to be frustrated by not being in a position to help as many people as I wanted to. Then, when some of my readers told me I'd made a difference in their lives, I realized I had already become a big success. What more could I ask for?

Another key assumption I hold is:

Having good intentions makes me a massive success.

Too often, we can be frustrated by our lack of results. But what if the key is not the results we obtain, but the intention behind our actions? Unfortunately, we don't have full control over the results we seek, but we can always choose our intentions. Why not see ourselves as a massive success for having noble intentions? After all, aren't we trying to do the best we can at our own level?

What about you? What makes you a big success? Who did you help? Perhaps you helped a family member when they were in trouble. Or maybe you coached someone and made a difference in his or her life. Or perhaps you're doing your best to educate your children. Take some time to acknowledge your accomplishments and accept the positive impact you're having on other people.

You can adopt the assumptions below:

By changing some people's lives, even in a minor way, I'm a huge success.

I have good intentions, therefore I'm a massive success.

Exercise:

Who did you help? Make a list of the people you helped in your life. Now, allow yourself to feel good for having helped these people. How does this make you feel? Aren't you already successful?

Negative assumption #29—I don't have enough

We live in a society where we never seem to have enough. While we enjoy more luxury than kings and queens did a couple of centuries ago, we behave as though we live in scarcity. This is simply not the case. We just lack perspective.

The United Nations Food and Agriculture Organization estimates that about 795 million people were suffering from chronic undernourishment in 2014-2016. Thats' one in nine! According to a 2005 United Nations report, across the world, 1.6 billion people are inadequately housed an 100 million are completely homeless.

In this regard, your current situation is probably not as bad as you think. What if you substitute your current assumption, "I don't have enough," for the formula, "Food + shelter = happiness + success." How much happier would this make you? The bottom line is you don't need to have more to be happier, you simply need to realize how much you already have.

Your new assumption:

Food + shelter = happiness + success.

Exercise:

Visualize all the things you ate today. Then, visualize some of your favorite dishes. Realize how blessed you are to have access to such a variety of dishes. Now, visualize yourself in the comfort of your bed. If that helps, remember a time when you felt so tired you couldn't wait to go to bed. Remember a rainy day or a cold day when all you wanted was to be warm at home. If you wish, you can do this exercise every day in the morning and/or in the evening.

Negative assumption #30—You can't have it all

We often say either something is too good to be true or that we can't have it all. It has to be either or. But is that true? Again, if you assume you can't have it all, how likely are you to do what it takes to attain it? For instance, perhaps you believe you can't both have a job you love and make good money. Or maybe you think you can't have both a successful career and free time to spend with your family. It has to be one or the other. Now, what if you could have a great job *and* make money; have a successful career *and* a lot of free time?

A great question to ask yourself is, "How can I get both? How can I have this *and* that?" Just by changing your assumption, you'll think differently and take actions that will help you achieve better results.

Your new assumption is therefore:

I can have it all.

Exercise:

Visualize what it would look like if you had it all (whatever that means to you). Keep that vision as a possible future. Hold the space for it in your mind.

Negative assumption #31 - I can't ask for what I want

You likely hold the assumption that you shouldn't ask for what you want. After all, when you were a kid, you wanted all kind of things but were told again and again:

"No, don't do this."

"Don't do that."

"You can't have this."

"Put that down."

As a result, by the time you reached your teenage years, you'd internalized the message that it's not okay to ask for what you want. Test it yourself. Do you ever ask for what you want right now in your life? Do you tell your spouse, your kids, your colleagues or your friends what you want?

By failing to ask, you limit your potential. What would happen if you took the risk to feel uncomfortable and started asking for what you want? What difference would it make to your intimate relationships, to your career, and to your friendships? Because I'm not (that) afraid to do so, I'm asking you to reclaim your asking power. Start asking for what you want, whether it is borrowing someone else's pen or getting a raise. Remember, when you don't ask the answer is always no.

When you fail to ask, you tell your subconscious you don't really matter and that your preferences and desires are unimportant. As you do so, you make yourself smaller and smaller, which erodes your self-esteem. Asking for what you want is a healthy sign you respect and value yourself. It demonstrates that you hold your space in this world, and you are not afraid to assert yourself. Below are some examples of simple things you can ask:

- Are you cold? Ask if you can raise the room temperature.
- Do you want to change seat in the bus/airplane/train? Ask the staff.
- Loved the dessert? Ask for more.
- Are you looking for a specific item in a store? Ask an employee where you can find it.
- Have a question? Ask!

These small requests may seem unimportant, but they aren't. If you're unable to ask for the simplest things, how will you muster the courage to ask for bigger things that genuinely matter to you? Remember, each time you fail to assert yourself, your self-esteem suffers.

Once you're accustomed to asking for small things, I encourage you to go one step further and ask for more than you believe you can receive. As you do so, you'll realize how much you've been limiting yourself by not daring to ask. Remember, you're not constraining anyone, you're merely asking. It could look like this:

Would you mind if ...

Do you think I could ...

I wanted to know if I could ...

I was wondering whether ...

May I have ...

Asking is a way to open yourself up to new opportunities. It allows you to expand rather than shrink yourself and, as such, it can be perceived as an act of self-respect and self-love.

Here is a new assumption you can adopt:

I allow myself to ask for what I want.

I talk in greater detail about the importance of asking and how you can overcome your fears of asking in my book, *The Passion Manifesto: Escape the Rat Race, Uncover Your Passion and Design a Career and Life You Love.*

Exercise:

Write down the top three things you wanted to ask but didn't. Ask yourself, what if I could ask these things?

Negative assumption #32—I already know that

Together with, "I can't," these four words form one of the most dangerous phrases in the English language. Have you ever been around people who seem to know everything, yet they fail to obtain any tangible results in "real" life? They read all the books on how to create more wealth but are still broke. They know all the theory on how to approach the opposite sex, but never actually do it. They've been to dozens of self-help seminars and read hundreds of books but are still in the same place they were before. They are the ones telling you, "I already know that," while they don't act on their so-called knowledge. They just think they do.

The truth is, most of the things you think you know, you don't. They're merely concepts; you haven't actually put them into practice or made them part of your identity. You can only master something by repeating it enough times to make it ingrained and easy. Only then can you say you know it.

Do you watch videos on how to become a better public speaker but have yet to try any public speaking? Do you believe you know everything about marketing because you went to business school, but haven't actually done any marketing? Then, you don't have real knowledge about these things.

When you believe you already know something, you close yourself off to change and miss opportunities for growth. You dismiss things you read or hear about since "there's nothing new here," and you keep looking for the magic pill that will give you results with minimum effort. However, in reality, you seldom need more knowledge—you already know what to do—you just need to embody what you know intellectually.

In effect, you need to apply what you learn.

Here is a more empowering assumption to adopt:

If I don't live it, I don't know it.

Exercise:

Write down ten things you believe you know but actually don't, (i.e., things you know intellectually but haven't actually applied in your life). The easiest way to do this is to look at results you're after but haven't been able to produce (yet).

Negative assumption #33—I've reached a plateau and can't improve anymore

While you may believe you can't improve at your job anymore or can't further develop any of your current skills, this is seldom, if ever, the case. Hitting a plateau is natural, but you have to remember you can always improve. There is no limit to what you can learn. Through constant self-reflection, repeated effort and continuous learning, you can improve on anything and thereby attain what you want in life. Having an average IQ cannot prevent you from becoming great at what you do. In fact, someone of average intelligence but who is curious, passionate and persistent will, in many cases, outperform a genius in the long term.

Your brain is malleable. You can rewire it and use it to learn anything you want. By using the power of repetition, you can internalize movements, tasks and ways of thinking. Repetition allows you to transfer your learning to your subconscious, making you feel almost as though you have superpowers—and you do. Take driving, for instance. The first time you took the wheel you were likely scared, unsure you would ever be able to drive. Years later, it has become effortless. You can now drive while talking to your friends or listening to music. The same process works for anything else you want to learn. Have you ever wondered why world-class athletes are so obsessed with nailing the fundamentals? This is because they must be able to execute key movements perfectly even under intense pressure. To do so, they must master the fundamentals until it becomes second nature. This is why you'll see world-class performers practicing the same movements over and over again. Basketball players repeat the same shots thousands of times. Tennis players practice their serve for hours. Golfers rehearse their swings over and over.

The bottom line is if you reached a plateau, it means you probably haven't fully integrated the concept of self-reflection, constant improvement and repetition. To progress at anything, you must isolate the key skills and tasks needed to improve your performance and master them by designing specific exercises you can practice consistently. Remember, to become exceptional at what you do, repetition is key. As Bruce Lee said, "*I fear not the man who has practiced ten thousand kicks once, but I fear the man who has practiced one kick ten thousand times.*"

What separates successful people from unsuccessful ones more than anything else is repetition, not IQ.

To learn more, you can refer to the chapters on skills in my books:

Upgrade Yourself: Simple Strategies to Transform Your Mindset, Improve Your Habits and Change Your Life, and

The One Goal: Master the Art of Goal Setting, Win Your Inner Battles and Achieve Exceptional Results.

You can adopt the following assumption:

Everything is learnable, and I can always improve.

Exercise:

Identify an area in which you feel stuck or fail to get the results you want. Ask yourself, what can I do to get unstuck?

6

ASSUMPTIONS ABOUT MONEY

Money is an important topic, and it is essential we spend some time uncovering your assumptions about it. In this section, I'll share with you disempowering assumptions commonly held and help you adopt more empowering ones that will allow you to think of money in a whole different way.

Negative assumption #34—Money is not important

A common assumption is that money is not important. Now, if you hold such an assumption, what are your chances of generating enough money to live in abundance? I would say zero or close to it.

Every time you hear someone saying that money is not important, you can be pretty sure they are broke or at least far from being what you would call wealthy.

Here's the truth people don't want to admit: *money is important.* Otherwise, why would most people trade forty-odd years of their lives to work at a job they hate? Isn't it so that they can pay their rent, put food on the table and send their kids to college? Now, if you had enough money to never have to work again, would you still be working at your current job? If not, I'm afraid money *is* important to you.

It is likely you also spend a lot of time thinking (or worrying) about money, as many people do. If so, saying money is not important is clearly BS. That's like being angry at someone and pretending everything is okay. You may try to convince yourself you don't care but, if in the back of your mind you can't stop thinking about someone or something, you probably do care.

Another way to assess whether money is important to you is by asking yourself, "Would I change my life drastically as a result of having more money in my bank account?" If so, whether you admit it or not, money is important to you.

To design a future where you go to work because you *want* to, not because you *have* to, it is critical you reassess your relationship with money. No, money is not everything. There are many things more valuable, such as time, friendship, love or health. However, accepting money is important is by no means dismissing the value of all these other things. As we discussed previously, it doesn't have to be either one or the other. You can have both. The truth is money can be a powerful enabler and, when used properly, it can do wonderful things.

There is one main reason I believe money is important: money buys time. And time, because of its scarcity, is more valuable than money. This is where most people get it wrong. They treat money as if it were scarce, and they waste their time as though time were abundant. Some surveys show that American adults watch TV five hour per day. If we extrapolate these results, it means people spend on average sixteen years of their lives watching TV. While I do enjoy watching TV from time to time, I'm not willing to waste a quarter of my life sitting on a couch mindlessly watching TV shows. I'd rather spend my life mindfully sitting in front of a screen—my computer—and do something more meaningful (hopefully).

The point is you don't create wealth by treating your time as a commodity. You create wealth by valuing your time more than anything else. If Bill Gates schedules appointments in six-minute increments, there must be a reason for that. Remember, you can double or triple your income, but you cannot double or triple your lifespan.

As a side effect of having more money and/or time, you also have the freedom to do whatever you want to do, whether it is spending time with your family, traveling around the world or doing charity work.

You can adopt the following assumption:

Money is important.

Exercise:

Answer the following questions with brutal honesty:

- If you had enough money to never have to work again, would you still be working at your current job?
- Do you often think about money? (Worrying, fantasizing about making more money etc.) What does this say about your relationship with money?
- Would you change your life drastically as a result of having more money in your bank account? If so, how?

Now, based on your answers, how important is money to you?

Negative assumption #35—Money is the root of all evil

Another common assumption is that money is the root of all evil. The truth is money is simply a tool—a means of exchange. In itself, money is neutral. It is neither bad nor good. When used wisely, it can do great things, when used poorly, it can do harm.

I suspect the reason money may seem like the root of evil, is because it tends to amplify who you already are. If you're generous it can make you more generous, if you're greedy, it can make you even greedier. In short, money gives you more room to express yourself. Thus, rather than seeing money as the root of evil, I encourage you to see it as a method for expressing yourself—in a positive way.

While many people see wealth as anti-religious or anti-spiritual, I've started seeing money as a spiritual thing. First, as Lynne Twist explains in her book, *The Soul of Money*, money can be used as a tool to express yourself. Second, the simple fact of giving yourself permission to accumulate wealth—or give it away—can be seen as a spiritual practice in itself. It requires that you conduct real inner work to remove any limiting beliefs and feeling of unworthiness or scarcity you may currently have. Sadly, many people—especially spiritual people—are afraid to charge for their work because of their beliefs about money. In addition to money being anti-spiritual, some common beliefs include:

- I want to charge more but I don't feel worthy of it.
- I feel as though I'm ripping people off.
- I'm afraid my clients can't afford to pay me that price.

The first thing you need to understand is that it's not your job to decide whether you're worthy of charging a certain price for your products or services. Charge what you think your products or services are worth and let your clients decide. The second thing to understand is that if you don't value yourself and respect yourself, your clients won't either, and you won't be able to make the amount of money you need to survive and thrive. Often, not charging enough can reduce the perceived value of your products and be detrimental to your clients or customers in other ways. Firstly, if they buy another, inferior product or service just because it's more expensive. Secondly, if they buy your product or service but don't use it as effectively because of its perceived low value (cheaper price).

Your ability to receive payment for what you're worth—and hence, your ability to earn more money—is also connected to *your* level of self-esteem. Choosing to create more abundance in your life forces you to face your inner demons and overcome some of your fears and insecurities.

In fact, you may hold many other assumptions about money. Perhaps you believe you shouldn't make more money than your parents. Or you may be afraid your family or friends will reject you if you become rich. You may also assume that making more money means you're stealing other people's wealth. And this is just the tip of the iceberg in terms of the money-related assumptions you may hold.

Part of your personal development journey is to remove all these assumptions and replace them with more empowering ones. Whenever you experience fear, shame or guilt in relation to money, you can be sure that you hold certain disempowering beliefs.

Whenever you have to deal with money, start observing what's going on inside you. How do you feel about investing in yourself? Are you scared of buying an expensive program that could make a big difference in your life? Notice this. What about charging for your products or services? Do you feel bad about doing this? Notice how it feels. Do you find it difficult to give money to charity because you live in scarcity? Take note of this as well.

Remember, whenever you face your fears and move beyond your comfort zone, you open yourself up to new possibilities. This goes for money-related fears as well. Whenever you stretch yourself and invest more in yourself than you feel comfortable doing, you grow. Whenever you give money to charity when you don't have much disposable income, you change your relationship with money and start removing some of your fears. Whenever you face discomfort and decide to charge for your work, you loosen some of your limiting beliefs about money as well. But more importantly, you signal to yourself that you value your work, which boosts your confidence and opens new opportunities for you.

As you can see, money isn't a bad thing, per se. Again, it's simply a matter of perspective. Some people want to make more money out of greed and fear. Instead, I suggest you use money as a way to remove your fears, expand your comfort zone and uncover your potential.

Whenever you witness certain patterns, such as constantly making and losing money, struggling to invest in yourself or always being in debt, look at some of your assumptions about money. In his book, *Secrets of The Millionaire Mind*, T. Harv Ecker explains how everybody has a money blueprint. Your blueprint is often inherited from your parents and tends to be either the same as your parents' blueprint or the exact opposite. See if you can find your own blueprint, whether it is saving a lot, overspending or refusing to charge enough for your work. What can you learn from this and what can you do about it?

You can adopt the following assumption:

I give myself total permission to give and receive money in abundance.

Exercise:

What is one small action you could take to change your relationship with money and extend your comfort zone (e.g., give money to charity, invest in yourself, charge more for your services, etc.)?

Negative assumption #36—Being poor is noble

You may believe being poor is a noble thing and feel good about yourself as a result. However, in reality, being poor in itself doesn't qualify you as a good or noble person. After all, it's the default position and requires no effort, does it? That's not to say there is anything wrong with it, though. There is just nothing fundamentally noble about being poor.

A major problem is that struggling financially doesn't help anybody. On the contrary, it drastically limits your ability to serve others. It is challenging to help others when you're struggling yourself and have little to no access to resources, such as money. You may already be helping many people and that's wonderful, but imagine how many more people you could help with more resources. Perhaps you could serve ten times or even a hundred times more people. Wouldn't that be better for everybody?

I hear you screaming, "But what about Mother Theresa? Wasn't she poor?" The major difference between Mother Theresa and most people struggling financially, is that she was poor by choice not by default. In fact, she was a fantastic fundraiser and raised millions of dollars for the poor, which is one of the main reasons she was able to make such a massive impact on the world. We could argue that if she wanted to, she could have been rich. One thing to understand is by serving a lot of people you often end up attracting money and support. It could be through people donating money, products and services or through companies/government sponsorship.

Now, I would like to ask, are you where you are financially by choice or by default? Do you pretend money is not important while knowing deep down this attitude is BS? In reality, you would probably like to earn more money, right? Nothing wrong with that (providing you acquire it honestly). Again, money is neutral and whether you have plenty or not enough, it doesn't say anything about you.

Also, did you know the real saying is not, "Money is the root of all evil", but, "*The love of money* is the root of all evil." Loving money to gain more power because of greed is a problem. Channeling money to help the world the same way Mother Theresa did, isn't.

Remember, money is simply a vehicle you can use to express yourself. What does money mean to you? How could you change your assumptions about money in a way that leads to positive changes in your life? And how will you use it in a way that is consistent with who you are?

Let me suggest you utilize the following assumption:

The more money I have, the more people I can help.

Exercise:

Spend a few seconds to write down the values you give to money, whatever they may be.

Negative assumption #37—Money is scarce

Do you think money is scarce? While people tend to give more importance to money than to time, in reality, time, due to its real scarcity, is far more precious.

Many people are ready to spend hours to save a few dollars, but wealthy people would rather spend their money to save time. I believe the transition from struggling financially to becoming wealthy begins when you realize time is far more precious than money, not the other way around.

The other day, I heard that at my local supermarket, people were almost fighting to get a discounted chocolate paste. They wanted to save a few bucks. Are these people likely to ever become wealthy?

Rather than trying to save a few bucks here and there, it is important to realize you can always find ways to make more money, but you can never get more time. Each second passed is forever gone. Contrary to what many people tend to believe, money isn't limited. It isn't a pie you need to get a slice of before there isn't any left. If that was the case, wealth creation wouldn't exist, and economic growth wouldn't be possible.

Money was first created in the human mind. This means you, like anybody else, have the ability to create wealth. You have the power to generate new ideas that you can turn into tangible things in the physical world. Because of this ability, the amount of wealth you can create is virtually unlimited. I believe that if people were in a position to utilize a mere five percent more of their potential, they could generate a staggering amount of wealth. In fact, when you look at countries like Japan after the Second World War, it becomes apparent that wealth comes first and foremost from the human mind. Few people would have expected a small group of islands with very few natural resources to become an economic superpower in a mere two decades.

The bottom line is, regardless of your external situation—unemployment rate, inflation, international financial meltdowns—

you can create wealth. Ask yourself, "In what way(s) am I limiting myself in terms of the amount of wealth I can create?"

What would happen if you decided to hold the assumption that wealth is unlimited, and you can always create more? What if you see yourself as the very source of wealth? How would that change the way you feel, think and act?

You can adopt the following assumption:

Wealth is unlimited, and I can always create more.

Exercise:

Take a few seconds to meditate on the fact that money isn't something external you need to earn or attract. It comes from within you as one manifestation of wealth.

Negative assumption #38 - Money doesn't grow on trees

Have you ever been told that money doesn't grow on trees? I actually believe money does grow on trees. But for that to happen, you have to plant the right seeds. The most important seed for wealth is your mindset, which is what this book is all about. For instance, if you hold the wrong assumptions, such as, "money doesn't grow on trees" or, "rich people are greedy," you're planting the wrong seeds and money will never grow. After all, why would you want to be rich if you believe rich people are greedy? Why would you want to be one of them? Simply by believing rich people are greedy, you dramatically reduce your chances of becoming wealthy. This is the power of assumptions.

Although this is not the specific topic of this book, you can sow other seeds to grow your money trees. Anything that allows you to leverage your work is a great seed. One obvious example is to utilize the internet, which works 24/7, doesn't require your presence and the products you put on it can be bought all over the world. Take this book as an example. It's available to download from Amazon 24/7. Not only that, but if it is ranked high enough, Amazon's algorithms will keep promoting it for free. Other seeds are outsourcing and delegating. By outsourcing some of your tasks, you can focus on the higher value tasks you are good at and enjoy doing. This is what valuing your time means. Yet another seed would be working with high-end clients or big corporations. In short, going where the money is. Again, no magic pill here. Wealth creation, like success, requires you to follow a specific process over an extended period of time. Certain things—such as building your own company—facilitate the accumulation of wealth. Other things—such as being an employee—make it very challenging.

If you want to learn more about wealth creation, I highly encourage you to check out MJ DeMarco's book, *The Millionaire Fastlane*, which outlines key principles and explains the mindset you need to adopt if you want to create more wealth.

You can adopt the following assumption:

Wealth creation is inevitable, I just have to sow the right seeds.

Exercise:

Write down twenty ways you could attract more money in your life.

Negative assumption #39—Wealth equals money

When we talk about someone being wealthy, we generally mean he or she has a lot of money in his or her bank account. But money is just one manifestation of wealth. What if wealth has nothing to do with money? What if wealth is not something outside you? Instead of thinking of wealth as something external you have to chase and could lose at any moment, imagine if you saw yourself as the very source of wealth. After all, if you removed all your limiting beliefs about money and had confidence in yourself and in your potential, couldn't you create more wealth? Ultimately, aren't you the source of your own wealth?

By choosing to believe you are the source of wealth, you can stop thinking of money as a limited resource. You will know that, by tapping into your resourcefulness, you can create wealth continuously throughout your life. Isn't that a more empowering belief to hold?

Here is the assumption you can adopt:

I'm the source of wealth, and I have enough resourcefulness to attract any resource I need to create wealth.

Exercise:

How resourceful are you? Write down all the qualities and strengths you have and could rely on to attract the resources you need to create wealth. This could be your motivation, passion, creativity, etc.

7

ASSUMPTIONS ABOUT EMOTIONS

The quality of your emotions largely determines the quality of your life. Imagine if you could better manage your emotions and experience more happiness and peace of mind. What would that do for you?

In this section, we'll discuss common assumptions about emotions, and we will offer new empowering assumptions to give you a new perspective.

Negative assumption #40—I am my emotions

Many people live their lives believing they are their emotions. When they feel anger, they react accordingly by yelling at people or taking reckless actions they may later regret. They're so caught up in their personal stories they fail to realize that emotions are only temporary visitors. The truth is, no matter how depressed, angry or despondent you are today, it doesn't make you less of a person than you were three weeks ago when you were feeling great. No emotions can ever affect the essence of who or what you are in the long term.

Think of the worst things that have ever happened to you. Perhaps you lost your job, or your boyfriend or girlfriend broke up with you. Or maybe you were depressed for months. But even the worse episodes of your life ended and, as time passed, you felt better, right?

Your emotions are little more than costumes you wear for a short while. They are clouds hiding the sun. While clouds will eventually disperse, you—the real you—will remain. Start seeing your emotions as temporary visitors or passing clouds. Don't try to change them or judge them. Avoid identifying with them. Just notice them.

Below, I've listed thirty-one simple coping strategies to deal with negative emotions short-term and long-term. These are from my book, *Master Your Emotions: A Practical Guide to Overcome Negativity and Better Manage Your Feelings*.

1. Short-term solutions

The following techniques will help you manage negative emotions as they arise. Try them out and keep the ones that work for you.

a) Change your emotional state

- Distract yourself: An emotion is only as strong as you allow it to be. Whenever you experience a negative feeling, instead of focusing on it, get busy right away. If you're angry about something, focus on an item on your to-do list. If possible, do something that requires your full attention. When you cross something off your to-do list, the positive energy you create will go a long way towards alleviating your negative emotions.
- Interrupt: Do something silly or unusual to break the pattern. Shout, perform a silly dance or speak in a strange voice.
- Move: Stand up, go for a walk, do push-ups, dance, or use a power posture. By changing your physiology, you can often change the way you feel.

- Listen to music: Listening to your favorite music may improve your emotional state.
- Shout: Talk to yourself with a loud and authoritarian voice and give yourself a pep talk. Use your voice and words to change your emotions.

b) Take action

- Do it anyway: Ignore your feeling(s) and do what you have to do. Mature adults do what they have to do whether they feel like it or not.
- Do something about it: Your behavior indirectly influences your feelings. Ask yourself, "What action can I take in today to change the way I feel?" Then, go do it.

c) Become more aware of your emotions

- Write it down: Take a pen and paper and write down what you worry about, why and what you can do about it. Be as specific as possible.
- Write down what happened: Write down exactly what happened to generate the negative emotion. Don't write down your interpretation of it or the drama you created around it. Simply write down the raw facts. Now ask yourself, in the grand scheme of your life, is it really that big a deal?
- Talk: Have a discussion with a friend. You may be overreacting to the situation and making things worse than they are. Sometimes, all you need is a different perspective.
- Remember a time when you felt good about yourself: This can help you return to the same, positive state and gain a new perspective. Ask yourself the following questions, "How did it feel?" "What was I thinking at the time?" "What was my outlook on life at the time?"
- Let your emotion go: Ask yourself, "Can I let that emotion go?" Then, allow yourself to release it.

- Allow your emotions to exist: Stop trying to resist your emotions or to change them. Allow them to be what they are.
- Embrace your emotions: Feel your emotions without judging them. Become curious about them. What are they exactly at their core?

d) Just relax

- Rest: Take a nap or a break. When tired, you are more likely to experience negative emotions than when properly rested.
- Breathe: Breathe slowly to relax. The way you breathe affects your emotional state. Use breathing techniques to calm yourself, or to give you more energy.
- Relax: Take a few minutes to relax your muscles. Start by relaxing your jaw, the tension around your eyes and the muscles on your face. Your body affects your emotions. As you relax your body, your mind will also relax.
- Thank your problems: Understand they are here for a reason and will serve you in some way.

2. Long-term solutions

The following techniques will help you manage your negative emotions long-term.

a) Analyze your negative emotions

- Identify the story behind your emotions: Take a pen and paper and write down all the reasons you have these emotions in the first place. What assumptions do you hold? How did you interpret what's happened to you? Now, see if you can let go of this particular story.
- Write down your emotions in a journal: Take a few minutes each day to write down how you felt during the day. Look for recurring patterns. Then, use affirmations, visualization, or a relevant exercise to help you overcome these emotions.

- Practice mindfulness: Observe your emotions throughout the day. Meditation will help you do this. Another way is simply to engage in an activity while being fully present. As you do this, observe what's going on in your mind.

b) Move away from negativity

- Change your environment: If you're surrounded by negativity, change your environment. Move to a different place or reduce the time you spend with negative people.
- Remove counterproductive activities: Remove or reduce the time you spend on any activity that doesn't have a positive impact on your life. This could be reducing the time you spend watching TV or surfing the internet.

c) Condition your mind

- Create daily rituals: This will help you to experience more positive emotions. Meditate, exercise, repeat positive affirmations, create a gratitude journal and so on. (The best time to deposit positive thoughts in your mind is right before going to sleep and first thing in the morning.)
- Exercise: Exercise regularly. Exercise improves your mood and is good for your emotional and physical health.

d) Increase your energy

- The less energy you have, the more likely you are to experience negative emotions.
- Make sure you get enough sleep: If possible, go to bed and wake up at the same time every day.
- Eat healthier food: As the saying goes, "You are what you eat." Junk food will negatively impact your energy levels, so take steps to improve your diet.
- Rest: Take regular naps or take a few minutes to relax.
- Breathe: Learn to breathe properly.

e) Ask for help

- Consult a professional: if you have deep emotional issues such as extreme low self-esteem or chronic depression, it might be wise to consult a professional.

You can adopt the following assumptions:

Emotions come and go. What I am, remains untouched forever.

To learn more about how to master your emotions, I highly encourage you to refer to my book, *Master Your Emotions: A Practical Guide to Overcome Negativity and Better Manage Your Feelings.*

Exercise:

Remember one of the worst things that ever happened to you. Now, notice how it has passed.

Negative assumption #41—My emotions dictate my actions

Have you noticed that the way you feel usually influences your actions? For instance, when you're angry, you may yell at someone or leave the room. Thus, it sounds reasonable to assume your emotions dictate your actions. However, in reality, *you* dictate your actions, not your emotions. You have the power to act despite your emotions. For instance:

- Being afraid of something doesn't mean you cannot do it.
- Being tired doesn't mean you can't work on your side business.
- Believing you can't do something doesn't mean you are actually unable to do it.

In short, you don't need to feel like it to do something. In fact, one of the major differences between successful people and others is that they do what they need to do whether they feel like it or not.

The idea you must feel like it to do something is a myth. That's why it's so important to rely on processes—a set of tasks you perform daily—to stay on track with your long-term goals. Processes allow you to remain consistent, regardless of what happens to you in the short term and how you feel inside. If you can install and follow processes, you can achieve anything you want.

You can adopt the following assumption:

I dictate my actions, regardless of the way I feel.

Exercise:

Knowing you dictate your actions, not your emotions, what will you start doing differently from now? What will you do whether you feel like it or not?

Negative assumption #42—I get upset because of something external

Another major assumption is that you become upset because something happens to you. The real reason you get upset is *not* because of what is actually happening, it's because of your *interpretation* of what is happening. Fundamentally, nothing can upset you. Let me give you an example:

Let's say you're about to leave for a picnic and it starts raining. You're now angry at the rain. But is it the rain that's the problem or is it the meaning you assign to it? While you're complaining about the rain, could it be that farmers somewhere are rejoicing?

Now, how would your life change if every time you get upset, you look at the meaning you give to the event rather than blaming external factors?

I recommend you use the following assumption:

Nothing outside me has the power to upset me.

Exercise:

Select something that upset you recently. Look at what happened objectively without adding your interpretation to the event. Notice how the issue probably isn't the event itself, but the story you've attached to it.

Negative assumption #43—I'm responsible for how other people feel

It's not your job to make other people feel good. I'm not saying you shouldn't be nice. I'm saying that you're not responsible for how other people feel. It's *their* job to control their emotions, *not* yours. In what world would we be living if we had to constantly watch our words lest we offend someone?

I believe that being offended is part of our personal growth. It's what allows us to remove our excessive attachment to our false sense of identity. It enables us to stop clinging so much to our physical attributes or beliefs about ourselves and the world.

I explain in more details how you can use feelings of defensiveness as a tool for your personal growth in my book, *Master Your Emotions: A Practical Guide to Overcome Negativity and Better Manage Your Feelings.*

Some people are easily offended, while others remain unaffected no matter what happens. This demonstrates it's not what you say that hurts people, it's their inability to deal with their emotions. Feelings of defensiveness are, in fact, incredible tools to help identify what you need to work on to become a more self-assured human being. Are you offended by comments people make about your body, the way you walk, or the way you talk? If so, what does it say about the relationship you have with yourself? What do you need to work on to avoid feeling the need to defend yourself? Or perhaps you're offended when someone criticizes some of your beliefs. It could be political or religious beliefs, or it could be beliefs about yourself. Remember, you are responsible for your emotional state. Similarly, other people are responsible for the way they feel.

Having said that, I don't recommend offending people on purpose, but I do encourage you to internalize the fact that, ultimately, you are not responsible for people's emotions. *They* are.

You can adopt the following assumption:

I'm responsible for how I feel, not for how other people feel.

Exercise:

Identify one situation where worrying about how others may feel prevents you from doing something you really want to do.

Negative assumption #44—Complaining is natural

Most people tend to believe that complaining is normal. Something bad happens to you, so you should complain, right? In reality, complaining is usually ineffective and doesn't help you create the life you want. If anything, it robs you of your power to make changes. I believe complaining is a habit and can be changed with practice.

Interestingly, when we complain about something or someone, we seldom complain about it to the right person—the person who can actually do something about it. When you're angry at your boss, you complain about it to your spouse, your colleagues or your friends. Yet, the best way to improve the situation is probably to talk to your boss directly.

One of the main reasons we complain is to avoid taking responsibility. Complaining is the easiest way out because it allows us to do nothing to improve the situation—nothing but complain. Many people complain about their current situation, saying they want to be somewhere else, do something else or become someone else, yet they do nothing about it. If you look at any situation in your life, you'll see that you only have three options:

- Complain
- Proactively do something to address/improve the situation, or
- Accept the situation.

Unfortunately, complaining isn't often a viable strategy which leaves you with two options:

- Do something about the situation.
- Accept the situation as it is.

Let me give you some examples:

Example 1: You're complaining because you believe you're not getting paid enough at work. You can:

- Keep complaining (but does that help you solve the problem?).
- Do something about it (ask for a raise, work overtime, change your job, start a side business etc.).
- Accept your current income without complaining.

Now, which option do you think is the easiest one? Complaining, of course. Most people choose the easiest path. But remember what the motivational speaker Les Brown said, *"Do what is easy, and your life will be hard. Do what is hard, and your life becomes easy."*

I wish everybody could earn ten times their current income, but that's not how reality works. As the motivational speaker, Jim Rohn, said, *"You can't get rich by demand."*

You can go on strike and complain as much as you want, but you're not going to double or triple your salary. Unless you have the power to change the entire economic system, your only choice is to take full responsibility for your life and make decisions that will allow you to make the amount of money you want to make. There is no point complaining, because the economic system is not answering your personal wishes.

Example 2: You're complaining because you're paying too much tax. You can:

- Keep complaining.

- Do something about it (find ways to pay fewer taxes, move to another country with more liberal tax laws, etc.).
- Accept your situation (and happily pay your taxes).

Example 3: You're complaining because you don't like your current life. You can:

- Keep complaining (and nothing will change).
- Do something about it (ask for advice, design your ideal life and take action etc.).
- Accept your current situation.

In short, complaining keeps you in a "victim mentality." In any situation, you can either do something about it or accept things as they are. Anything else—such as complaining—is not only ineffectual, it is insanity.

Your assumption:

Instead of complaining, I either do something about my situation or fully accept it.

Exercise:

For one full day, refuse to complain about anything. If you want, you can extend this challenge for as long as you like. A great book to read on the topic is Will Bowen's, *A Complaint Free World: How to Stop Complaining and Start Enjoying the Life You Always Wanted.*

8
ASSUMPTIONS ABOUT WORK

You'll spend a large part of your life working. Now, would you rather do something you enjoy or something you hate? Unfortunately, people often hold limiting beliefs that prevent them from having the fulfilling career they love. In this section, we'll challenge a few common assumptions that could stop you designing your ideal career.

Negative assumption #45—I can't find a job I love

Do you dread Monday mornings and celebrate Friday afternoons as though you were a kid on Christmas Day? One day, my supervisor told me we didn't have to love our job. He thought a job was merely a way to earn a living. I almost believed him, but something didn't seem quite right to me so I didn't. Now, can you imagine what would have happened if I had listened to him and believed I couldn't find a job I love? For a start, I wouldn't have written this book!

What about you? Do you believe you're not supposed to enjoy your job? Do you find it acceptable to hang around for years at the same job because people told you this is the way it has to be?

What if you replace your assumption, "*I can't find a job that I love,*" with "*I can find (or create) a job I love. And I will!*" What effect will this, apparently minor, revision have on your life? What will you start doing differently today?

Adopt the following assumption:

I can find a job I love, and I will!

To learn how to find what you love and make a career out of it, refer to my book, The Passion Manifesto: Escape The Rat Race, Uncover Your Passion and Design a Career and Life You Love.

Exercise: What does your ideal job look like? Write it down.

Negative assumption #46—I can't make money doing what I love

Do you believe it's impossible to make money doing what you love? If so, how likely are you to ever work at a job you actually enjoy?

It is *absolutely* possible to make money doing something you love. In fact, millions of people enjoy their job—though they sometime have to do it secretly to avoid annoying the majority of people who hate what they have to do to earn a living.

I'm not saying finding the perfect job is easy, but I am saying it is possible. And if you're willing to do what it takes, you *will* eventually find a satisfying job. Millions of people have done this before you and so can you. There is no doubt about it.

Now, what if you hold the following assumption:

I can absolutely make money doing what I love.

Exercise:

Write down twenty ideas on how you could make money doing what you love.

Negative assumption #47—I have to work forty plus years and retire at sixty-five

The common view is that we're supposed to work forty plus years, eight hours (or more) per day until we can finally retire at sixty-five. This assumption often remains unchallenged, but is it the only option? What if you want to take a long break, work less or retire early? It is important you stretch your thinking and consider other possibilities that may better suit you. There is no rule that says you have to work from 9 to 5, five days a week. The eight-hour day was originally designed for factory workers who would work in shifts. In many cases, it is not the most productive way to work.

In today's world, the possibilities are limitless. You can decide how you want to work. The key is to have clarity. The more you know what you want, the easier it will be to design your ideal career. While vague goals lead to vague results, crystal-clear goals create extraordinary results.

Your assumption could be:

I have the power to design my career the way I want to.

Exercise:

Where would you like to be professionally in five years? Write down what your ideal career would look like.

Negative assumption #48—I work hard now so I can enjoy my life once I finally retire

Many people are willing to endure years at jobs they hate in exchange for a reward called "retirement." This is a completely terrible idea.

First, there is no guarantee you will live long enough to retire. Many people die before they reach their sixties. Second, at sixty-five you might not be as healthy as you imagine. You might even be unable to do all the wonderful things you planned for your retirement. This is what many people discover when they retire. Third, believing you'll be living happily ever after can lead you to make wrong career choices. You may work hard trying to make money to find yourself sick or depressed at sixty-five.

A wonderful question I encourage you to ask yourself right now is: "Assuming I could never retire and had to work until the day I die, would I still be doing what I'm currently doing?" If not, you might need to change something. The good news is that you now have new powerful assumptions to support you:

1) *I can find a job I love. And I will!*

2) *I can absolutely make money doing what I love.*

3) *I have the power to design my career the way I want to.*

Rather than assuming you will retire one day, I suggest you live your life as if retirement wasn't an option. It doesn't mean you should spend all your money recklessly not saving for your old age; it simply means you must find a job or career you don't want to escape or retire from.

You can adopt the following assumption:

I proactively design a career I love, and I enjoy life now.

Exercise:

Answer the following question, "Assuming I could never retire and had to work until the day I die, would I still be doing what I'm currently doing?"

9

ASSUMPTION ABOUT TIME

Time is one of the most important resources we have. In this section, we'll cover two major assumptions that could prevent you from making the most of your time.

Negative assumption #49—I don't have enough time

Do you struggle to find time to do the things you want to do? We all have twenty-four hours each day. Some people use their time to achieve all their goals and dreams, sometimes they even exceed their expectations. These individuals often accomplish more in one year than most people do in ten. Others stay at the same place all their lives not achieving any of their dreams.

For most people, the issue is not lack of time, but lack of priority and clarity. People who achieve their goals know exactly what they want and work on making it a reality every single day. These individuals have a vision for their lives and make sure what they do every day is aligned with their long-term vision. They are proactive.

Other people are reactive. They wake up every day without having a clear vision of what they want to accomplish by the end of the day, let alone the end of the year. As a result, they waste time on activities that contribute nothing to the life they aspire for. They engage in gossiping, waste hours in front of the TV or spend much of their time on unproductive tasks.

In reality, you *do* have time.

What if you ditch the excuse "I don't have time," for the following assumption:

I make the time to do whatever I'm committed to

Did you notice the word "committed" there? Committing presupposes that you know exactly what you want (clarity) and you resolve to make it happen (priority). These two components are essential to ensure you use your time effectively. So, decide what you want, and make it an absolute priority in your life.

Your assumption therefore is:

I make the time to do whatever I'm committed to.

Exercise:

For an entire week, write down every activity you do at work and at home. Now, look at all your tasks. Which ones are really productive? Do you really not have time to strive for your goal in life?

Negative assumption #50—Money is more valuable than time

While most people treat money as if it were more important than time, we've seen it is not the case. *Time is way more precious than money.* It is one of the scarcest resources you have. Dying billionaires would probably give away all their money to live a few more days, wouldn't they?

Sadly, many people manage their time extremely poorly. They give it away as if it were free and abundant. In many regards, they behave as if they had an infinite amount of time. They happily offer their time to anybody who asks for it. Some will even wait hours in line to save a few bucks.

Other people may expect you to give your time freely—because they do so themselves—but that does not mean you should. You must protect your time and use it wisely. Whether you're asked to join a cause, organize an event, or take on an extra project at work, be willing to say no when it doesn't align with your values and vision. Remember, once time is gone, it's gone forever.

The reason people waste so much time is because they don't have a clear sense of direction and, thus, they have no priorities. In some cases, they don't even know what spending their time efficiently would look like. In short, they have no clear vision for their lives. And people who have no vision can often end up helping other people—who do have one—achieve it. Is that what you want? Are you giving your time to other people to help them live a great life? Or would you rather spend your time strategically and design *your* ideal life?

A great question I like to ask myself is, "If I keep doing what I'm doing today, will I end up where I want to be in ten years from now?" This is a fantastic way to check whether you're using your time wisely or wasting it. Try it.

The bottom line is that, to succeed in life, having a long-term vision is *essential*. You don't build a house without a clear blueprint first, do you? No. You create a detailed plan. You must do the same with your life. You must see a decade or two—or even longer—into your future and decide how you want your life to be. Then, once you have a crystal-clear vision, you can determine what you need to do today, this week, this month and this year to move closer to that ideal vision.

Now, you might think I'm asking you to time everything you do to the second and avoid wasting time at all cost. No, I'm not asking you to drink less water, so you can go to the bathroom less often to save a few minutes. I'm not saying you shouldn't spend hours chatting with friends either. What I'm suggesting is you start using your time more deliberately.

While people tend to believe that productivity is about producing more in less time, I believe the real meaning of productivity is to spend most of your time doing what you want to do, whether it is working a job you're passionate about, meeting your friends or spending time with your family. You can be the most productive person in your company, but if you spend seventy hours a week at a job you hate until the day you retire, that's not what I call being productive. It might be productive for your company, but not for you or your family.

Successful people value time more than money and, as a result, they can create more money if they choose to. They use their money to save time, not their time to save money. Start thinking and acting like them. Value your time more! By doing so, you'll develop more self-respect, become more productive and, as a result, you will create more freedom in your life.

Your new assumption:

I value my time because I value myself.

Exercise:

Write down all the tasks you could stop doing because they aren't aligned with your vision or aren't productive.

To learn more about productivity, I encourage you to refer to my book, *Productivity Beast, An Unconventional Guide to Getting Things Done.*

PART III

CREATING NEW ASSUMPTIONS

Now we've reviewed and torn apart common assumptions, it is time to look specifically at your assumptions and make sure you replace them with more empowering ones.

You may be familiar with the concepts of affirmation and visualization, but we're going to go one step further here. We don't merely want to repeat some affirmations, we want to have a look at your current web of beliefs, or "life assumptions," and replace them with more empowering beliefs, ones that will allow you to design the life you want. We want to create your "Identity Map 2.0."

The sum of all your assumptions forms your programming, that is, how you think, feel and act. And, since your Identity Map determines the actions you take, it determines the results you obtain.

- If you believe rich people are greedy, you'll never become wealthy yourself.
- If you believe you're not good enough or can't do something, you'll give up prematurely.

- If you believe you're a dunce, like Victor Serebriakoff did, you may give up on yourself.
- If you believe success is an event rather than a process that includes countless "failures," you will never achieve your most exciting goals and dreams.
- If you believe your emotions dictate your actions, you won't discipline yourself enough to do the necessary work to achieve the results you desire.
- If you believe it's normal to hate your job, you probably won't do what it takes to design a career you love.

We all have different assumptions. Among the assumptions we discussed previously, you may have found new empowering assumptions you can't wait to adopt in your life. You may also decide not to adopt some others, and this is perfectly fine.

The most important thing is for you to start selecting the most empowering assumptions, ones that will support you in creating the kind of life you dream of living.

10

MOVING FROM WHO YOU ARE TO WHO YOU WANT TO BE

In this section, we're going to craft your Identity Map 2.0 by adopting new empowering assumptions that will help you change your life. We will remove weeds from your garden and sow powerful new seeds that will transform your life.

Imagine how your life would change if you could remove, one by one, all the limiting beliefs that have been destroying your potential and, instead, implement powerful beliefs that will serve you for the rest of your life.

While most people react to life based on the unconscious assumptions they hold, I want you to select empowering assumptions that strongly resonate within you and implement them in your life. These empowering assumptions will become the core beliefs that dictate your actions and shape your destiny.

Selecting your core life assumptions

Let's start by unearthing your major assumptions about life.

We introduced the following assumptions earlier:

- *Life is easy. And I do whatever I can to keep it this way.*
- *I'm as happy as anybody else.*
- *As I change, my environment changes.*
- *I create my own reality. What others believe I can or cannot do is irrelevant.*
- *By giving more, I open myself to receiving more.*
- *Having problems is normal. The less attached I am to them, the more irrelevant they become.*
- *In any problem lies opportunity.*
- *I fully accept what is, and I can create what will be.*
- *Every day I start anew, free of any burden from the past.*
- *I'm good enough for now.*
- *I'm perfect in my imperfections.*
- *My intent is pure.*
- *I matter.*
- *I believe it, and therefore I'll see it.*
- *Because I start before I'm ready, I can achieve anything I want faster than I ever thought possible.*
- *I ask for whatever I want, regardless of how I feel.*
- *I'm the scriptwriter of my life, and I can rewrite my story at will.*
- *I'm motivated because I have a motive for action.*
- *Self-discipline equals freedom. With enough self-discipline, I can achieve anything I want.*
- *I take care of me for my family and friends.*
- *I'm never too old to do what I want to do.*
- *I help others and myself grow by telling the truth whenever possible.*

To begin with, select only five assumptions from this list. If you were to adopt them, what five assumptions would make the biggest difference in your life?

Selecting assumptions in major areas of your life

Now you have selected your top five life assumptions, let's look at some major assumptions you could adopt in various areas of your life.

Below is a summary of the assumptions we introduced previously:

Success

- *Success is inevitable.*
- *Success is not about what I have, it's about who I become.*
- *I happily fail my way to success. I fail faster and better each time.*
- *I'm successful because I'm making progress toward my goal.*
- *I create my own success regardless of external circumstances.*
- *I'm already there, and I'm more than enough for now.*
- *By having changed some people's lives, even in a minor way, I'm already a huge success.*
- *I have good intentions, therefore I'm a massive success.*
- *Food + shelter = happiness + success.*
- *I can have it all.*
- *I allow myself to ask for what I want.*
- *If I don't live it, I don't know it.*
- *Everything is learnable, and I can always improve.*

Money

- *Money is important.*
- *I give myself total permission to give and receive money in abundance.*
- *The more money I have, the more people I can help.*
- *Wealth is unlimited, and I can always create more of it.*
- *Wealth creation is inevitable, I just have to plant the right seeds.*
- *I'm the source of wealth. I have enough resourcefulness to attract any resources I need to create wealth.*

Emotions

- *Emotions come and go. What I am, remains untouched. Forever.*
- *I dictate my actions, regardless of the way I feel.*
- *Nothing outside of me has the power to upset me.*
- *I'm responsible for how I feel, not for how other people feel.*
- *I refuse to complain. I do something about it or I accept it.*

Work

- *I can find a job I love, and I will!*
- *I can absolutely make money doing what I love.*
- *I have the power to design my career the way I want to.*
- *I proactively design a career I love and enjoy my life now.*

Time

- *I make the time to do whatever I'm committed to doing.*
- *I value my time because I value myself.*

Now, let's see how you can start creating a new identity by using some of these empowering assumptions.

11

CREATING YOUR IDENTITY MAP

You become what you believe. No matter where you are now in life, you can change your environment by changing your beliefs. You can create a brand new identity and become more confident, determined, motivated and powerful than you can ever imagine. Remember, you already have everything you need to achieve anything you want. You just have to remove the filters preventing you from shining.

Whatever disempowering assumptions you hold, you can remove.

Whatever fears you have, you can overcome.

Whatever habits or skills you need, you can develop.

It's now time to rewire your brain and create a new identity that will allow you to obtain the results you want in life. We'll create your Identity Map 2.0 using your free action guide here. Alternatively, you can use a separate sheet of paper.

In the middle, write down, "My best self." Then, create branches for each area in which you want to implement new empowering assumptions. I recommend you use the same categories we use in this book. Feel free to add, remove or alter categories to fit your personal needs. Remember, this is all about *you* and the life you want to create for *yourself*.

Start with the questions: "Who do I want to become? If I were to adopt them, what new empowering assumptions would allow me to be that person?"

Strengthening your new identity

Now you've created your Identity Map, you can start adopting the new empowering assumptions you've selected. You can use two things to rewire your brain: repetition and emotion. By having the same thought over and over again and charging it emotionally, you create new neural connections for that specific thought pattern and, by doing so, you strengthen it. You physically change your brain! Remember, your brain is malleable. You can create new neural connections and implement/remove any belief you desire. And you can do so, whether you're fifteen or seventy years old.

How to change your identity

To make your new assumptions part of yourself, you must focus on them as often as possible. Dedicate time each day to repeating them. I recommend you spend five minutes each morning when you wake up and five minutes each evening before falling asleep. Make your assumptions the first thing you think of in the morning and the last thing you think of at night, which is when your subconscious mind is at its most receptive.

At first, refer to your mind map and repeat each assumption you've written aloud. Repeat them multiple times. As you do so, try to associate images with your assumptions. If your assumption is "success is inevitable," envision what success means to you. What specific goal or vision will you inevitably achieve? Can you visualize specific situations? Perhaps you are standing in front of a large audience, delivering a speech with ease and confidence. Or maybe you're traveling the world. Whatever your vision of success might be, envision as many relevant situations as possible.

Coming up with additional reasons

The next step is to ask yourself why your assumption is true. As an example, let's use: "Success is inevitable."

By coming up with more and more reasons your assumption is true, you reinforce it and make it easier to believe in. Below are some examples of answers.

Success is inevitable for me because:

- I have an incredible ability to learn.
- There is no limit to how much I can grow.
- I have access to all the information in the world.
- I will never give up.
- Other people have done it before, and so can I.
- I'm willing to work hard on myself.
- 7.5 billion people on earth are willing to help me.
- My mind is more powerful than I can ever begin to imagine.
- I'm committed to doing whatever it takes to achieve my goals.

Using anchoring to energize your assumptions

Engage your emotions. Now you know success is inevitable, how does this make you feel? Are you filled with joy, excitement, confidence? Are you proud of yourself? Feel all these emotions. Mix them together.

Then, ask yourself how you can amplify these emotions. You can engage your body and talk out loud to create what the world-famous coach, Tony Robbins, calls, "incantations."

Additional tip:

Listen to music and/or watch videos to help you. Select music/videos that match the belief you want create. You could select motivational videos that give you a sense of confidence or beautiful songs that evoke feelings of gratitude in you. Use whatever works for you.

Linking your assumptions to concrete actions

Your beliefs influence the way you feel and the actions you take. As you change your belief system by adopting new assumptions, the action you take will also change. To begin the process, imagine what some of your actions would be. Make sure they are as specific as possible. Your subconscious loves clarity. Consider the following reasons and add specific examples relevant to your situation.

Success is inevitable therefore:

- I enjoy the process and stay confident no matter what (define the process, which could be specific habits you do every day such as writing, eating a certain type of food or working out).
- I move toward my goal with absolute certainty (state your goal).
- I see "failures" as the feedback I can use to adjust my plan (identify potential failures).
- Nobody can talk me out of my vision (mention specific people who may be holding you back).

Creating reminders

Now you have your Identity Map, put it somewhere you can see it every day. I recommend you put it on your wall, on your desk and/or in a notebook you carry with you. When it comes to adopting new assumptions, repetition and daily exposure is key.

Remember, your mind is very similar to software—you have the power to reprogram it to achieve the results you want.

To ingrain your new assumptions further into your mind, write your assumptions on flashcards. Read your flashcards multiple times every day. This will remind you to feel and behave in accordance with your new assumptions. You can read them at home, during your daily commute or when you go to the bathroom.

Your thirty-day challenge

If you don't live it, you don't know it. Dedicate the next thirty days to implementing new and empowering assumptions. Go through the process described above every single day. Aim to spend at least ten minutes focusing on your new assumptions (five minutes in the morning and five minutes in the evening). Whenever you have free time during the day, think of your assumptions. A good time to do so is when you're taking a shower or commuting.

Additional tips:

Another great way to make your new assumptions part of your identity is to do the thirty-day challenge with your partner or a friend. By doing so, you can validate each other's assumptions—and have fun doing it.

Let's see how you can do the exercise. For example's sake, let's use the assumption, "Success is inevitable."

Step #1 - Say your assumption aloud. *Success is inevitable.*

Step #2 - Have your partner/friend ask why. Make sure you repeat the original assumption to strengthen it. Ask the question three to five times. *Why success is inevitable for you?*

Step #3 - Have your partner/friend ask you to describe in detail what it means. *What exactly does "success is inevitable" mean to you?*

Step #4 – Have your partner/friend ask how you feel about it. *Knowing success is inevitable for you, how does it make you feel? How can you amplify the feeling?*

Personalize your Identity Map

By now, you should have an Identity Map with all your amazing assumptions. Feel free to personalize it. You can add pictures and color to it.

Overcoming fear

As you create your new identity and write down empowering assumptions, you may experience some internal resistance. If so, this means you have some fears and self-doubt about certain assumptions. This is normal. The first step toward overcoming these fears is to notice the resistance. Usually, it manifests somewhere in your body. When you feel resistance, ask yourself where exactly you feel it in your body. Is it in your neck? Is it in your stomach? In your chest?

Once you've located the feeling, observe it. Don't judge it. Don't try to make it go away. Don't try to run away from it. Instead, stay with it. Now ask yourself, where is the most intense part of this feeling? Focus on this part to the best of your abilities. Again, don't judge it. Be present with it. Send love to it. It's not your enemy. Keep focusing on it until the feeling becomes less and less intense. If the feeling moves to another part of your body, repeat the same process.

Note that you may need to go through the same process several times until the fear dissolves. Then, repeat your assumption one more time and see if the fear is still there. By now, the negative emotion should be less intense and, if you keep practicing this exercise, the fear will eventually dissipate.

This process will work for any fear you may have. It could be fears around money or it could be fear of not being good enough. As you repeat your assumptions every day, be mindful and, whenever you feel resistance, deal with it using the above exercise.

Step-by-step method to creating your new identity

Below is a summary of the step-by-step method you can use to create your new identity.

- Create an Identity Map

- Select your core life assumptions.
- Select assumptions in each area of your life.

- Repeat your assumptions each day for at least ten minutes (five minutes in the morning, five minutes in the evening). Follow the process below:

- Repeat your assumptions (in your mind or out loud).
- Ask yourself why it is true.
- Energize your assumptions by engaging your emotions.
- Envision the concrete actions you can take.

- Check how you feel. If you feel resistance, work through it.

- Identify where you feel the emotion in your body.
- Stay present with it until it starts dissolving. Focus on the most intense part of the emotion.
- Repeat this process as many times as necessary for the fear to dissipate.

- Create reminders

- Put your mind map on your wall, desk and/or in a notebook you carry with you.
- Write down your assumptions on flashcards and review them several times each day.

12

ASKING "WHAT IF?"

To gain new perspectives, you must create thoughts that never crossed your mind before—thoughts that are so big they scare you, so far out of your current model of reality you have a hard time conceiving them.

The truth is you limit yourself in many ways. There may be things you can't do yet. But if you really wanted to, you could probably do most of them. For instance, you may believe you can't speak in front of a large audience, approach someone to initiate a new relationship or change careers. But all these things are possible.

In this section, I invite you to entertain the idea that some of the things you can only envision in your wildest dreams *are* possible. To do so, I'm going to introduce you to two magical words that will open an entire new world of opportunity. These two words are:

"What if?"

I love these two words because they are reassuring and inviting.

What if you could speak in front of a large audience? *What if* you could approach people in the street? *What if* you could change your career? Maybe it doesn't seem possible to you right now, but just entertain the idea that it could be possible. So, *what if?*

An effective way to stretch yourself beyond your comfort zone is to look at each of the following areas of your life and ask yourself, *"What if?"*

- Career
- Family/friends
- Finance
- Health/fitness
- Relationship
- Personal growth

Answer the following questions:

Career

What if I could have the perfect career?

Family/friends

What if I could experience and share more joy than I ever have with my family and friends?

Finance

What if I could double my income by the end of the year?

Health/fitness

What if I could have lots of energy and feel great every day?

Personal growth

What if I could overcome my fears and grow beyond my imagination?

Relationship

What if I could take my relationship to a whole new level?

Visualize what your life would look like in each of the above situations.

Going beyond your realm of possibility

Did you complete the previous exercise? If so, how did it make you feel?

Now, when you answered the previous questions, you were probably still limiting yourself. Let's think bigger. Let's go over each area one more time and do it for real. I'll provide you with some possible questions, but I want you to come up with your own. Entertain ideas that make you feel really uncomfortable and maybe even a little scared.

Whatever goals you had until now, multiply them by two, then by two again. Then, double or even triple that. Do this until you feel uncomfortable and scared. Dare to explore possibilities you've never thought of before. See if you can stretch yourself and start believing you can make the impossible, possible.

Career

What if I could have the perfect career in exactly the way I want it?

What if I could change my career within twelve months? Six months? One month?

What if I could change my career this week?

Family/friends

What if I could experience ridiculous levels of bliss and joy in the presence of my family and friends? What if I could feel total gratitude for every person who ever showed up in my life?

Finance

What if I could double my income within a year? Within six months? Within thirty days?

What if I could generate ten times my income within a year?

Health/fitness

What if the level of joy I've experienced so far is just a fraction of the level my real self can experience?

What if I could experience intense feelings of bliss as never before?

Personal growth

What if I'm currently just a tiny fraction of the person I could be?

What if I'm just scratching the surface of what is possible for me in this world?

What if I could remove any fear, self-doubt and limitations in any areas of my life and move freely in this world?

Relationship

What if I could take my relationship to a whole new level and one I didn't even know existed?

Committing to the impossible

Let's take this exercise one step further. For each area, ask yourself, "If I had to achieve this crazy vision, what would I do?"

How could you increase your income tenfold within a year? How could you change your career within six months? How could you experience more joy than you ever had before?

Play along and imagine you had to achieve your goals at all cost. Force yourself to think in a way you've never thought before. For the sake of this exercise, stretch yourself as much as you can. The point is not necessarily to achieve all these huge goals but to start moving beyond the limitations you've set for yourself through the assumptions you hold.

If you've completed this exercise, you should have experienced fears and discomfort, which is normal. To achieve a new goal, you have to move from Identity A, the person you are now, to Identity B, the person you need to become to achieve that goal. This entails changing your current assumptions and replacing them with more empowering ones.

A great question to ask yourself when working toward a stretch goal is, "What do I need to believe to achieve this goal?" Answering this question will allow you to discover the new beliefs (assumptions) you can implement to achieve that goal.

Putting things together

One of my main assumptions is that everything is possible. I refuse as much as I can to limit myself or to put other people into small boxes. I believe holding space for anything to happen is extremely important. This is because I understand whatever you think you can't do, you can't. As soon as you judge something as impossible, you exclude it from your field of potentialities. That is, you add an artificial filter and, by doing so, you limit your potential.

Why not assume everything is possible? Can you change the entire world? Maybe. Can you heal yourself? Why not? Is it possible to end wars and end poverty? Perhaps.

In fact, when you look at history, people who ended up changing the world were visionaries who saw things that people believed impossible. If people from the past were to look at today's technologies such as the internet, smartphones or airplanes, how do you think they would react? They would look at these things in disbelief.

Thus, I encourage you to adopt the ultimate assumption: "Everything is possible."

- Can you design your dream career? Yes, everything is possible.
- Can you attract your ideal partner? Yes, everything is possible.
- Can you impact the lives of millions of people around the world? Yes, everything is possible.
- Can you overcome your deepest fears or traumas and live in peace? Yes, everything is possible.

As the famous coach, Tony Robbins, says, "The quality of your questions determines the quality of your life."

As you hold the space for what is possible, I encourage you to keep the following words: "What if?" "Why not?" and "How?"

Below is an example of how you can use these magical worlds:

- What if? What if I could design an amazing career that I love?
- Why not? Why not design a great career I enjoy?
- How? How can I create an exciting career?

Remember: Life is easy, and everything is possible. Success is inevitable. Wealth is unlimited. You can have it all. You can create your own reality and start every day anew, free of any burden from the past. By changing yourself, you can transform your environment. By disciplining yourself, you can achieve anything you want. Nothing can upset you. You're good enough for now. And these are just a small sample of the beliefs you can develop.

I would like to remind you, nothing changes until you do. And more importantly, nothing changes until you take action. For your new assumptions to become part of who you are and allow you to achieve more than you ever thought possible, you *must* take action. While it is true your beliefs largely dictate your actions, it is also true your actions strengthen your beliefs.

A great example is confidence. The more you take baby steps toward your goals and stay consistent long term, the more you build confidence. As you attain more and more goals, you feel better about yourself. You start respecting yourself more, and you will develop a deeper sense of self-trust. You weren't born lacking confidence. Low self-confidence is a result of social conditioning. Or put it differently, low self-confidence is nothing more than an idea in your mind, an assumption you unconsciously adopted. It is by no means who you are. In the same way, you're not shy, you're not lazy or "not good enough."

Another main reason taking action is so important is because it expands your field of possibility. Remember, action cures fear. It cures the false assumptions and the wrong ideas you have about yourself. Your lack of confidence or shyness doesn't stand the test of truth. Action destroys the person you think you are and enables you to reveal who you really are. As the saying goes, everything is hard before it's easy. Many things are outside your comfort zone until they become part of it. The same way driving was once challenging but became effortless, one day public speaking, talking to strangers or anything else you're afraid of can be within your comfort zone.

CONCLUSION

I would like to congratulate you for reading this book until the end. This shows your desire to improve your life and design a brighter and more exciting future.

My sincere hope is the information within this book allows you to shift your perspective and open yourself to new possibilities. You have an almost limitless potential and you can make an infinite number of choices every day. Refuse to confine yourself and refuse to make yourself smaller than you are. Instead, hold the space for more, and see yourself as you could be, rather than as you believe yourself to be right now. Whenever you catch yourself saying, "I can't do this or that," take a deep breath and ask yourself, "What if? What if it's possible? Why not? How could I do that?"

Keep removing disempowering assumptions and replace them with assumptions that give you more freedom and power to change your life and the lives of others. And, more importantly, take action. Move beyond your comfort zone. As you do so, you'll be amazed at the wonderful things you can achieve. Review your empowering assumptions every day and keep refining them until you have a solid web of beliefs that will allow you to design the life you want.

Finally, never stop believing in what's possible. With an unshakable belief in yourself and in your vision, you can do extraordinary things.

If you want to share your story or ask me any questions, please feel free to contact me at: thibaut.meurisse@gmail.com. I always love hearing from my readers.

I wish you all the best,

Thibaut Meurisse

Founder of Whatispersonaldevelopment.org

BOOK 3 - SUCCESS IS INEVITABLE

17 LAWS TO UNLOCK YOUR HIDDEN POTENTIAL, SKYROCKET YOUR CONFIDENCE AND GET WHAT YOU WANT FROM LIFE

Why Should You Read This Book?

Have you ever set a goal you failed to achieve? Now, imagine what would happen if you had the perfect understanding of how success works and could rely on a set of specific rules to help you achieve any goal in any area of your life? Excited yet?

Often, the reason people fail to achieve their wildest goals and fail to live the life they want long term is their lack of understanding of how success works. Having no clear map to guide them, they feel lost in the sea of information, unable to identify exactly what they need to do to reach their goals. This misunderstanding leads them to live far below their potential and accomplish far less than they otherwise could.

This book will help you gain a crystal-clear understanding of how success works and will provide the tools and the habits to help you develop the mindset you require to achieve your goals in every aspect of your life.

You will greatly benefit from this book if you recognize yourself in one or more of the following statements:

- You want to understand how success works in order to achieve any future goal.
- You want to master each area of your life and design the life you desire within the next few years.
- You want to make a living from your passion—whatever that may be.

If any of the above statements apply to you, order a copy of this book and start your personal transformation today.

How to Use This Book

I encourage you to read all the way through this book at least once. After that, I invite you to revisit the book and focus on the section(s) you want to explore in greater depth.

In this book, I include a number of exercises. Although I don't expect you to work through them all, I hope you will choose your favorites and apply them in your life. Remember, the results you obtain from this book depend on how much time and effort you're willing to invest.

If you feel this book could be of any use to your family members or friends, make sure you recommend it to them.

INTRODUCTION

What if you could live your life as though success was inevitable? What if you knew with absolute certainty you would achieve most of your goals no matter how many times you fail along the way? How would that change the way you think, feel and act every day?

This is the concept I invite you to explore in this book.

The truth is, when it comes to transforming your life, your belief in yourself and in your vision is far more powerful than anything else. Extraordinary people don't become that way because they are geniuses; they are often ordinary people with an extraordinary mindset and a desire to fulfill their destiny no matter what obstacles may stand in their way. Successful individuals hold themselves to a high standard and see themselves for what they could become, not what they currently are. They maintain the vision of a compelling future where they are confident, happy and successful. And more importantly, they *believe*. Successful people believe they can achieve the results they want in each area of their lives whether it is their career, their relationships, their finance or their health.

World famous guru, Tony Robbins, says that in any interaction, people who display the most certainty have the most influence over the other(s). And in many cases, this is true. Now, what if *you* could be the person with the most certainty? What if you could develop the rock-solid confidence that success is not only inevitable for you, but also for everybody around you?

This book invites you to do just that. **It invites you to live your life as though success is inevitable for you.**

In these pages, I'll challenge you to make that conviction your main focus until it becomes a rock-solid belief that affects everything you do. I want you to hold that belief and remind yourself of it as often as possible, whether it is when you wake up, take a shower, drive to work or go to sleep. I want you to develop a level of confidence and certainty you've never experienced before, and I want to help you *expect* success and happiness to manifest in your life.

Imagine how much better your life would be if you understood and felt that, at a deeper level and in the long term, success is inevitable for you.

What new actions would you take? How much more confident would you be throughout your day? With such a belief, how would your life change over the next six months? What about the next twelve months? The next decade?

Success is inevitable if you are willing to:

- **Take the time to identify what you really want**
- **Work hard on yourself** and transform your mindset
- **Work hard on your craft** and develop all the skills you need to achieve your goals
- **Get rid of all excuses** to the best of your ability and take one hundred percent responsibility for your life no matter how hard it may be.
- *Never* **give up, and**
- **Believe that success is inevitable.**

The point of this book is not just to tell you success is inevitable. It is to explain *why* this is the case. To do so, we'll discuss at length how success works, and I'll show you a specific model you can use to achieve your future goals in any area of your life.

In **Part I**, we'll define success. I will introduce you to the power of responsibility and you will discover why belief, clarity and passion are critical to your success. I will explain in detail how you can develop these qualities.

In **Part II**, you will learn how to use the power of commitment to achieve success. You will learn why being committed—and not merely interested—is one of the prime keys to changing your life.

In **Part III**, I will demonstrate why trusting the process is critical to long-term success. You will learn the laws of success and how to develop the mindset needed to achieve each of your goals.

In **Part IV**, we will discuss the importance of building emotional resilience. You will discover why controlling your emotions is incredibly important, and you will also learn how to do so effectively.

In **Part V**, we will see how you can relate to others in a way that will guarantee your long-term success.

Finally, in the **Bonus** section, you will discover the additional core beliefs you can develop to achieve success. You will be introduced to some of the most powerful beliefs that, when developed over time, will allow you to raise your game and achieve more than you can ever imagine.

Are you ready?

YOUR FREE ACTION GUIDE

To help you take action on what you'll learn in this *"Success Principle Series"* I've create free action guides. If you haven't yet, you can grab them at the URL below:

https://whatispersonaldevelopment.org/success-series

PART I

MASTERING THE FOUR POWERS THAT ENABLE SUCCESS

1
SUCCESS IS A MINDSET

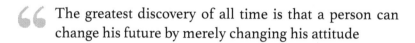 The greatest discovery of all time is that a person can change his future by merely changing his attitude

— OPRAH WINFREY, HOST OF THE OPRAH WINFREY SHOW

Success is a mindset. Working hard isn't enough. Unless you develop the mindset required to achieve your vision, you'll probably never turn your vision into a reality. To achieve extraordinary results, you need to develop an extraordinary mindset. Developing such a mindset requires you to utilize the four fundamental powers for success:

1. Responsibility
2. Belief
3. Clarity, and
4. Passion

If you picture success as a pyramid, the power of responsibility is its foundation on which everything else rests. The second layer is made up of three blocks: the power of belief, the power of clarity and the power of passion.

Defining success

Before I talk in greater detail about success and before I introduce the power of belief, clarity and passion, I will define what I mean by success.

Though money may be part of it, success is not solely defined in terms of the size of your bank balance. Being rich and famous doesn't necessarily guarantee you a happy life. Many wealthy people live miserable lives. In fact, you're probably better off than many rock stars or movie stars you might look up to.

Before we go further, I want you to develop your own definition of success. Too often, we fail to realize the extent our definition of success has been influenced by society or by our family and friends. It is extremely important you take a step back and ask yourself what you *really* want from life. You must do this with brutal honesty. Don't worry, you don't have to share your definition of success with anybody else. Feel free to go wild.

I define success as living life on my own terms. That is, doing something I love, surrounded by people I love, while having the money and/or time to do the things I want. After all, isn't that what everyone looks for?

For you, success might mean working only twenty-five hours a week to allow yourself plenty of time to dedicate to your hobbies and/or family (even if this means making less money). Alternatively, success could mean working sixty hours a week or more doing something you really enjoy and, in doing so, making good money so you can afford the things you want.

So, how you would define success? Are you living up to that definition right now?

* * *

Action step

Write down your personal definition of success using the free **Action Guide** (*Part I. Mastering the Four Powers That Enable Success*).

2

THE POWER OF ABSOLUTE RESPONSIBILITY

> Take full responsibility for what happens to you. It's one of the highest forms of human maturity ... It's the day you know you have passed from childhood to adulthood.
>
> — JIM ROHN, MOTIVATIONAL SPEAKER.

The key to achieving anything you want and to making your success inevitable is to take absolute and total responsibility for your life. This is by far the most powerful thing you can do to change your life. You must accept responsibility for all your actions and accept that you are mainly where you are because of who you are and what you do.

If you want to be somewhere else five years from now, how you think and the way you act will have to change. Your core belief will have to change. What you do every day will have to change.

As you start thinking and acting differently—and I cannot stress this highly enough—you cannot fail to alter the course of your destiny.

Remember, human beings are the only species on earth with the power to design the future they want to live in.

Why taking responsibility is critical

People like to blame others or bad luck for their situation in life. And sometimes, it is undeniable that an event or situation may have been caused by external factors, at least to some extent.

No wonder the urge to blame external factors can be so strong, especially when these same external factors might be partially responsible for your life circumstances. The real meaning of taking responsibility, however, has nothing to do with apportioning blame or being right. You're not looking at who is to blame for a particular situation. You're not searching for a culprit.

To be honest, it doesn't matter who was right and who was wrong *in the past*. To achieve success *in the future*, you need to take one hundred percent responsibility for your life right now.

It's about taking absolute control over your life so you can achieve anything you've ever wanted to achieve. It's about reclaiming the power to transform your life. It's about making your long-term success and happiness an absolute priority.

As we'll see in more depth with *The Law of Humility*, your ability to set aside your ego and take responsibility for your life will greatly improve the results you achieve in every area of life.

Without responsibility no change is possible

The more responsibility you take for your life, the more power you have to change it. This is a universal law.

Why is this the case?

Imagine you're in an unsatisfying relationship. Naturally, you believe your partner is wrong while you're mostly, if not completely and consistently, right. In such a situation, how much power do you think you have to improve the relationship?

Since you believe you're not responsible for the quality of the relationship, not much.

Now, what if you were to take one hundred percent responsibility for your relationship? How much power would you have to change it?

Perhaps you could listen to your partner's complaints, determine whether there is some truth there and do something about it. Perhaps you could ask your partner what you could do better. Perhaps you could express the way you feel, instead of hiding your resentment. Or perhaps you could choose to separate if it's obvious the relationship is not working and has no chance of working in the future. As you accept full responsibility, the choices you can make dramatically increase. Also, the more options you have, the more power you have to change your life situation.

Taking extra responsibility

Taking absolute responsibility for your life means you're willing to accept as much responsibility as you possibly can.

Let's imagine you delegate a task to someone and the job isn't done properly. Your first reaction might be to blame the person for his or her incompetence. Instead, you should ask yourself, "How could I be responsible in this situation?" For instance, perhaps you asked the wrong person to complete the task. Maybe you didn't give them the right instructions. Or you may have failed to follow-up and monitor the progress of the project. As you can see, even in this specific situation you are responsible for the outcome of the task.

In fact, when you trace a problem back to its origins, you'll often find you could have avoided it if you had taken more care. Maybe you could have taken more time to plan or could have asked for advice. Or maybe you could have been less complacent. To address this issue, I encourage you to work through the following exercise:

1. Look at one thing that currently bothers you—the challenge.
2. Go back in time and try to find the root cause.

3. Then, decide what you could have done differently to prevent the challenge from happening in the first place.

By completing this exercise, you may realize how much overall responsibility you had for the outcome. One benefit of taking extra responsibly is that you will become better at anticipating problems. As you regularly ask yourself, "How am I responsible here," you will train your mind to look for ways to think and act differently. This, in turn, will allow you to prevent similar problems from happening in the future (e.g., asking the wrong person to do a task in the first instance).

Accepting what you can't change

Taking absolute responsibility also entails accepting things you cannot change. If you lose your legs in a car accident and end up in a wheelchair, you might not be able to do much about it, but you can accept your situation one hundred percent. The motivational speaker, Nick Vujicic was born with no arms or legs. As you can imagine, he was angry about his situation for years. He thought he would never be able to find a job or get married like "normal" people. He could have remained bitter for his entire life, but at some point, he decided to accept his disabilities and make the most of his challenges. He then became a successful motivational speaker and a father of two. Now that is what I call a real success story.

The bottom line is you are responsible for how you react to life's events. Blaming others won't help you. The blame game will only succeed in making you unhappy.

What about you? How would your situation change if you decided to take one hundred percent responsibility for your life?

Now, look at each area of your life. How could you improve each one by taking absolute responsibility for them?

Take more responsibility for your life than anybody else and you'll see that, in the long run, your life will dramatically improve.

Remember, nothing in your life can change until you do. If your life is going to change, the change will have to start with you.

***

Action step

Using your **Action Guide**, answer the following question: What is the one thing you could start doing today to get better results in one particular area of your life? (*Section I. The Power of Absolute Responsibility*).

3

THE POWER OF BELIEF

> If you limit your choices only to what seems possible or reasonable, you disconnect yourself from what you truly want, and all that is left is a compromise.
>
> — ROBERT FRITZ, AUTHOR OF THE PATH OF LEAST RESISTANCE.

The ability to believe is one of the most fundamental components of success. It opens the door to limitless possibilities and allows you to turn all your dreams and desires into reality. Belief enables you to develop your skills, abilities and talents to the highest degree possible, and it helps you make your biggest contribution to the world.

Your level of belief in yourself and in your overall vision acts as a filter to determine what you can and cannot do in life. Lack of self-belief erodes your potential and severely reduces what you can accomplish. As Henry Ford once said, *"Whether you think you can, or you think you can't—you're right."*

Failing to believe in something almost automatically removes that thing from your reality, making it almost impossible for it to manifest in your life. For instance:

- If you believe you can't find the job you love, you'll never design a career you're passionate about.
- If you believe you can't improve, you'll continue to live far below your potential.
- If you believe you can't develop a healthy self-esteem, you'll live the rest of your life with low self-confidence, which will negatively affect your well-being and your potential. It could even prevent you from attracting your ideal partner or designing a meaningful career.

We *must* believe in something before we can see it. It doesn't work the other way around. This is what makes human beings different from every other animal on the planet. We can use our imagination to turn the invisible—an idea—into the visible. With strong belief, we can have a tangible result in the real world.

Unfortunately, most people struggle to reach a level of belief that will allow them to transform their life. Instead, they search for leaders and gurus to tell them how to think and behave. Psychological experiments have shown how easily we can be influenced.

For instance, the Milgram experiment revealed how most people blindly obey individuals perceived as authority figures—in the Milgram test, this was the man with a white coat. In this well-known experiment, participants were led to believe they were administering electric shocks to "students" to study how people learn. The real purpose of the experiment, however, was to see how participants would react to orders when it went against their conscience. In many cases, the participants blindly followed the so-called doctor's orders, even when the "students" (who were, in fact, actors) explicitly demanded they stop, mentioning a heart problem. In short, under the instructions or commands of the so-called doctor, many participants were willing to endanger the lives of the "students" rather than disobey orders from an authority figure.

The Asch conformity experiments is another example of how easily people can be influenced. In these experiments, a group of participants were each given two cards; one card displayed a single line, the other showed three lines, A, B and C, each of different lengths. The group of participants was, in turn, asked to say aloud which of the three lines on the second card (A, B or C) matched the length of the line on the first card. Among the eight participants, seven were actors and only one was the actual participant. In this experiment, the actual participants gave wrong answers 36.8% of the time (as opposed to 1% of participants in the control group, without the actors).

After seeing the majority giving incorrect answers one after the other, some participants concluded that the majority must have been right. In short, they knew the correct answers, but didn't have the confidence to contradict the group majority.

These two classic and well-cited experiments show how our lack of self-belief can lead us to make wrong and even harmful decisions under the pressure of a single authority figure or a group of people.

While these are only experiments, they reflect how society works. Society tends to act as an invisible force that pulls us toward mediocrity. The authority figures (our parents, teachers and the media) and our peers (friends and colleagues) constantly remind us our goals are impossible, and thereby dissuade us from pursuing our dreams successfully.

If you put a group of crabs in a bucket, none of them will survive. Whenever a crab tries to escape, others will grab it and drag it back down. As you climb your way toward greatness, you may feel as though you are trying to escape from a bucket, with everyone pulling you back. This is especially true if you happen to live in a toxic environment with no successful role model to look up to.

In truth, you will certainly fail to achieve your goals many times, but this is how you grow and learn. Through repeated "failures" you'll learn from your mistakes and end up achieving far more than you can ever imagine. This is how your mind works. Unfortunately, most people will never reach this stage because they don't believe in themselves enough to dare to fail enough times. As a result, they give up too soon.

To succeed in life, you must learn to develop an unshakable belief in yourself and in your vision. You need to reach a point where your self-belief exceeds the lack of belief other people have in you and in your vision. Whenever possible, you should avoid spending time with negative people who do not believe in you or your ultimate success—they will only drag you back down into the bucket of obscurity.

How to believe in yourself and in your vision

In his book, *6 Months to 6 Figures,* Peter Voogd wrote, "*There is nothing more powerful than self-confidence in multiplying your income by two, by three, by five, and then by ten.*"

Think about this for a moment. What if Peter Voogd is correct? How magical would that be?

Self-confidence is one of the key factors to success. In this section, we'll see how to develop a rock-solid belief in yourself and in your vision.

My friend, Mike Pettigrew, author of *The Most Powerful Goal Achieving System in the World*, explains how his low level of self-esteem directly impacted his business and his life. His business was losing money, primarily because he priced his service too low. Facing bankruptcy, he doubled his prices. Surprisingly, none of his customers left. In fact, some of them even told him his services had been too cheap in the first place. What do you think his main reason was for not charging enough money? Yes, that's right—it was his lack of self-confidence.

Self-confidence will not only affect your bank account, it will also affect other areas of your life. Low self-confidence may prevent you from going after the job you really want. It may stop you from asking out the person you like. Finally, low self-confidence can make you feel bad about yourself.

No matter what your level of self-confidence is now, I'm about to show you how you can boost it to give yourself a better chance to create the life you really want.

The Self-Empowerment Triangle

For the most part, what you think, feel and do determines your level of confidence. When your thoughts, feelings and actions work together to create the identity of a highly confident person, your confidence will grow naturally and exponentially. In other words, success most definitely breeds success.

Unfortunately, we often fail to make the connection between self-discipline (what we do consistently), and self-esteem/self-confidence (how we think and feel about ourselves). Self-confidence and self-esteem are largely determined by our ability to complete and achieve our goals. The more self-discipline we develop, the more we respect ourselves and the more confident we feel as a result. This is what I call the *Self-Empowerment Triangle*.

The *Self-Empowerment Triangle* works as follows:

As we discipline ourselves to finish small tasks to the best of our ability (self-discipline), we feel better about ourselves (self-esteem). By repeatedly doing so, we learn to trust our ability to achieve our future goals (self-confidence).

Another key element required to make the *Self-Empowerment Triangle* work is self-compassion, which is the glue that binds self-discipline, self-confidence and self-esteem. Self-compassion enables self-empowerment and makes it durable. If we keep beating ourselves up whenever we "fail," our self-esteem and self-confidence will suffer. We'll talk about self-compassion in more detail in a separate section (see *Cultivating self-compassion*).

Now, for clarity sake, here is a brief definition of each of the elements constituting the *Self-Empowerment Triangle*:

- **Self-discipline:** the ability to do what you should do, when you should do it, whether you feel like it or not.
- **Self-esteem:** the respect you have for yourself.
- **Self-confidence:** the inner knowledge that you can cope effectively with life's challenges and, by doing so, you will achieve your goals.
- **Self-compassion:** the deep understanding that you're *exactly* where you're supposed to be at any given moment and that you have a total love and acceptance of the current situation.

Self-Empowerment Triangle

Now, let's see how you can use the *Self-Empowerment Triangle* to generate success.

Building self-discipline

Your ability to do what you should do when you should do it, whether you feel like it or not, will, for the most part, determine your future success. To develop more self-discipline, you must start by completing small tasks consistently. As you do so, your self-esteem will grow, (see also **Part IV: Overruling your feelings**).

Fortunately, you don't have to start big. Consistency is more important than magnitude or intensity. By setting small, achievable goals you will find it easier to remain consistent over the years and therefore are more likely to be successful. Take New Year's

Resolutions as an example. At the beginning of the year, the nation's gyms become crowded with new members who are inspired by their resolutions. A couple of months (or weeks) later, gyms are empty again and exercise classes return to their standard occupancy. Needless to say, setting large, unrealistic resolutions (goals) is not how to build confidence and achieve great results.

Rather than trying to accomplish massively ambitious tasks, choose a simple target and commit to completing it every day. Select a task linked to one of your major long-term goals. Perhaps you could complete a certain number of press-ups every morning. Or maybe you could jog a certain distance. Alternatively, you could write a specific number of words or read a few pages of your favorite inspirational book. Simply completing one simple thing each day will enhance your self-discipline and your self-confidence, and it will help make you feel better about yourself.

In my book, *Habits That Stick*, I offer a list of the seven most powerful habits you can adopt. These habits will have a profound impact on your life in the long run, and they include:

Setting daily goals

Setting your goals every single day will boost your productivity. To set your goals, take a pen and paper and make a list of three to five tasks you want to accomplish. Then, prioritize these tasks in order of importance. Complete your first task before moving on to the next one. Repeat the process until all the tasks are done.

Meditating

Meditation provides many benefits, which include:

- Reduced worry
- Enhanced self-esteem and self-acceptance
- Improved resilience against pain
- Heightened/Enriched mood
- Increased focus, and
- Improved blood pressure.

If you want to learn more, check out the article the following article: http://liveanddare.com/benefits-of-meditation. It mentions over seventy-six scientific benefits of meditation. There are many ways to meditate, but it can be as simple as closing your eyes and focusing on your breathing. You can begin by spending just a few minutes on this each day.

Practicing gratitude

Practicing gratitude is a powerful way to enhance your overall happiness. To learn how to cultivate gratitude refer to the section, *Practicing Gratitude* in **Part IV**.

Consuming motivational books and videos

No matter how exciting your goals may be, there will be times when you won't feel like doing anything. Feeding your mind with inspirational material on a daily basis will help you stay motivated for the long haul.

Daily exercise

Studies have shown that moderate exercise has a positive impact on both your physical and mental health. According to research published in PLoS Medicine, two and a half hours moderate exercise each week could add more than three years to your lifespan. As for the benefits of exercising on your mood, they are both immediate and long term. Professor of psychology, Michael Otto, says people usually derive a mood-enhancement effect within five minutes of partaking in moderate exercise.

To learn more about the power of mini-habits, check out Stephen Guise's book, *Mini-Habits*.

* * *

Action step

Write down one thing you could start doing consistently every day for the next thirty days. And then, most importantly, *do it!* (*Part II. The Power of Belief*)

How to boost your self-esteem

As you adopt one simple daily habit and stay consistent with it, you will boost your self-esteem. This is one of the main reasons daily self-discipline is so important.

How often have you felt guilty because you didn't do what you planned to do? This is when self-compassion is so valuable. A healthy dose of self-compassion is far more powerful in helping you stay on track with your goal than constant self-criticism. In the section, *Cultivating Self-Compassion*, we will learn about the concept in greater depth. We will also learn what you can do to cultivate self-compassion.

Additionally, self-discipline helps you build momentum. Have you ever felt good after completing a task you have been delaying for a while? And, after completing the chore, didn't it make you want to tackle similar tasks? This is known as the power of momentum.

However, developing more self-discipline is only one way to boost your self-esteem. Below are a few effective ways to enhance your self-esteem:

Acknowledge your small wins. While things may not always go as planned, we can choose to focus on all the things we're doing well. This is what confident people do. They blow their own horn, if you will. Conversely, people with little self-confidence tend to dwell on their failures. No wonder they feel inadequate. How about you? Do you acknowledge your small wins?

Reinterpreting your past. Instead of focusing on negative events, make sure you remember events that make you feel good and ignore all the negative ones. You'll notice that the things you refuse to focus on no longer exist and, from your mind's perspective, this is absolutely true. The less you think about something, the less power it has to generate negative feelings. And if you think that this is "cheating" please note, the human mind does this naturally. We tend to embellish past memories and often end up fantasizing about them. We remember how happy we were, dismissing all the little things that annoyed us at the time. This is a healthy process. You can take the same process one step further by consciously remembering positive events and discarding negative ones. Or you can give past events an entirely new meaning as I'll demonstrate in the next point.

Reframing your past. You can choose to interpret your past differently. Rather than focusing on your mistakes, learn to show compassion toward your younger self and acknowledge your noble intentions. Realize your past is not set in stone, at least not in the way our brain interprets it. After all, we only remember fragments of our past, and we filter these memories based on our own changing belief system and self-image. As David J. Schwartz wrote in his excellent book, *The Magic of Thinking Big*, "*Much lack of self-confidence can be traced directly to a mismanaged memory.*" As you learn to manage your memory better, your self-esteem will naturally grow alongside it.

Here are some practical exercises to boost your self-esteem:

1. What three things do you want to acknowledge yourself for? They can be simple things such as eating healthily, helping a friend or waking on time. The idea is to learn to focus on the things you're doing well.

Another quick tip: make sure you acknowledge yourself for the things that matter to you. For instance, I dread administrative tasks and it can sometimes take me weeks just to fill in a form that requires a few minutes to complete. I like to celebrate these types of accomplishments because they are meaningful to *me*.

2. Write down all your accomplishments. Don't be shy, write down all your past accomplishments—small and big. This exercise works best when done once in a while. After you have done so, allow yourself to feel proud of these past accomplishments. Mix them together and, if it helps, listen to songs that elicit feelings of gratitude while doing so.

3. **Reward yourself.** Make sure you celebrate every important milestone. For instance, I celebrate each time I release a new book. I also set specific rewards for major goals. Ideally, the reward should be something you genuinely want. It could be going out for dinner, eating your favorite cake or buying a long-awaited book.

4. **Record every positive thing people have said about you.** In a journal, write down all the positive things people tell you. For instance, it could be a compliment your colleagues give you on your hairstyle. Or it could be something nice your spouse tells you. This process will train you to look for the positives in your daily life. I created such a journal a few years ago and go through it on a regular basis, updating it whenever necessary.

These two things alone—developing self-discipline and acknowledging your small wins—will go a long way in increasing your self-esteem. The key is to be consistent.

* * *

Action step

Complete at least one of the four exercises above using the **Action Guide** (*Section II. The Power of Belief*).

Building self-confidence

The daily discipline of achieving small tasks and acknowledging your wins will boost your self-confidence over the long term. And the more confident you become, the more likely you are to achieve your goals which will, in turn, further enhance your confidence. I consider this one of my virtuous circles.

Understanding success

Learning about the mechanism of success will allow you to develop even more confidence, which is what this book is mainly about. It will make you realize that success is inevitable through a clear understanding of how success works. As you build a better mental representation of the process called "success," you will feel far more confident in your ability to achieve your goals long term.

Having integrity

Another key to building deeper self-confidence and self-respect is having integrity in everything you do. This means telling the truth to yourself and to others and doing what you know is right. This implies knowing your core values, beliefs and personality traits and being able to identify your strengths and the areas of interest you wish to pursue. We'll talk about that in more detail in the following sections when we discuss the power of clarity and passion.

Finally, remember you can learn to believe in yourself. Nobody is born with self-confidence and self-belief. Confidence is something you acquire over time. Thus, if you've been struggling with confidence issues, don't assume anyone but you can build self-confidence because of X, Y or Z. You *can* become more confident and you *will*. In fact, like success, self-confidence is inevitable. There is no reason you can't develop more self-confidence in the long term.

By now, you should understand why believing in something is critical in helping you achieving anything you want in life.

* * *

Action step

Complete the corresponding exercises in the **Action Guide** (*Section II. The Power of Belief*).

4
THE POWER OF CLARITY

> It's a lack of clarity that creates chaos and frustration. Those emotions are poison to any living goal.
>
> — STEVE MARABOLI, MOTIVATIONAL SPEAKER AND AUTHOR.

The third step to creating a successful life is to know exactly what you want. In his excellent book, *High Performance Habits*, Brendon Burchard identifies "seeking clarity" as one of the six fundamental habits used by high achievers. It sounds obvious, but you cannot fulfill a vision you don't have. Most people achieve mediocre results simply because they don't really know what they want. These people wake up every day with no clear objective. They have no goal for the year. Neither do they have a specific vision for each area of their lives. As a result, they get no closer to their ideal life.

But why wander through life hoping for success when you can decide exactly what you want and take positive daily action to make your vision a reality?

Remember, you can use your imagination to design the life you want, and this is what differentiates you from any other living thing on earth. Creating a clear picture of your ideal future is critical. You *must* seek clarity to design a better future. You must work on refining your vision continuously by asking yourself, "What do I really want?"

Once you have determined your life goal, it becomes easier to focus your time, effort and resources on the desired outcome. Instead of being "all over the place," you will be able to zero-in on your vision and act with laser-sharp focus. This, in turn, will stop you wasting time on trivial tasks and will significantly increase your performance and improve your ultimate chance of success.

The bottom line is that wanting to make more money, to be successful or to be happy aren't goals. They are merely wishes or fantasies. You must become crystal clear and define what you want as specifically as possible. For instance:

- Exactly how much money do you want to make?
- What does success look like to you?
- What does happiness mean to you?

Unless you can answer these questions, you risk spending most of your life chasing the wrong things. To avoid this outcome, make sure you know who you are and what you want from life.

1. Defining what you want

The best way to identify what you want is to have an honest look at each area of your life. How close are you to your ideal in the following areas of your life? Consider the following aspects:

- **Career/mission:** do you wake up excited about your goals? Do you feel as though you're making a difference in your own unique way?
- **Family:** do you spend enough quality time with your family?
- **Finance:** do you make enough money to do what you want in life or do you struggle to make ends meet?

- **Health (Physical):** do you have a healthy body?
- **Health (Emotional):** how good is your emotional wellbeing?
- **Personal growth:** do you feel as though you're growing into the person you want to become?
- **Relationship:** is your relationship with your partner the best it could be?
- **Spirituality:** do you feel a sense of connection with God/the universe?

Rank yourself on a scale of 1 to 10 for each of the areas above, where 1 means you are miles away from your ideal, and 10 means you have it exactly the way you want.

Now for each area, take a few minutes to visualize in detail what your ideal vision looks like. See yourself as being already at a 10 in each area and answer the following questions:

- **Career:** what contribution are you making to society and the world in general? What does your day at work look like?
- **Family:** how are you interacting with your family on a day-to-day basis and how does that make you feel?
- **Finance:** how much money are you earning each month? What are you doing with this money?
- **Health:** how do you feel every day? What does your diet look like?
- **Personal growth:** what three words best describe you? What do you think people say about you when you're not there? What message are you spreading to the world?
- **Relationship:** what emotions are you experiencing daily? How do you treat your partner? And how do they feel as a result? How does your partner treat you?
- **Spirituality:** how do you serve God or the universe? What spiritual qualities do you embody?

If you can define what you want in each area of your life, you're already ahead of most people.

Writing down what you want

Now you have defined what you want in each area of your life, let's try to be even more specific. Remember, *clarity is power*. For each area, write down a short statement that defines how your ideal self feels, thinks and acts. This represents your vision for each specific area.

Below are two tips to help you design an effective vision statement.

1. It must be inspiring when you read it. Write something that resonates with you and that motivates you to take action. Make your statement as short and concise as possible.
2. You must be able to visualize the outcome. Add specific visions to give your statement more power. What are you doing? Who are you surrounded by? How do you feel?

Here are some examples of vision statements:

Career/mission:

I wake up every day with a clear purpose and a deep sense of responsibility. I have an unshakable belief in myself, an unwavering commitment to change people's lives, and my love for others allows me to transform countless people's lives.

Finance:

I create wealth. I manifest abundance in my life by serving people all around me and inspiring them to become the best they can be. I can buy all the things I need, do all the things I want, and become all I can become.

Health:

My body is my temple. Every day I nourish it with incredibly healthy foods that give me abundant energy to take care of my family, do amazing work and make each day memorable. I'm excited about living a long, happy and healthy life, savoring each moment with a deep sense of gratitude and love. The healthier I am, the happier I become.

Personal growth:

I'm totally confident in my ability to achieve anything I want. Every day, I become better, stronger and wiser. By who I've become, I inspire everybody around me to be who they've always wanted to be. I'm overcoming my fears and limitations so I can love more, live more and serve more. My compassion toward myself and others has no limit. My determination to be all I can be has no boundary. I am unlimited potential and pure love.

These are merely examples. The key is to make sure your vision statement inspires you. The more you imbue it with your values and use words that strike powerful chords, the better.

For instance, if you want to become healthier, you have to determine why it matters to you. You can sometimes pursue the right goal for the wrong reasons. While your focus may be on losing weight, what you really want is to stay healthy until old age so you can watch your great-grand children grow. This simple reframing can help boost your motivation and increase your likelihood of success.

This isn't an easy exercise so don't worry about coming up with the perfect vision statement. You can always refine it over time and will probably need to do so as you evolve over the years. At this stage, having some clarity is far better than having none at all.

Knowing your core values

Unless you know what drives you deep down, you'll have a hard time designing a life you truly enjoy. What do you value most? Truth? Freedom? Relationships? Learning? Creativity?

What are values?

Values aren't things you believe you should do because society or your family said so, but they are what you're naturally drawn towards. For instance, perhaps you have a love for learning, a yearning for truth or a craving for more freedom.

Think of your core values as the principles that determine whether you live your life with integrity. That is, whether you're acting every day as, deep down, you know you should. When you fail to act with integrity, you'll experience resistance and suffering. This is usually a sign you're not living up to your true values.

Of course, we all have many values that are important to us. The key to success, however, is to identify those which are truly the most important.

Take a few minutes to write down your top ten core values. Again, don't try to come up with the perfect answers, simply trust your intuition and write down what feels right to you at this moment.

The importance of self-awareness

Cultivating self-awareness, defined as "the ability to learn about yourself every day and self-reflect," is essential to help you identify who you are and what you want. It is difficult to live a great life without true self-awareness. While you may have a seemingly successful career, without self-awareness, you run the risk of living an unfulfilled life that fails to reflect your core values or personality. Here are some examples of what self-awareness encompasses:

Being able to identify your core values and live by them. Refer to the previous section on discussing values.

Knowing your weaknesses. Identify your weaknesses and find ways to cope with them. This could be by working on them, having someone else support you or simply ignoring them. Some weaknesses can act as bottlenecks that prevent you from reaching higher levels of success and happiness, while other weaknesses may be irrelevant (which is often the case). I recommend you work mostly on weaknesses that may prevent you from achieving your long-term visions—your bottlenecks—and ignore the others. Meanwhile, work on your strengths to become truly exceptional at what you're doing.

Understanding your core beliefs and the way they affect your behaviors and actions. Do you hold disempowering beliefs relating to money? Do you believe you can improve in any area you want (growth mindset) or do you believe you're doomed to stay at your current situation (fixed mindset)? Reading this book will allow you to develop new empowering beliefs, but only if you take action to change for the better.

Identifying the recurrent thought patterns that prevent you from reaching your potential. What negative emotions do you experience on a regular basis? Do you often think you're not good enough? Do you keep beating yourself up? If so, what major thoughts or circumstances trigger these patterns? A great exercise is to write down the emotions you experience during the day every night for a week. It will help you identify some of your most common thoughts and emotions.

Identify your "zone of genius," i.e., what you're doing better than anybody else. What are some of the things only you can do? Don't dismiss anything. Perhaps it is your incessant desire to learn. Perhaps it is your ability to influence people. Perhaps it is your exceptional memory. Seemingly unimportant strengths can make a huge difference in your life when you leverage them to the maximum. A great exercise to help you identify your strengths is to send an email to your family, friends and/or colleagues and simply ask them what they believe your particular strengths are. Another tip is to look at the tasks you find so easy you can't understand why other people find the same tasks difficult.

Knowing whether you're an extrovert or an introvert and understanding all the implications. The key difference between extroverts and introverts is in the way they recharge their batteries. Extroverts need to be around people and live in stimulating environments to feel energized. Introverts, on the other hand, feel most energized when they are in quiet environments by themselves or with a few people. To learn more about introversion, I invite you to refer to my book, *The Thriving Introvert: Embrace the Gift of Introversion and Live the Life You Were Meant to Live.*

Being able to monitor your emotions and avoid reacting mechanically. Your ability to control your emotions greatly determines your happiness and your overall performances. In **Part IV**, we'll discuss in great length what you can do to manage your emotions better. You can learn more about emotions in my book, *Master Your Emotions: A Practical Guide to Overcome Negativity and Better Manage Your Feelings.*

Identifying your blind spots and seeking new perspectives. You can easily get stuck in the same old paradigm of thinking and end up unable to see new perspectives. Take note of when you lose sight of the big picture and seek the help of people who can give you some perspective. This could be by hiring a coach or talking to a friend.

Being able to listen to your intuition. You're here to live *your* life, not the life other people want you to live. Your ability to listen to your intuition can be developed in different ways. For instance, you can start making decisions based on your intuition rather than doing what other people expect of you. You can also spend more time alone to reduce external influences, whether they be your family and friends or the media. Additionally, asking your subconscious mind questions such as, "What am I supposed to do?" or "What do I really want?" can also help. The best time to do this is before going to sleep, which is when your subconscious mind is most receptive.

Self-awareness leads to clarity. Realize that the cultivation of self-awareness is an on-going process and continuously seek clarity by identifying what matters most to you (your core value) and how you want to express yourself to the world (your purpose).

People who know exactly what they want to do tend to achieve far more than people with no clear vision. This is because they can move toward their vision with laser-sharp focus rather than scattering their energy.

* * *

Action step

Complete the corresponding exercises in the **Action Guide** to gain clarity on what you really want (*Section III. The Power of Clarity*).

2. Setting crystal clear goals

Gaining clarity regarding who you are and what you want to be or do happens at a macro level. You must also gain clarity at the micro level, by setting crystal clear and specific goals.

Most people only have vague goals. There are several reasons for this. One obvious reason is they don't know what they want. Another is probably that they have a fear of failure. After all, if they set a goal and fail to achieve it, they consider themselves a "failure." Yet another reason is that they were never taught how to set goals. Sadly, there is no course on goal setting at school. As a result, most people will graduate from school or university without having learned how to set clear goals and achieve them.

What goals are

Goals are desirable results you want to achieve at some time in the future. Ideally, they are aligned with your values and part of a bigger vision or purpose. Setting goals is like entering a destination into your GPS. Goal setting gives clarity and allows your subconscious mind to work on your goals 24/7. In the same way that you can't type the name of a city and expect to arrive at the specific address, you can't set an ill-defined goal of, say, making more money, being happy or losing weight and expect to achieve the tangible results you're after. You must know precisely what you want to achieve in order to create a plan and enable your subconscious mind to guide you.

Let's see how you can set goals effectively.

Setting SMART goals

You may be familiar with SMART goals, but it won't hurt to review the process quickly.

In this instance, "SMART" stands for:

- **Specific:** what exactly do you want? What are you trying to achieve?
- **Measurable:** can you assess the progress toward your goal easily? How will you know whether you've achieved it?
- **Achievable:** is the goal achievable? Is the timeframe realistic? Can you put in the effort required, despite your other responsibilities?
- **Relevant:** is the goal in line with your core values? Does it excite you?
- **Time-bound:** does your goal have a clear deadline?

Below is one example of SMART goals. It's actually one of the goals I set at the beginning of 2018.

My goal: I will complete eight books by December 31st, 2018.

- Is it specific? Yes, I have to write eight books within twelve months.
- Is it measurable? Yes, I can break down my goal into eight, six-week-long milestones, and make it easy to assess whether I'm on track.
- Is it achievable? Yes, I've been able to write books in short periods of time before, so I know I can do it again. I have the time and willingness to do so.
- Is it relevant? Yes, I like writing inspirational books. The goal is aligned with my mission of helping people become their best self.
- Is it time-bound? Yes, there is a clear deadline, which is December 31st, 2018.

You want your goals to be at least this specific.

Breaking down your goals

No matter how big your goal is, you can always break it down into smaller tasks. A yearly goal can be broken down into a 90-day goal, a monthly goal, a weekly goal and even a daily goal. For instance, a goal of writing eight books in one year can be divided into eight projects of smaller sub-tasks such as creating an outline, completing the first draft, completing the second draft, et cetera.

Then, for each goal, you can identify several key tasks you must work on every single day. Knowing what you have to do every day is invaluable as it sharpens your focus and makes it far more likely you'll achieve your long-term goal. We'll see how to identify key tasks in more detail in the upcoming section, *The Law of Effective Action*. In my case, an example of a key task would be writing every day.

Now you understand the importance of belief and have gained more clarity regarding who you are and what you want, let's look at the power of passion.

To learn how to set exciting goals and discover the SMART Goals Method in greater detail, I encourage you to refer to my book, *Goal Setting: The Ultimate Guide to Achieving Goals that Truly Excite You*.

* * *

Action step

Set at least one SMART goal and break it down in the **Action Guide** (*Section III. The Power of Clarity - Setting Crystal-clear Goals*).

5

THE POWER OF PASSION

> When you catch a glimpse of your potential, that's when passion is born.
>
> — Zig Ziglar, salesman and motivational speaker.

Are you passionate about what you're doing, or do you constantly rely on willpower alone to complete your tasks?

Highly successful people tend to be passionate, perhaps even obsessed, about what they're doing. They have a compelling vision, and they can't wait to make it happen. When you're deeply passionate about what you're doing, your chances of success long term are significantly increased. You have far more energy and enthusiasm, and you are able to persevere longer than the average person will. To paraphrase Steve Jobs, you must have a lot of passion for what you do because it's so hard, if you don't, any rational person would give up.

While there are heated debates on whether or not you should follow your passion, I believe that, to truly excel at what you do, you'll need to be extremely passionate about it.

As an example, I would probably have given up writing books a long time ago if I weren't obsessed about what I was doing. My level of obsession and my passion are the prime reasons you're able to read this book.

Defining passion

Before we explore the power of passion further, let's define what we mean by passion. While it can mean different things to different people, some of the following characteristics can be useful when trying to identify your specific passion as something that:

- **Naturally appeals to you:** when you're passionate about something, you're naturally drawn toward it. Look at what you're doing whenever you have free time. Are you losing track of time? That's a sign you're passionate.
- **Energizes you:** your passion should energize you. If you constantly have to motivate yourself, either your passion is not the right one for you, or it must be refined to energize you more effectively.
- **Stems from your life purpose:** a passion becomes even more powerful when it is linked to a broader mission or a life purpose. If your passion is impacting other people's lives in a positive way whether by entertaining them, helping them or touching them in some way, you might be onto something.

Now, let's have a look at six questions you can ask to help find your passion.

1. What did you enjoy doing when you were a young child? Often, what we do as kids reveals certain aspects of our personality. As time passes, we tend to become distracted by life (school, sport, work or even video games). When I was a kid I usedr to read a lot. Sometimes, I read most of the day. I even remember writing short stories when I was eight. Ironically, it took me more than twenty years to return to writing, and this is something I would never have predicted.

2. Who do you envy? What are the people you envy doing? I used to

be jealous of successful personal development bloggers. I wanted to do the same thing they were doing.

3. If all your family members, friends and people you know were no longer around and you were completely alone, what would you start doing? This situation allows you to think about what you want to do in this world without worrying about familial or societal pressures.

4. If you had all the time and money in the world, what would you do? (After partying and drinking cocktails on the beach got boring!) This situation removes issues you might have, like lack of time and lack of money, and gives you an opportunity to think about what you want to do more creatively and without boundaries.

5. If you had complete confidence and were already your absolute best self, what would you be doing with your life? This helps you envision your best self and removes any sense of limiting fear. It can also help you find clarity on what you really want to do in life.

6. How do you want to express yourself to the world? Do you want to entertain, educate, inspire, heal, teach or create? What emotions do you want people to feel as a result of the work you're doing? This question helps you clarify your means of expression and how you want to serve the world.

Being passionate gives you tremendous energy and makes it far more likely you'll achieve your goals long term. However, passion is not the only tool to rely on when designing an exciting future. Another way to generate energy is to identify compelling reasons why your goal *must* become a reality.

To learn how to find your passion, I encourage you to read my book, *The Passion Manifesto: Escape the Rat Race, Uncover Your Passion, and Design a Career and Life You Love.*

* * *

Action step

Uncover your passion using the corresponding section of the **Action Guide** (*Section IV. The Power of Passion*).

Strengthening your "whys"

While passion motivates you to engage in a specific activity you enjoy, it's not always effective in helping you achieve tangible results. For instance, perhaps you have a passion for cooking and want to open a small restaurant. However, opening a restaurant requires a lot of work completely unrelated to cooking. It's easy to use this as an excuse to give up and return to cooking as a hobby unless you have specific reasons why you *must* absolutely open that restaurant.

Similarly, you may love writing, but you *must* have specific reasons why becoming a full-time writer is a must. Otherwise, you'll continue to write as a hobby.

Don't get me wrong. Passion is powerful and will give you an edge, but you'll also need other powerful reasons to help you keep going when times are tough.

Looking for specific reasons to strengthen your ability to persevere is what I call *Why Stacking*.

For instance, one of my passions is studying the human mind to help people reach their full potential. My goal related to that passion is to make a living publishing books to help people become their "best self."

Now, to boost my motivation and ensure I achieve this specific goal, I developed inspiring reasons why my vision *must* become a reality. In the case of self-publishing books on Amazon, the benefits are straightforward and relate to:

- Being my own boss
- Having the freedom to work whenever I want
- Being able to travel whenever I want, and
- Having the ability to increase my revenue.

By *Why Stacking* all these benefits together and combining them with my passion for writing and helping others, I have boosted my motivation and persevered far more than I otherwise would.

You should consider doing the same thing with your passion by stacking as many "whys" as possible. The more compelling reasons you can come up with, the more likely you are to succeed long term. The key is to be specific and to make sure your "whys" speak to you at an emotional level. Let's see what this looks like by using the above examples. Specific reasons why being my own boss appeals to me are:

- It allows me to avoid the rush hour traffic. I can't stand crowded places and can't imagine having to use public transport every working day for forty years.
- I can work from home. At heart, I'm a real introvert and I like working from home. I'm far more productive when I'm by myself in a quiet environment, and that's what I enjoy the most.
- I don't like being told what to do. I've always been far more motivated when I'm doing things on my own rather than when a teacher or a boss issued instructions.
- I'm in charge of my own destiny. I experience a stronger sense of autonomy and control when I work for myself.
- I always have work to do. I will never again be in a position where I have no work but have to stay at the office because the rules force me to.
- I can focus only on what is productive. I don't need to attend unproductive meetings or work on low-value tasks that don't fundamentally improve the business.
- I can have integrity. In one of my previous jobs, I had to cold call companies and lie about who I was and what my intentions were just to obtain information.

Here are some specific reasons why having the freedom to work whenever I want is important to me:

- I can take breaks whenever I fancy.

- I can work as little or as much as I need to.
- I can wake up late or work until late at night if I wish.

And now for a number of specific reasons why being able to travel whenever I want is a must:

- I can visit my family when I choose to do so.
- I can attend interesting workshops or seminars without having to take days off or begging my boss for the leave.
- I can live and work in any country I choose. I love learning languages, and I'm interested in exploring different countries. To be able to do so, working for myself is an absolute must.

And finally, here are some specific reasons why having the possibility to increase my revenue is appealing:

- I am rewarded whenever my revenue increases which is highly motivating.
- If I grow my business, I know I will reap all the financial benefits. On the other hand, if, as an employee, I help my company make a million dollars, I will get little or no reward other than the occasional "thank you," if I'm lucky.

This is just the tip of the iceberg in terms of reasons why my goal of making money from my writing is essential for me. To be honest, when I discovered I could make money online doing what I love, I knew I had to make it happen no matter what obstacles stood in my way. As we'll see in the next section, this level of commitment and determination is a major component of success.

The different levels of "whys"

I believe four main motivators drive our behavior: Pain, pleasure, ego and love. When you are in control of your destiny, you can use these motivators to help you identify your "whys." Here is a brief description of each:

Pain: is what you want to shy away from. Wanting to avoid painful situations will compel you to take action. In the previous examples, pain includes:

- Commuting
- Spending my life doing something I don't enjoy
- Having little or no freedom, and
- Having a boss tell me what to do.

Pleasure: is what you want to gravitate toward, which is basically the opposite of pain. For me, pleasure includes:

- Being able to work from home
- Doing what I love, and
- Having freedom to act and do as I please.

Ego: is the desire to develop or maintain your sense of pride. For instance, it could be making your parents proud, being admired for your work or proving naysayers wrong. For me, it's a healthy dose of each.

Love: is the desire to contribute to something bigger than yourself. You can think of it as being akin to your "life's purpose." This could be a desire to make a difference in the world and to feel good as a result of it. For me, it is receiving emails from people telling me I helped changed their lives in some way.

As it happens, these four motivators are not equal in weight or importance. Whenever possible, I advise you to focus mostly on love and pleasure and use ego and pain whenever you need a short-term motivational boost. For instance, I often relied on ego and pain after a long day of work when I needed a spurt of motivation to work on my online business.

Please note, the more aligned you are with your purpose, the more you will rely on love as your main motivator. Similarly, a good understanding of your core values and personality traits will help you leverage the pleasure motivator more effectively.

* * *

Action step

Why Stacking: Write down all the reasons your goal is an absolute must for you in the **Action Guide** (*Section IV. The Power of Passion - Strengthening Your Whys*).

Bonus tip: whenever you feel your motivation is waning, take a sheet of paper and write down why the goal is important to you. Reignite the passion by reminding yourself why you even set your goal in the first place. Visualize all the wonderful things that will happen when you reach your goal. You might also want to go through your list of whys on a regular basis.

Turning your passion into an "obsession"

Being passionate is not enough. You must develop a healthy obsession or, as Napoleon Hill wrote in *Think and Grow Rich*, a "burning desire" to achieve your goal.

More recently, Angela Duckworth, in her book, *Grit: Why Passion and Resilience are the secret to success*, also stresses the importance of obsession. I believe obsession is a combination of passion and perseverance. When you are really passionate about something, you don't give up easily, do you?

Now you have written down all the reasons you must achieve your goal, you should feel more motivated to do whatever it takes to achieve it. Most people believe passion is something you either have or don't have. While certain people are definitely more passionate than others, I believe we can all strengthen our passion over time. You can actually *choose* to become more "obsessive." As a rule of thumb, the more committed you are to your vision—and the more compelling reasons you have to achieve it—the stronger your passion will grow.

How perseverance can lead to intense passion

Note that the intensity of your passion further grows as you keep persevering in the face of multiple setbacks and disappointments. Each time you refuse to give up you will develop more determination. Whenever you encounter intense setbacks, you will be forced to reconnect with your initial passion and to ask yourself why you even started along the route in the first place. This repeated questioning and continuous search for clarity and meaning will lead you to develop a burning desire.

For this reason, instead of thinking of passion as something you either have or don't have, I encourage you to see it as the natural process you go through as you progress toward your goal. Whenever you face setbacks, use this as an opportunity to strengthen your passion and seek clarity and meaning.

Now you have developed a stronger belief in yourself and in your vision, you've clarified what you want and have defined your passion, you're ready to take the next step. You are ready to **commit**.

PART II

ACTIVATING THE POWER OF COMMITMENT

6

ARE YOU COMMITTED OR ARE YOU MERELY INTERESTED?

> The difference between involvement and commitment is like ham and eggs. The chicken is involved; the pig is committed.
>
> — Martina Navratilova, former professional tennis player.

Most people never really commit to anything. They never make their goals a *must*. Instead, they look for ways out and keep Plan B in the back of their mind. While having a backup plan is smart, to achieve challenging targets that will transform your life, you must be willing to commit wholeheartedly to your goals.

Commitment is the key difference between success and failure and will often determine whether you achieve your wildest dreams or live a mediocre life. When you fail to decide what you want and fail to commit to it, your mind wanders around, jumping from one goal to another, your focus becomes blurred and your confidence wanes.

Conversely, when you commit to achieving a specific goal and eliminate all your excuses, you access the power of your mind. You become more resourceful, your confidence grows, and your focus is where it should be—on your goal. You progressively remove the uncertainty most people experience by deciding success has to happen no matter what.

Remember, committing is never casual. As Jim Rohn said, "*Casualness leads to casualty.*" The path to achieving the life you need must start with commitment. Great athletes, CEOs and other high performers are not just interested, they are committed to their goals, and you should be, too.

Whenever you find people who fail to achieve their goal, you'll generally find they lack commitment. Human beings have the incredible power to achieve extraordinary feats, but to do so they must be fully committed. In general, people struggle with commitment because:

- They don't truly believe their goal is possible (lack of belief)
- They don't know what they want and therefore feel stuck (lack of clarity), and
- They haven't come up with enough compelling reasons to motivate them to take action (lack of passion).

Look back at a time in your life where you failed to achieve a goal. Be honest with yourself. Were you one hundred percent committed to the goal or were you uncertain, indecisive and unmotivated?

Fortunately, once you know what you want (power of clarity), develop the belief you can do it (power of belief) and create enough compelling reasons for achieving your goal (power of passion), you'll find it relatively easy to commit fully to your goal.

Being committed to your goal means:

- **You're willing to learn whatever you need to learn to get where you want to be.** You never stop learning and are willing to set aside your ego to absorb any information that will help achieve your goal. You don't tolerate excuses like, "I

don't know how to do it." Instead, you commit to learning whatever you need to (see *The Law of Humility*).
- **You refuse to give up until you attain the results you want.** You persevere for years and commit to your goals long term. Even better, you write down a specific date a few years in the future and resolve to keep going until you reach that date. Whenever you feel like giving up, you remind yourself of the set date and refocus on your goal. This will help you focus on your major goal(s) and can prevent you from feeling overwhelmed or discouraged (see also *The Law of Perseverance*).
- **You constantly seek to raise your standards.** You ask yourself how you can improve. You look back at what didn't work and learn from your mistakes.
- **You swallow your pride.** Instead of becoming defensive when people criticize you or tell you to do things differently, ask yourself, "Is there any truth in that?" You accept feedback and, as much as possible, you learn from your mistakes. Again, you're committed to do whatever it takes to achieve your goal.

The bottom line is you *must* be committed. You've never heard of people becoming the best in their field because they showed a mere interest in it. People who design the life they want, do so because they are totally and utterly committed to it.

If you are committed to your goal, you will find a way, otherwise, you'll find an excuse.

* * *

Action step

Complete the exercises in the corresponding section of the **Action Guide** to assess your level of commitment (*Part II. Activating the Power of Commitment*).

PART III

MASTERING THE LAWS OF SUCCESS

7
UNDERSTANDING SUCCESS IS A PROCESS

To be successful, you must understand what success is and how it works. Most people hold misconceptions and often fail to realize what it really takes to succeed.

Success follows a specific process and requires you adopt a different mindset from the norm. While successful people understand that success is a process, most people believe success is an event that can happen almost overnight. They buy into the idea of a magic pill, a lottery win. Unfortunately, they won't lose forty pounds in thirty days by buying a $29.99 course. Neither will they be making $10,000 per month in thirty days with little effort for just $49.99. In short, there is no "magic bullet."

Anything of value—whether it is developing an intimate relationship or building a heart-centered business—takes a great deal of time and effort. This is what makes them so valuable. Needless to say, hard work is one of the prerequisites to success. It may seem common sense but it's worth repeating because most people largely underestimate the amount of work necessary to achieve their goals. In many cases, people give up before the game even starts, taking far less action than necessary to achieve their targets.

Let me give you an example. When I lived in Japan, many people asked me how I learned to speak Japanese so well. Many wished they could speak English as fluently as I speak Japanese. I told them the truth: I worked hard. But it didn't seem to be a convincing answer to these people. They assumed it must have been something else. They assumed I must have been a gifted linguist.

Surprisingly, I've rarely, if ever, seen someone wishing to speak a language—or achieve any other goal—do the required work to achieve the results they say they want. Most people seem to believe that by studying merely fifteen minutes a day for a few months they should be able to speak a language. When they can't, they assume something is wrong with them. I spent over ten thousand hours studying Japanese while living in Japan for almost a decade. Do you call that being a gifted linguist? No, I just followed one fundamental rule for success. I applied consistent effort over a long period of time.

This example clearly illustrates how most people hold unrealistic expectations. They assume success should come quickly and easily, which leads them to take insufficient action and give up prematurely.

Success takes time and effort because, for most endeavors, there is a significant learning curve and limited spots available. For instance, whenever a new business offers promising opportunities, people rush to buy shares in the company, which leads to fierce competition and an increase in the share price. In 2010, you could have made a lot of money publishing crappy e-books on Amazon. In 2018, that's impossible, because more people have entered this market, and Amazon's sales algorithm has become smarter.

Usually, the lower the barrier to entry, the fiercer the competition will be. Self-publishing on Amazon in 2018 is a great example. The barrier to entry is extremely low. If you can create your own cover—which you can do for free—you could technically release a book without spending a dime. However, the poor quality e-book probably won't sell. These days, to be successful as an independent writer, you need to develop a whole set of skills and arm yourself with patience, which is no different from any other businesses or meaningful goal in life. To succeed, you must (among other things):

1. Write quality books that people want to read
2. Create covers that actually sell your books
3. Write book descriptions that actually sell
4. Understand Amazon's sales algorithm (most indie authors earn a majority of their income from selling books on Amazon)
5. Market your books effectively, which can be done in multiple ways (Amazon ads, Facebooks ads, posting on social media, etc.), each method having its own learning curve
6. Develop relationships with authors in your niche, and
7. Brand yourself so that you stand out from the crowd, etc.

To sum up, you need to develop a deeper understanding of how success works and go through several years of hard work before you can achieve your goal, whether the goal be personal or professional.

Now, let's dive into *The Seventeen Laws of Success*. Each law, when applied individually, will increase the odds for success. As you combine them and practice them consistently, you'll dramatically increase your chances of success long term.

8
THE LAW OF HUMILITY

> Pride is pleasure arising from a man's thinking too highly of himself.
>
> — Baruch Spinoza, philosopher.

The Law of Humility states that, by swallowing your pride and accepting the requirement to change everything needed to achieve your goals, you will dramatically increase your chances of success.

Swallowing your pride

Have you ever watched the show called *The Profit*?

In this fascinating show, serial entrepreneur, Marcus Lemonis helps struggling businesses, by offering his own money in exchange for an equity share of their businesses.

What surprised me the most in the show was how defensive many business owners were. Their behavior and attitude seemed to be the main reason they were struggling. They were:

- Unwilling to reconsider the way they do business and let go of things that clearly didn't work
- Unwilling to take responsibility for their poor results. Instead, they blamed employees, customers, suppliers or external circumstances
- Unable to let go of control and allow employees do their job, and
- Unable to empower employees and nurture an environment in which they could grow.

I encourage you to watch the show. You'll find a few episodes on YouTube.

Here is another example of the role pride plays in someone's success. The internet marketing guru, Dan Lok, once complained to his mentor about his lack of success. Despite having started many different businesses, he was always struggling.

"I'm not making enough money, I'm struggling. I don't know why. My customers, they are like, cheap. They are really difficult to deal with. Oh man I don't know. The economy kind of sucks. And I think I'm paying too much taxes."

His mentor asked him to stop and said, *"It is very simple Dan. Let me teach you something. If your business sucks, it's because, as a business person, you suck."*

Ouch!

One of the major reasons people fail to achieve their business goals (and other goals), is they are unwilling to look in the mirror and accept the need to change everything that doesn't help them achieve the results they want.

For instance, many authors say they want to sell more books, but:

- They cling to their original cover ideas because the cover looks beautiful, even though the cover doesn't sell
- They are unwilling to lower the price of their books or offer temporary discounts because they spent so much time writing their book, and
- They shy away from promoting their books, believing that if they write a great book, readers will come by some form of thought osmosis.

I take authors as an example but the same goes for any profession. Your ability to swallow your pride and take responsibility for where you are now will largely determine your chances of success. Being humble enough to realize you may be wrong and accepting you don't know everything is a critical component of success.

In the end, the key question is whether you're getting results. Results don't lie. Ask yourself:

1. Is your business generating revenue?
2. Are you making money from your side business?
3. Did you win the competition?
4. Have you lost weight?
5. Are you happy?

To succeed long term, you must be willing to look at the harsh truth and make changes when necessary. You must be radically honest with yourself and take responsibility, even when you're only partially responsible.

Perhaps you believe you excel at what you do while reality shows a different picture. Or you may think your business idea is amazing, but it only works on paper. If so, you need to take a step back and ask yourself whether you are *really* doing what it takes to achieve success. If you keep doing what you've done today, this week or this month, will you achieve that specific goal? If the answer is no, you're going to have to change something!

Remember, the more you take responsibility for your life, the more likely you are to succeed. For instance, you can't improve your intimate relationship if you believe you're right and your partner is wrong. My gut tells me Dan Lok's mentor would say the following, "*If your intimate relationship sucks, it's because you suck as a partner.*"

You must let go of pride and accept one hundred percent responsibility for your life. Only then, can you make the changes you need to create the life you want.

Fighting complacency

Complacency is a major reason people fail to achieve their goals in the long term. It generally results from the belief you don't need to improve anymore because you're already doing a good enough job. While there is great value in celebrating your wins, you also run the risk of slackening off.

Remember, since success is a process and not an event, you must embody the process every day. Resting on your laurels is the antithesis of what success is. You can't expect to have a fulfilling marriage if you stop putting in the effort after getting married. Neither can you expect to have a thriving business that remains prosperous for decades if you're not working on it consistently. Yet, this is what many people tend to do.

To maintain success long term, you must try to improve each and every day, continuously. To learn more about the importance of continuous improvement, refer to *The Law of Mastery* and *The Law of Continuous Learning*.

In your field, you can always learn something new to help you perform at a higher level and make a bigger contribution. If you feel you already know enough, you're probably overconfident. And it might be time to humble yourself and become obsessed with improving your skills.

To achieve the result you want in any area of your life, swallow your pride, stop being complacent and change *everything* you need to change to be where you want to be in the future.

* * *

Action step

Write at least one reason pride could stand in your way. Answering the following questions in the **Action Guide** might help you (*Part III. Section I. The Law of Humility*):

- How can pride prevent me from achieving the results I want in life?
- Do I refuse to ask for help?
- Am I unwilling to change things that don't work?

9
THE LAW OF MASTERY

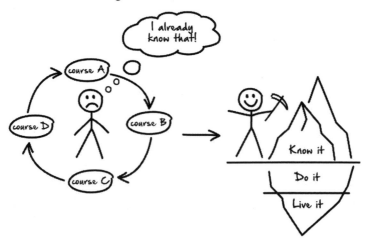

> A woodpecker can tap twenty times on a thousand trees and get nowhere but stay busy. Or he can tap twenty thousand times on one tree and get dinner.
>
> — Seth Godin, The Dip.

The Law of Mastery states that if you apply anything you learn and delve as deep as you can, you will inevitably generate positive results over the long term.

Developing a mastery mentality

To reach your goals, it is essential you develop a "mastery mentality," which means the ability to master any area you choose to focus on. Most people just scratch the surface of any given subject. These people adopt a short-term mentality, trying to achieve results as quickly as possible. They fail to go deep enough with their new ventures and keep jumping from one opportunity to another. They don't take their relationships to a new level because they're afraid of showing vulnerability. Or they give up learning a new skill after repeated failure.

If you look at one area of your life in which you're struggling, you'll probably notice that you failed to adopt a mastery mentality. The key characteristics of the mastery mentality are:

1. Focusing on one thing at a time
2. Practicing what you know intellectually, and
3. Repeating the process until you reach a high level of skill.

For instance, let's say you've tried to create an online business for the past three years. You may have tried to shoot video on YouTube, sell products on Amazon, do affiliate marketing, or publish Kindle books. Now, you may wonder whether any of these things really work.

However, the real question is, do other people have real success with these businesses? If so, how come you don't?

Often the problem isn't whether something works, but whether you will *make* it work. Will you learn to master the process, so you can achieve the results you want, or will you dabble and barely scratching the surface of the new challenge?

* * *

Action step

Complete the following exercises using your **Action Guide:**

1. On a scale of 1 to 10 (1 being false, 10 being true), evaluate yourself on the following points:

- I easily avoid jumping from one opportunity to another.
- I put into practice everything I read or learn about.
- When I'm learning something new, I keep practicing until I reach a high level of mastery (*Part III. Section II. The Law of Mastery - Developing a Mastery Mindset*).

2. Look at one area of your life in which you aren't satisfied. How much of what you know have you actually put into practice? Have you mastered the fundamentals in this area?

1. Focusing on one thing at a time

Have you ever jumped from one training course to another or tried several diets without seeing positive results? If so, you're a victim of the so-called "Shiny Object Syndrome." This syndrome stems from the false idea that success is an event, not a process, and thus should come easily and quickly if you can only find the "right method" for you. In reality, as we've already seen, anything of value takes *a great deal of time* and *a great deal of effort* and must involve a specific process.

I've seen high achievers trying to do multiple things at the same time. Unfortunately, I've seldom witnessed people succeeding in doing so. Most of the time, these individuals work hard just to get mediocre results at best. The truth is, you don't need to be a genius to achieve great results, but you need to focus on one thing (or a very few things) and go as deep as you can with it until you master it. Only then should you consider moving on to the next thing.

Remember, perseverance is key.

Below are some examples of what focusing on one training course or program at a time actually means:

- Choosing the best diet and sticking to it long-term until you actually lose weight
- Focusing on one or two skills needed to further your career and becoming proficient at these skills, and
- Promoting your business only on one or two social media platforms until you achieve tangible results.

This is not to say you can't succeed in multiple areas of your life, create several businesses or learn dozens of new skills, because you definitely can. But, it's far more effective to do so by mastering one new skill at a time.

Although you might have hundreds of items on your to-do list, I encourage you to select a couple of things you're really excited about and focus on these for the next few months. Once you have made demonstrable and consistent progress, you can focus on other things on your to-learn list. This approach is usually less overwhelming and, I promise you, far more effective over the long term than trying to do everything at once.

To give you a personal example, at one point I was doing all the following activities:

- Shooting YouTube videos
- Creating video courses
- Doing "Facebook Lives"
- Posting daily on Facebook
- Blogging
- Guest posting, and

- Writing books.

I was working hard but not seeing much progress. One day, I decided to eliminate the things that failed to produce satisfying results such as the YouTube videos, "Facebook Lives" and the guest posts. Instead, I focused almost entirely on three things:

- Writing more books
- Marketing using PPC ads, and
- Connecting with other authors in my genre.

Suddenly, my whole business process felt less overwhelming.

What about you? If you were to focus on only two specific actions, which ones would be most likely to pay off?

For more on the importance of focus, refer to *The Law of Focus*.

***

Action step

Look at all the projects and goals you're working on right now. Select the one you're the most excited about and write it down using your **Action Guide**. Turn it into a SMART goal and spend most of your effort on it over the next few weeks or months until you obtain the results you want (*Part III. Section II. The Law of Mastery - Focusing on One Thing at a Time*).

2. Practicing what you know intellectually

Because you think you "know" something intellectually, it doesn't mean you actually know it. This is a dangerous assumption that prevents many people from achieving the results they want. "Knowing" a topic is almost useless without experience. For instance:

"Knowing" everything about nutrition doesn't help unless you eat more healthily.

"Knowing" the entire content of this book is useless unless you actually apply the knowledge.

"Knowing" how to approach a man or a woman with a view to building a relationship is irrelevant if you don't actually make the approach.

Many people know the theory but fail to take action. This is the main reason they fail to make changes in their lives. Simple yet true. They're the ones who "already know that," and for whom "there is nothing new." When it comes to achieving any goal, however, what matters is the ability to execute. Intellectual knowledge is of little help if action isn't taken. If I had merely read self-help books without applying what I'd learned, my life wouldn't have changed much.

* * *

Action step

Write down all the things you know at an intellectual level but haven't truly mastered **in your Action Guide**. That is, things you've read or heard about but haven't really applied in your life (*Part III. Section II. The Law of Mastery - Practicing what you know intellectually*).

3. Repeating the process until you reach a high level of mastery

True knowledge requires repetition. Every master of every craft is a master of repetition, be it a martial arts expert, a successful writer or an accomplished comedian. Anything not practiced consistently and fully integrated at the subconscious level remains purely intellectual. You can't learn to drive a car by reading books. You must practice over and over until you internalize all the different skills and moves required to be a good driver. Nor can you become a public speaker without actually practicing speeches in front of an audience over and over again.

Don't dismiss the power of *The Law of Mastery*. This law, when applied consistently, will massively improve your long-term success rate.

Coach and online entrepreneur, Stefan Pylarinos, breaks down mastery into three levels: *knowing*, *doing* and *living*. *Knowing* is when you only know something intellectually but have little or no experience doing it. *Doing* is when you're actually performing the skill or task. *Living* is when you've become a living example of it.

Below is a concrete example:

- Knowing level: reading a book on nutrition.
- Doing level: Changing your diet to eat more healthily.
- Living level: Eating healthily every day as an ingrained way of life.

Go deep with whatever you need to learn to achieve your goal. Find a great training course or program and apply everything consistently until it becomes second nature. Keep doing this and return to the fundamentals when you struggle, and you'll achieve far better results long term. Also, remember, the mastery mentality is a way of thinking. Once you understand it (by living it), you'll be able to use it for all sorts of goals.

* * *

Action step

Answer the following question in your **Action Guide**:

If you were to master one thing to make the biggest impact in your life, what would it be? (*Part III. Section II. The Law of Mastery - Developing a Mastery Mindset*).

10

THE LAW OF FOCUS

> I focus on one thing and one thing only—that's trying to win as many championships as I can.
>
> — KOBE BRYANT, PROFESSIONAL BASKETBALL PLAYER.

The Law of Focus states that intense focus on the most important area of your life right now will yield great results while positively impacting most of the other areas of your life.

If you're like most people, you want an exciting career, a good paycheck, a healthy body and plenty of time to spend with your family.

However, the reality of the day-to-day living seldom provides us with such a harmonious life. To make major changes in your life, I encourage you to let go of the idea of "balanced life." Instead, realize that you must often accept living an unbalanced life in the short term to design your ideal life in the long term.

The same way you can't build four successful businesses at the same time, you can't transform all the areas of your life at once. You must take a more focused approach.

I believe there are five major areas in life:

- Career
- Finance
- Health
- Personal growth, and
- Relationships

With a balanced approach to life, you would spend roughly twenty percent of your time and/or effort on each of these areas. Now, what kind of results do you think you would get under these conditions? Ask yourself if you could be successful with all the following goals:

- Build your ideal career (career)
- Get your finances right (finance)
- Lose weight (health)
- Change yourself (personal growth), and
- Find your soul mates (relationships)

If you're doing well in each of these areas, it may work temporarily. But if you're like most people, you'll probably find it difficult to achieve the results you want in all the areas simultaneously.

What if you're overweight, single, broke and hate your job?

Do you think spending only twenty percent of your time and effort on each of these challenges will allow you to overcome them?

A better strategy would be to focus a majority of your effort—eighty percent or more—on one major area. For instance:

- If you're currently overweight and at risk of becoming severely ill, you should probably focus most of your effort on improving your diet, losing weight and, as a result, improve your overall health.
- If you hate your job and wake up depressed every day, you should probably focus on changing your career.
- If you've been single for a long time and feel lonely, perhaps starting a relationship or making new friends should be your immediate priority.
- If you're broke and can't afford to buy healthy food or go on a date, you should probably gear most of your efforts toward improving your financial situation.

Success and balance don't work well together. It is unlikely you'll be able to design the life of your dreams without a certain level of obsession. This is because success tends to like intense focus sustained over an extended period.

After you make satisfying progress in one specific area, you can move on to replicate the same process for other areas of your life.

You can change your life faster than you think

We grossly overestimate what we can do in six months, but largely underestimate how drastically we can improve our lives in five or ten years. In five years, you can change one or two key areas of your life.

In ten years, you can transform most or all of them. That's why it's so critical to adopt a long-term mentality and learn to remain consistent over the years (see also *The Law of Long-Term Thinking*).

As you learn to focus most of your efforts on one major part of your life, you'll start seeing noticeable changes not only in that area, but also in other areas, too.

For instance, when you find a job you love, you'll probably experience less stress which may lead you to feel better. As a result, you might have more motivation to make changes in other areas of your life.

My point is, every area of your life is interdependent, and changing one will often change the others.

Give yourself enough time, stay focused and remain consistent while being kind to yourself, and you'll be amazed at what you can accomplish in a few short years.

* * *

Action step

Answer the following question in your **Action Guide**: Among the five areas—health, finance, relationships, career, personal growth—if you were to focus most of your effort right now on only one, which would most help transform your life? (*Part III. Section III. The Law of Focus*).

11

THE LAW OF EFFECTIVE ACTION

> Efficiency is doing things right; effectiveness is doing the right things.
>
> — Peter Drucker, management consultant and author.

The Law of Effective Action states that success becomes almost inevitable when you identify key actions and focus on them daily.

Sometimes, we work hard but fail to realize that what we do is highly ineffective. On my website, I used to have banners redirecting visitors to my books' sales pages on Amazon, hoping they would generate sales. But did you know the average click-through rate for this type of banners is a pitiful 0.03%?

This means only three out of 1,000 people who visit my website will click on the ad banner. Even worse, among this three, on average only four percent will buy the book. Assuming my blog generates 10,000 unique visitors this month, the banners will generate a mere 1.2 sales. This demonstrates that relying on banners is the perfect example of an ineffective action.

Identifying the process

It doesn't matter how badly you want to land your dream job, lose weight or become wealthy. Unless you put in place a specific and successful process, you won't achieve your goal. The process is what you do every day to reach that goal. It entails answering "yes" to the following question:

"If I keep doing what I'm doing today, will I achieve my goal?"

The better you can identify the most effective process to get from point A, where you are now, to point B, where you want to be, the higher your chances of reaching your goal.

To design the optimal process, you must identify the best strategy possible. It isn't nearly as complicated as it sounds, though. Some people have already achieved the same goals you are targeting. Thus, all you need to do is to identify these people and reverse-engineer what they did. There is no need to reinvent the wheel. For instance, as Brendon Burchard explains in his book *High*

Performance Habits, he discovered that to become a number one best-selling author, he would likely have to focus on the following tasks:

- Finish writing a good book (sounds obvious).
- Find an agent (for a major publishing deal) or self-publish.
- Build an email list of subscribers (using social media and blogging).
- Create a book promotion page and offer great bonuses to encourage people to buy the book, and
- Get five to ten people with a big email list to promote the book.

These are the five core tasks he chose to focus most of his time on to publish a number one best-seller (which he did).

Similarly, you'll notice there are usually a few strategic moves—generally between three and five—that will allow you to achieve your goal with the minimum effort and the maximum impact. Make sure you spend time identifying these moves. Doing so will save you a great deal of time and effort down the line.

Here are some tips to help you discover your strategic moves:

Identify role models who have achieved the results you desire and observe what they're doing. What actions do they take every day? What are their core beliefs?

Interview people who have achieved your goal and ask them what they would do if they were in your position. You will be surprised how many successful people will be willing to help. Consider asking them the following questions:

- What do I need to do to be in your position? What skills do I need to develop? What mindset do I need to adopt?
- What is the secret to your success?
- What is your daily routine? What key tasks do you perform every day?

- Knowing what you know now, what would you do to go from where I am today to where you are now as quickly as possible?

Brainstorm strategic moves. Write down all the things you could do to achieve your goal. Come up with a list of at least twenty things. Now, ask yourself:

- If I could do only one task every day to achieve my goal, what would it be? If I could do a second task what would it be? Repeat the process until you have your three to five core tasks.

Hire a coach. A coach might be expensive, but they can allow you to reduce your learning curve and save you months or even years of struggle (among other benefits).

* * *

Action step

Using the tips above and your **Action Guide**, write down what you could do to identify the strategic moves you need to adopt to achieve your goal (*Part III. Section IV. The Law of Effective Action*).

Using the 80/20 Rule

The 80/20 rule states that twenty percent of your actions will yield eighty percent of your results. Regardless of your goal, there are always a few things that will produce greater results than all the other things combined. Make sure you identify these key tasks and focus most of your time on them.

The 80/20 rule works in many situations and can help you achieve all sorts of goals with significantly less effort. Here are some examples:

- Want more fulfilling relationships? A few friends bring you eighty percent of your happiness. Spend more time with them.
- Want to make more money? About twenty percent of your clients bring you eighty percent of your revenue. Identify these high value clients and find a way to serve them better and therefore sell them more products.
- Stressed by your current job? Identify the twenty percent of the tasks that are generating eighty percent of your stress and see if you can delegate them, do fewer of them or approach them in a different way.

Note that the accurate ratio might not necessarily be 80/20. It could be 90/10 or 70/30, but the principle is the same.

* * *

Action step

Complete the following exercise in your **Action Guide** to help you identify the few things that really move the needle up the success slope (*Part III. Section IV. The Law of Effective Action*).

1. What three to five strategic moves do you need to focus on to achieve your biggest goal?

2. Select one of the areas below and apply the 80/20 rule:

- **Relationships:** Who are the few people who bring the most of your joy? How could you spend more time with them?
- **Happiness:** What few things do you derive most of your happiness from? What could you do to make them your main points of focus?
- **Work:** What few tasks really move the needle toward success? How can you make them your priority?
- **Thoughts:** What few thoughts generate most of your joy and

excitement? What practice will allow you to focus on these thoughts more often?
- **Worries:** What few worrying things generate most of the stress in your life? How can you eliminate these worries from your life?

12
THE LAW OF DELIBERATE PRACTICE

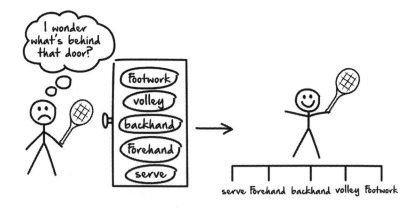

> Practice does not make perfect. Only perfect practice makes perfect.
>
> — VINCE LOMBARDI, AMERICAN FOOTBALL COACH.

The Law of Deliberate Practice states that you'll become far more competent at what you do if you design effective practices aligned with your goals.

Why do some people consistently make progress while others stay at the same level of competence for years? The former individuals practice with a specific aim in mind while the latter keep doing the same thing without an effective practice in place.

According to researchers at Harvard Medical School, doctors with decades of experience don't seem to provide better patient care than those with just a few years of experience. You would expect a doctor with decades of experience to be significantly more skilled than one who's just getting started, but that doesn't appear to be the case. It also applies to nurses, and I suspect, the same goes for many other professions.

In short, the main reason most people are stuck at a certain level of expertise is not that they lack intelligence or talent, but that they fail to make the necessary efforts to improve their performance.

What exactly is "deliberate practice"?

In their book *Peak, Secrets from The New Science of Expertise*, Anders Ericsson and Robert Pool state that deliberate practice:

- Builds skills for which effective training techniques have already been established.
- Takes place outside of people's comfort zone, requires significant effort and is generally not enjoyable.
- Involves specific, well-defined goals.
- Requires a person's full attention and conscious actions
- Entails regular feedback
- Both creates and relies on effective mental representation, and
- Almost always involves working on existing skills or building new ones by focusing specifically on some aspect of those skills that need to be improved.

As you can see, deliberate practice is quite different from the way most of us practice our craft. In fact, I would suggest that most people have never applied deliberate practice before.

The famous novelist, Stephen King, wrote, *"If you want to be a writer, you must do two things above all others: read a lot and write a lot."* He has a good point but what if it's more complex than that?

Benjamin Franklin felt he needed to do more than merely read and write a lot. He focused on improving three specific skills: his writing style, his vocabulary and his sense of organization. In a nutshell, here is Benjamin Franklin's schedule for deliberate practice:

- **Writing style:** He made notes on articles from *Spectator*, a high-quality newspaper, which he would use to rewrite the articles a few days later. He would then compare his version with the original article and modify it accordingly.
- **Vocabulary:** He rewrote *Spectator* essays in verse and then in prose, to compare his vocabulary with the original article.
- **Organization:** He wrote summaries of every sentence in a particular article on separate sheets of paper. He would then wait a few weeks before challenging himself to write the article in the correct order and compare his work to the original.

How you can apply "deliberate practice"

To help explain *The Law of Deliberate Practice*, I'll use tennis to demonstrate how practicing deliberately differs from playing casually. To do this, we'll review each characteristic of deliberate practice.

Deliberate Practice builds skills for which effective training techniques have already been established.

Chances are the goal you are trying to reach has already been achieved by someone else. As we've seen when we discussed *The Law of Effective Action*, there is no need to reinvent the wheel.

If you wish to become a professional tennis player, why not copy the practices used by people who have already reached that status? This might entail hiring a coach, reading sports magazines or watching training videos on YouTube.

The same goes for any other area in which you want to improve your skills. Whether you want to create a business, become a musician or enhance the quality of your relationships, you will find people who have already achieved these goals. They will be able to show you the way.

In an interview, Arnold Schwarzenegger recalls how one day he saw the whole blueprint for becoming a bodybuilder in an article featuring Reg Park, a bodybuilder, actor and three times Mr. Universe. He used the same blueprint to start his training. Could it be that simple?

Sometimes however, the path toward your goal is unclear. Perhaps there isn't any proven method to achieve your goal. If so, do some research and try your best to design your own blueprint. You can always refine it over time.

Deliberate practice takes place outside your comfort zone, requires significant effort and is generally not enjoyable.

If you keep doing the things you already know how to do, your progress will slow, and you'll eventually reach a plateau, being unable to improve your performance.

Playing tennis with your friends every Sunday might be fun, but how much progress can you reasonably make? On the other hand, practicing your serve for two hours is tedious, but when done right, will turn you into a better player.

Deliberate practice involves specific, well-defined goals.

Working on your first serve is a specific and well-defined goal. Playing with your friends on Sundays isn't, since you probably won't be working on a specific skill, you'll just be having fun.

To give another example, merely rehearsing a speech will be less effective in the long term than focusing on a specific skill, such as voice projection, body language or rhythm.

Deliberate practice requires an individual's full attention and conscious actions.

If you practice serves with focus you will improve. However, if you go through the motion mechanically—as you would when washing the dishes—your progress will be slower and you'll reach a plateau very quickly.

Deliberate practice entails regular feedback.

For instance, as you practice your first serve, you receive instant feedback on the results. In addition, if you work with a coach, they will point out what you need to focus on in order to improve. As you make adjustments based on that feedback you will almost inevitably improve.

Deliberate practice both creates and relies on effective mental representation.

Deliberate practice and repetition creates a mental representation of patterns of information held in long-term memory. These patterns contain various elements—facts, images, rules, muscle memories or relationships—organized in a coherent way. Deliberate practice leads to the creation of effective mental representations which, in turn, enhance performances. For instance, mental representation allows taxi drivers to find their routes in complex cities and enables chess masters to play blindfolded.

A tennis player who has practiced the same move repeatedly will have a far more effective mental representation of the action than someone who plays tennis as a hobby.

Deliberate practice almost always involves working on existing skills or building new ones by focusing on a specific aspect of those skills.

When you play tennis with your friends on Sunday, you're generally not trying to improve any particular skill. You may improve your game slightly over time, but your progress is likely to be slow and rather random.

On the other hand, when you apply deliberate practice, you break down a skill or a craft into different components. Tennis can be seen as one skill that encompasses a whole set of other skills. Some of those skills are first serve, second serve, forehand, backhand, volley, footwork and so on. If we further break down these macro skills, sub-skills might involve isolating a muscle via a well-defined exercise to improve a certain shot or practicing a specific exercise to increase your stamina.

Therefore, if you want to improve, identify a few key sub-skills and work on them deliberately and consistently until you see some improvement.

*　*　*

Action step

Look at one particular goal you would like to accomplish in the near future. What skills do you need to develop to achieve that goal? And what specific exercises do you need to perform/practice to make progress as quickly as possible? Go through each characteristic of deliberate practice as identified by Anders Ericsson and Robert Pool, and write down your answer in your **Action Guide** (*Part III. Section V. The Law of Deliberate Practice*).

13

THE LAW OF CONSISTENCY

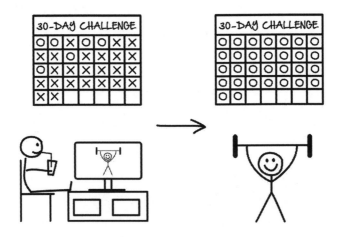

 It's not what we do once in a while that shapes our lives. It's what we do consistently.

— Tony Robbins, motivational speaker.

The Law of Consistency states that simple daily habits repeated for a few years lead to exceptional results.

Success is a process that requires both repetition and regularity. To increase your chances of success long term you must learn to develop consistency. Here are some examples of consistency:

- The Olympic swimmer, Michael Phelps, only missed five days of swimming in a seven-year training program.
- The famous writer, Stephen King, writes every day, including his birthday and during Christmas. He aims to write six pages a day.
- Russian author, Leo Tolstoy, wrote every day, saying: "*I must write each day without fail, not so much for the success of the work, as in order not to get out of my routine.*"

Consistency is one of the best predictors of success because, in the end, your ability to do something consistently whether you feel like it or not will determine whether or not you achieve your goals. There will be days when you don't want to do the work, but if you can force yourself to work anyway, your chances of success will increase significantly.

Consistency is more important than intensity

People largely underestimate the power of consistency while they overestimate the power of intensity. They tend to believe they can change in a matter of days or weeks just by working hard. Who is more likely to obtain the best results long term—the person who commits to running two minutes every day for a year, or the person who goes to the gym four times a week for two hours and gives up after a month?

Becoming a high performer doesn't require you do great things; it requires you do small things *consistently* every day to the best of your ability. These small things build over time and, as you keep transferring new habits to your subconscious mind, you will become far more effective. If you are a regular driver, think back to the first time you drove a car. I bet it felt overwhelming and a little scary. Today, after practice and years of experience, the act of driving has become effortless.

Remember, consistency is more powerful than intensity. Starting small not only reduces the risk of procrastination, but it also boosts your self-esteem and helps you generate momentum (see *The Law of Momentum*).

Adopting daily habits

By now, you should have identified your three to five key moves. If not, return to the section, *The Law of Effective Action*.

Now, look at your strategic moves. How could you turn them into daily practices? If you were to perform certain moves every day, which ones would allow you to make the most progress toward your goal?

For instance, if you're an aspiring writer, you could block a specific amount of time every day to write or decide on a number of words to crank out daily. Also, you could connect with other authors in the same genre by emailing one new author each day. Marketing would probably be another strategic move. Jack Canfield, author of the popular series, *Chicken Soup for The Soul*, did five things every day for over a year to promote his book. Perhaps, you could do something similar.

The bottom line is that identifying your strategic moves and turning them into consistent daily habits is one of the most important things you can do to promote success.

How to become more consistent

One of the most effective ways to develop consistency is to implement a morning ritual. Morning rituals have been popularized by Hal Elrod in his book, *The Miracle Morning*.

A morning ritual can serve two main purposes. First, it can help prime your mind by deciding how you want to feel. For instance, this can be done by performing gratitude exercises, by listening to music or by using visualization and affirmations. Second, it can allow you to work consistently on key tasks by making them part of your morning ritual. For instance, when I was an employee, I would spend thirty to forty-five minutes writing before going to work.

A crash course in creating a morning ritual

You can create your own customized morning ritual to help you condition your mind and get rid of limiting beliefs. In my book, *Wake Up Call*, I present nine steps to help create a morning ritual that will support you in achieving your goals. They are:

1. **Clarifying your "why".** Make sure you have a clear objective in mind when you create your morning ritual. You might want to experience particular emotions, or you might want to focus on a specific goal, using affirmations or visualization.
2. **Getting excited about your morning ritual.** Drink your favorite coffee, read your favorite book, or spend time with your family. Do whatever excites you.
3. **Identifying obstacles and preparing yourself mentally.** Look for potential hurdles you may encounter as you create your morning ritual. If you failed to implement a morning ritual in the past, ask yourself why.
4. **Selecting the components of your morning ritual.** For a more balanced morning ritual, select activities that will feed your body, mind and soul. Try exercise, meditation, journaling and things of that nature.
5. **Deciding how much time you have available.** It could be as little as ten minutes or as much as an hour, but be consistent.
6. **Removing roadblocks and distractions.** Prepare everything you need the night before. Go through your morning ritual first thing in the morning to avoid procrastination.

7. **Setting yourself up for success.** Make sure you get enough sleep. If necessary, create an evening ritual as well. Whenever possible, go to bed at the same time every night. You can also set your intentions the night before and visualize the tasks you want to work on the next day.
8. **Committing one hundred percent.** Commit to your morning ritual. Don't be casual about it.
9. **Undertaking the Thirty-Day Challenge.** To strengthen your commitment, dedicate at least thirty days to your morning ritual.

If you want to learn more about how to create an exciting morning ritual, check out my book, *Wake Up Call: How to Take Control of Your Morning and Transform Your Life.*

* * *

Action step

Complete the exercises below using the **Action Guide** (*Part III. Section VI. The Law of Consistency*).

1. Look at the three to five strategic moves you've identified previously. Now, what could you do to turn them into daily habits?

2. Select the one move you could do first thing in the morning to help you achieve your main goals. Stick to it for at least thirty days.

14
THE LAW OF IDENTIFICATION

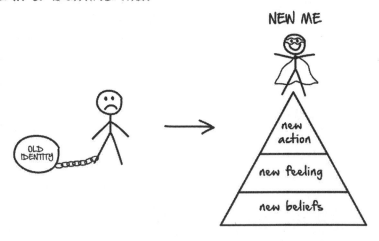

> Your main job in life is to create the mental equivalent within yourself of what you want to realize and enjoy in your outer world.
>
> — EMMET FOX, AUTHOR.

The Law of Identification states that the more you think, feel and act like the person you wish to become, the faster you'll achieve your goals.

What a goal really is

Have you ever wondered why some people achieve their goals while others fail? Is it because they work harder? Well, hard work can't be the only answer, otherwise, all hard-working people would reach their goals. To answer this question let's consider the following example:

Imagine you are currently fifty pounds overweight and have been struggling to lose weight for years. Now, put yourself in the shoes of someone with the "ideal weight" such as a personal trainer. Imagine you—as a personal trainer—wake up one day carrying an extra fifty pounds of unwanted weight. How would you react?

I'm betting you would be shocked. You would think, "This is not who I am. This is unacceptable," and you would instantly start transforming your body. You would remove all junk food from your house and exercise daily until you returned to your ideal weight. And you would do it as quickly as possible. It would still be hard, but you would do it regardless. This is inevitable.

Why is it inevitable? It's because you have a specific image of what your body *should* look like and a specific idea of your health. This image is so closely linked to your identity you would inevitably return to your original weight. The only unknown is how long it would take.

Money is another good example. There are many stories of multi-millionaires who lose all their money and make it back, seemingly in a heartbeat. Why is that? It's because they have a multi-millionaire identity. They perceive money in a different way from the rest of us and, while $20,000 feels like a lot of money for most people, for them it's no big deal. As a result, they are comfortable negotiating huge deals or borrowing large sums of money. The difference in mindset goes far beyond their perception of money, however. Their relationship with failure, the way they interact with people and how they think is also different from the majority of the population. It is no wonder that even when bankrupt, they behave differently from other people in the same financial situation. This is inevitable.

This example leads to the following question:

What if reaching your goal isn't so much about going from point A to point B, but more about shifting from Identity A, who you are, to Identity B, who you need to become to achieve your goal?

I believe both approaches are interconnected. By taking the necessary actions to move from point A to point B, you become a new person. And by shifting your identity and focusing your effort on becoming a different person, you support the actions needed to move to point B.

Shifting your identity

Think of one of your goals. What shift in identity would need to happen for you to achieve this particular goal? How different would you be as a person?

The first step to shifting your identity is to think of what the personal development blogger, Steve Pavlina, called the "side effects" of having achieved your goal. Or, to put it another way, what would be different about your life once you've achieved your goal? Ask yourself:

- What would be your core beliefs about yourself and about the world?
- How would you think differently?
- How would you feel?
- What would you do differently?
- What new habits would you have developed?
- What old habits would you have rejected?

If you're unsure of the side-effects of your career goal, talk to someone who has achieved your goal and ask them the following questions:

- What do I need to believe to be in your position?
- What habits would I need to develop?

To achieve your goal, your beliefs and actions must match those of people who have achieved this goal. Now, it won't happen overnight. The key is to start closing the gap by progressively shifting your identity over time.

For instance, let's say my goal is to be a successful non-fiction writer. What would be the side-effects?

- I would write every single day as do most successful writers.
- I would introduce myself as a writer without feeling embarrassed.
- I would contact other successful writers like me.
- I would expect to sell a lot of books.
- I would find it normal to be invited to speak at events or even on TV or radio.
- I would expect to be paid a lot of money to speak at events.

Action step

Write down the side effects of having already achieved your goal using the **Action Guide** (*Part III. Section III. The Law of Identification*).

15
THE LAW OF CONDITIONING

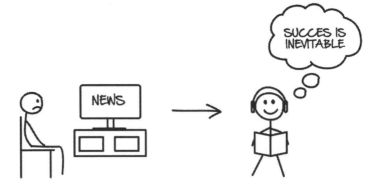

> A human being always acts and feels and performs in accordance with what he imagines to be true about himself and his environment.
>
> — Maxwell Maltz, author of Psycho-Cybernetics.

The Law of Conditioning states that you can train yourself to experience any emotion if you focus on feeling that particular emotion for long enough.

You have the power to recondition your mind to experience more positive emotions. In many regards, your mind works like an app which you can program to do whatever you want it to do. The major problem is that many people, instead of doing the programming themselves, let other people or their environment do it for them. They feed their mind with negative news and disempowering beliefs. This daily exposure to negativity generates toxic thoughts that become their default position. Not surprisingly, these people experience far more negative emotions than they otherwise would.

Here is the truth: if you don't program your mind, someone else will. Therefore, it is your responsibility to take control of your thoughts and choose the information you feed your mind every day.

The best way to condition your mind is to adopt powerful daily rituals. One example would be to create a morning ritual (see *The Law of Consistency*). Another way to do this is to set specific intents as you move from one segment of your day to another. When performed consistently, these small rituals will, in the long term, have far more impact than you might imagine.

Successful people adopt daily rituals to condition their mind and perform at their best. Here are some ways you can condition your mind:

- Adopting a gratitude practice every morning.
- Having the intent to be fully present when you greet your spouse after returning from work.
- Focusing on three things you're proud of before going to bed.

Remember, the more often you feel a certain emotion, the easier it will be for your brain to reproduce it.

The bottom line is that through conscious repetition and clear intent, you can train your mind to generate positive emotions. Make sure you use *The Law of Conditioning* to help you achieve your goals.

* * *

Action step

Select one daily habit that will help you condition your mind to experience more positive emotions in your life. If you can, make it part of your morning ritual by combining it with the thing you committed to doing in the **Action Guide** section, *The Law of Consistency (Part III. Section VIII. The Law of Conditioning)*.

16

THE LAW OF ATTRACTION

> The key to success is to focus our conscious mind on things we desire, not things we fear.
>
> — BRIAN TRACY, AUTHOR AND MOTIVATIONAL SPEAKER.

The Law of Attraction states that the more you focus on something, the more likely you are to attract that thing into your life.

You may have heard of *The Law of Attraction* before, but in this section, we'll introduce a simple and straightforward version of it.

1. Focusing on what you want

To activate *The Law of Attraction*, you must constantly focus on what you want. Many people say they want to make more money, be happier or have better relationships, but they never make it their focal point. I believe you *cannot* fail to make progress long term if you keep focusing on what you want. Define exactly what you want and make it your main focus. Remember, clarity is power.

Here is what success expert, Brian Tracy, wrote is his book *Goals!*

"Many thousands of successful people have been asked what they think about most of the time. The most common answer given by successful people is that they think about what they want—and how to get it—most of the time."

Note, you must focus on what you want, *not* on what you don't want. It may seem like there isn't much of a difference, but the difference is significant. When you focus on what you don't want, your focus is on the negative things you want to prevent from happening. And we've already learned that whatever you focus on, you tend to attract. It also generates negative emotions and puts you in a disempowering state of mind.

Look at the examples below and see which options are the more empowering:

- Ruminating on your lack of money.
- Or thinking about all the positive aspects of making more money in the near future.

- Reading news about the poor shape of the economy.

- Or reading books written by wealthy people with an "abundance mindset."

Remember, whatever you choose to focus on consistently, you will eventually attract in the long term. Money is just one of many examples. Thus, make it a habit to think of what you want as often as possible and commit to making it a reality (see *Power of Commitment*).

Please note, you can condition your mind to experience positive emotions by implementing daily habits such as consuming motivational materials or eliciting feelings of gratitude through various exercises.

2. Appreciating what you already have

There are a myriad of things for which you should be grateful, such as your overall health, your ability to walk, talk, hear, feel and taste or having access to the countless services available in the Information Age. Learning to experience a deep sense of gratitude for all the things you already have is a powerful activator of *The Law of Attraction*. Conversely, failing to count your blessings generates feelings of scarcity and prevents you from unlocking the resourcefulness and optimism required to improve your life.

We'll discuss in more detail how to cultivate gratitude in the section *The Law of Gratitude*.

3. Activating the power of your subconscious mind

Your subconscious mind is the most powerful mechanism on earth. To achieve the success you want in life, you must leverage its power on a regular basis. One of the reasons *The Law of Attraction* can be so effective is precisely because it allows you to use the power of your subconscious mind to a greater extent than most people manage.

Here are a few key characteristics of your subconscious mind:

It records far more information than the conscious mind

Your subconscious takes in far more information than your conscious mind ever could. It is also in charge of regulating bodily functions. Imagine how exhausting it would be if you had to consciously remind yourself to grow your hair, make your heart beat or regulate your body temperature. Fortunately, the subconscious takes care of all these things for you.

Have you ever experienced buying a new car and then seeing the same make and model everywhere as you drive around?

It's not because there are more cars of that same type now than before. It's just that you didn't notice them before. But your subconscious mind did. Now, take a moment to complete the following exercise:

1. Look for any red item in your room for about five to ten seconds.
2. Now, close your eyes.
3. Try to remember any blue item in the room.

You probably had a hard time coming up with even one blue item. This shows that whatever you're looking for, your subconscious mind will help you find it by processing information available in your environment. This is another reason to clarify what you want. By doing so, you tell your subconscious mind what it should be looking for.

The subconscious cannot discern what is true from what is false

Your subconscious mind isn't judgmental and has no ability to assess whether something is true or not. It will inevitably accept what you have been told repeatedly. In fact, by age seven, you will have already built your own model of reality from beliefs you've accepted as true.

More interestingly, your subconscious mind cannot tell the difference between your imagination and what actually happens, which is why athletes, chess players and musicians use visualization to improve their skills.

For instance, in the 1960s, an experiment was conducted to evaluate students on their ability to make free throws in basketball under various conditions. Students were divided into three groups. The first group was asked to train twenty minutes a day for twenty days, a second was asked not to train at all and the third was asked to imagine themselves making free throws twenty minutes a day for twenty days. Ultimately, the group of students who practiced only in their imagination performed almost as well as those who practiced in reality. Specifically, those who practiced in reality improved their scores by twenty-four percent, while those who practiced in their imaginations improved by twenty-three percent. Students who refrained from both visualization and physical training showed no improvement. This experiment has been replicated many times since and has continued to produce similar results.

The bottom line is that your subconscious mind will accept anything as true provided you repeat it enough times and/or emotionalize your vision correctly.

The same process is used to indoctrinate religious extremists. Once people have been told the same thing a million times, they lose their ability to even question the validity of a so-called fact. Because they're convinced their beliefs are facts, no one can question those beliefs without triggering their inbuilt defense mechanism.

Here's another example. Imagine your parents have been telling you that you will never amount to anything. How likely are you to achieve great things in your life? Now, the statement, "you'll never amount to anything" is *not* a fact, it is an opinion. The fact is, human beings can always grow and improve, and we can certainly outgrow these limiting beliefs.

The subconscious is more powerful than your conscious mind

Whenever there is a conflict between your subconscious mind and your conscious mind, the former always wins. This is because your conscious mind is just the tip of the iceberg, while your subconscious mind is the submerged part that drives most of your thoughts and behaviors.

By turning your attention to what you want as often as possible using visualization, you will reprogram your subconscious mind (i.e., you will modify the invisible force that drives most of your thoughts and behaviors). As you do so, you will shift your beliefs and generate new thoughts. These thoughts will drive new behaviors and allow you to obtain better results.

As you focus consistently on what you want, you cannot fail to change your life in the long term. So, whether you want more money, deeper fulfillment or better relationships, keep thinking about those things and never cease to clarify exactly what they mean to you. Meanwhile, consume materials that expose you to the new mindset you want to adopt.

* * *

Action step

Complete the following exercise using the **Action Guide** (*Part III. Section XI. The Law of Attraction*).

- Spend as much time as possible focusing on the main area you wish to make a change in (see *The Law of Focus*). Throughout your day, keep thinking of the ideal results you want to achieve in that specific area.
- Adopt a gratitude practice each morning (see *The Law of Gratitude*).

17
THE LAW OF RESET

LAW OF RESET

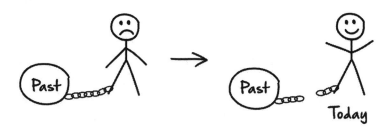

❝ Create your future from your future, not your past.

— Werner Erhard, author.

The Law of Reset states that every day is a new day, completely independent of the previous one.

If you have been carrying the weight of the past on your shoulders, how would you feel if you could reset your life and start afresh today? Wouldn't this make you feel lighter? Well, it is entirely possible. In fact, it's inevitable if you choose to live in the present rather than in the past.

While many of us become stuck in the past, the truth is our *present* determines our future not our past. Nothing prevents you making different decisions today compared with the ones you made yesterday and, by doing so, you will create a different—and better—future. Every day you receive a credit of 86,400 seconds. It's up to you to seize this new opportunity to become the person you want to become and to design the life you want to live.

Bear in mind, if you don't do what's necessary to move toward your vision today, you probably won't do it tomorrow either. Studies show that we tend to perceive our future self as having more discipline and being better in many ways than our current self. However, the truth is your future self will *not* change unless your present self makes the change.

What you do *today*, not what you've done in the past or what you think you'll do in the future, will allow you to live the life you want, and I can't emphasize this enough.

Making different decisions

We are largely creatures of habit. We have our own routines and tend to feel, think and act the same way every day. Because we've been doing the same things for so long, we tend to be blind to all the possibilities and opportunities in front of us, which makes us feel stuck. In short, we lack an overall perspective.

Life, however, is like a chess game, each moment offering an opportunity to make different decisions when faced with an almost infinite number of possibilities. In truth, we only feel stuck because we start our day with the same beliefs and ways of thinking we had yesterday and the day before. However, as we change the way we think and act, new opportunities cannot fail to arise.

Consider the following: on average we make 35,000 decisions each day. Now, how many of these decisions do you think you need to change to start altering your whole existence? Remember, just a couple of habits repeated consistently every day will yield huge results.

In effect, your past is almost irrelevant and does not have to determine your future. Your future is the result of what you do today, not what you have done in the past, and not what you say you'll do tomorrow.

***

Action step

Complete at least one of the following exercises using the **Action Guide** (*Part III. Section X. The Law of Reset*).

1. **Brainstorming exercise:** Write down everything you could do differently. Could you do something different upon waking up? Adopt at least one new positive habit in your life? Contact someone you haven't contacted for a while? Start journaling?
2. **7-Day Challenge:** For the next seven days, begin your day as though you have been born again, and feel the field of possibilities ahead of you.
3. **Visualization exercise:** Forget about everything—who you think you are, your past, your future et cetera—and reconnect with the present moment. Close your eyes to do

this exercise. Now, spend a couple of minutes envisioning your future and the life you wish to create.

18

THE LAW OF INTENT

> Everything that I do is with a purpose and intent of wanting to make a difference.
>
> — Katrina Adams, professional tennis player.

The Law of Intent states that the more purposeful you are during your day, the better results you will achieve.

Developing the habit of "setting intent" will radically transform your life. Before starting a new activity simply ask yourself, "What's my intent here?"

Imagine if you were to ask yourself that question on a regular basis, how much more deliberate would your actions be? How much more would get done?

Setting the intent before a new activity is what Brendon Burchard refers to as "managing transitions." This means you make a conscious effort to separate your day into different segments. For instance, you may have had a bad day at work, but it doesn't mean your bad mood has to spill over into your home life. Setting a clear intent before a new segment of your day is an effective way to live a more deliberate life. This will allow you to achieve better results in every area of your life.

Setting intent in your daily life

Look at your current life. How much intent is there behind the things you do every day?

Do you choose how you want to feel and think before going to work? Do you consciously choose to switch your energy and mood once your working day is over?

Imagine if you decide to set clear intents every day. How much will your life change over the coming months?

Identify key transitions

We can see our day as a succession of segments and choose to move from one to the next with a clear intent. Some key daily segments are:

- Waking up
- Eating breakfast

- Leaving home
- Arriving at work
- Eating lunch
- Going home after work
- Eating dinner, and
- Going to bed.

While most people go through their day largely without a conscious plan (without intent), you have the power to decide how you want to feel during any part of the day.

- You can wake in the morning excited to start your day and with a deep sense of gratitude.
- You can eat breakfast intending to be fully present and available to your spouse and your kids.
- You can arrive at work with a clear intent to be as productive as possible and focus on the things that matter.
- You can eat lunch with the intent of releasing all the tension developed from work and decide to relax fully.

As you choose your intent for specific segments of each day, and consistently and consciously choose how you want to feel, after a few weeks, these feelings will become natural, and everything will start to happen almost automatically.

So, what about you? What are the key transitions in your daily life? Start asking yourself the following questions:

- What do I want my intent to be here and now?
- What am I trying to do here?
- How do I want to present myself in this segment of my day? Excited? Confident? Loving? Determined?

* * *

Action step

Think of your typical day. Use the **Action Guide** to decide: which one segment of your day could you bring a specific intent to, that will have the most positive impact? For the next seven days, resolve to set your desired intent before moving to that specific segment of your day (*Part III. Section XI. The Law of Reset*).

19
THE LAW OF CONTINUOUS LEARNING

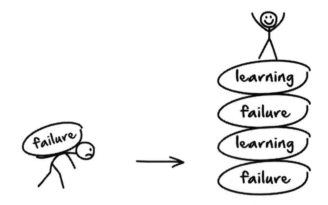

> If you leave your growth to randomness, you'll always live in the land of mediocrity.
>
> — BRENDON BURCHARD, HIGH PERFORMANCE COACH AND MOTIVATIONAL SPEAKER.

The Law of Continuous Learning states that getting better is inevitable if you keep acquiring new skills and learning from failures.

Developing the habit of continuous learning

It is your responsibility to educate yourself continuously after you graduate school and land your first job. See yourself as the CEO of your own life. Take responsibility for learning everything you need to learn to achieve your goals. Remember, nobody cares as much about you as you do yourself. Don't delegate the role of educating yourself to your company or society.

The sad truth is, many people stop educating themselves once they leave school. According to a 2018 survey conducted by the Pew Research Center, twenty-four percent of Americans say they haven't read a book in the past year. Many people will seldom or never read a book after they graduate. Don't be like them. Instead, continuously seek new knowledge until the day you die. Continuous learning allows you to improve and increase the value you can provide to your company, your family and friends, and society as a whole. The more you educate yourself, the more doors will open for you.

Nowadays, with the internet, you have access to a vast amount of information, and you can use it to learn anything you want. You have no excuse not to educate yourself.

The Law of Continuous Learning also states that the more you struggle in life, the more you must make learning a priority. As the motivational speaker, Jim Rohn, said, *"Miss a meal if you have to, but don't miss a book."* You cannot afford not to learn. The long-term consequences are too severe.

Failure and success—same things?

Have you ever considered that failure and success may actually be the same thing? As a result of the way failure is perceived in most societies, we tend to see failure as the opposite of success. However, that's total rubbish. The only true failure is when you refuse to learn lessons from your so-called failures.

- Is an entrepreneur who failed in multiple businesses before creating a multimillion-dollar business a failure?
- Is someone who went on hundreds of dates and suffered hundreds of rejections before finding the love of their life a failure?
- Is a writer who received hundreds of rejections before winning a major publishing deal and becoming a best-selling author a failure?

Again, success is a process. You don't succeed by avoiding failure, in fact, *you fail your way to success!* Failure is thus part of the success process, not separate from it. Continuous learning involves regular "failures" before your ultimate and inevitable success.

I've witnessed countless people being held back by their fear of failure and, as a result, they don't live the life they want. I don't want that to happen to you. Here is how I encourage you to see failure:

As a feedback mechanism and part of the process called "success."

Airplanes are a great example of how this feedback process works. An airplane will drift off track during most of the flight. Without constant intervention and adjustment, either by the pilot or his buddy, the auto-pilot, the airplane would never reach its destination. The tiny adjustments made during the journey ensure the plane reaches its final destination rather than landing hundreds of miles away. "Failures" work the same way. They serve as feedback by letting you know when you need to make adjustments to reach your final destination.

Your ability to learn from your mistakes and make adjustments as you proceed is key to achieving your goals.

The bottom line is, by continuously educating yourself and learning from your mistakes, you maximize your chances of success (see also *The Power of Reframing*).

* * *

Action step

Commit to learning. Use the **Action Guide** and dedicate at least ten minutes every day to reading educational material that will help you achieve your long-term vision (*Part III. Section XII. The Law of Continuous Learning*).

20
THE LAW OF PERSEVERANCE

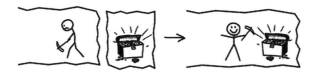

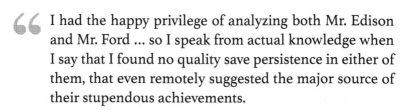

> I had the happy privilege of analyzing both Mr. Edison and Mr. Ford ... so I speak from actual knowledge when I say that I found no quality save persistence in either of them, that even remotely suggested the major source of their stupendous achievements.
>
> — NAPOLEON HILL, AUTHOR OF THINK AND GROW RICH.

The Law of Perseverance states that you can and will achieve far more than you can ever begin to imagine if you keep persevering and refuse to give up prematurely.

Perseverance is one of your most undervalued assets. Use it to your advantage and learn to stick to your goals *until you attain the results you want*. When most people reach the stage when they would give up, you must keep going. When you decided to pursue your goals you probably didn't think, "I'll just give it a try and give up like everybody else as soon as the going gets tough," did you? No! You were committed to achieving your goal. So, keep this in mind while you progress toward your goal.

The 90% rule

This rule states that around 90% of people will give up too soon to ever be in competition with you.

To illustrate this rule, let's return to our previous example of Kindle Publishing. Let's say out of 10,000 people who want to make a living writing and publishing books on Amazon, only ten will succeed (quite close to actuality I would suggest). It sounds incredibly competitive, doesn't it? Among these 10,000 people, how many are actually committed to doing what it takes to succeed? What percentage of them will still be writing and publishing after three years? A rough estimate is that ninety percent of them will see writing as a hobby and won't make it full time.

Among the 1,000 people left, ninety percent will have disappeared within twelve to twenty-four months and won't be willing to do what it takes to succeed. This leaves only one hundred people.

Among these one hundred people, between half and two-thirds will not succeed because of their inability or unwillingness to learn from their mistakes. For example, they probably won't do what's necessary to sell more books such as temporarily lowering their prices or learning to do effective marketing (see *The Law of Humility*).

We are now left with only thirty to fifty people. Among these burgeoning authors, the ones who adopt the principles described in this book are much more likely to succeed. Because these individuals think long term and understand it takes time to get results, they will persevere and overcome challenges and disappointments along the way. They will improve continuously and put into practice everything they learn. As a result, they will achieve results long term even in such a hugely competitive market.

Of course, these are rough estimates. The aim here is to help you understand the role that perseverance plays in success.

The relationship between luck and perseverance

As I've already stated, success is a process, not an event. You don't become successful because you get lucky (except on some rare occasions such as winning the lottery). While luck can certainly play a role in someone's success, luck (both good and bad) tends to average out over the long run. You may be out of luck for a few months or even a few years, but if you stay focused on your goals and follow the process laid out in this book, you are likely to "get lucky." The key is to remain consistent over the long term, work hard and never give up. Obvious, right?

The truth is, the more action you take, the more likely you are to find something that works. If you take five times more action than the average Joe and keep focusing on your goal for three years while he gives up after four months, which of you is more likely to succeed?

In my personal and professional life, I've seen that perseverance often pays. For instance, I noticed that in one of my previous jobs, if I "cold called" enough people and for long enough, I would generally end up talking to the right people. As you learn to persevere, in many situations you'll be able to figure out ways to achieve your goal.

It might also help to think of perseverance as part of the natural process of selection. If one hundred people want the same thing, why should you be the one getting it? Why not see each obstacle as a test designed to assess your degree of motivation? Temporary setbacks, discouragement and self-doubt are part of life's selection process.

The relationship between commitment and perseverance

A commitment is a declaration to yourself and to others that you will reach your goals and stick to your promises. When you commit, you activate your perseverance muscles and make it far more likely you'll reach your goals. In short, commitment puts you in the top five percent of people who will not give up prematurely. For more see *Part II. Activating the Power of Commitment*.

To strengthen your perseverance muscles, you must regularly:

- Recommit to your goal
- Reignite your passion and the whys behind your goal
- Strengthen your beliefs, and
- Seek clarity regarding what you want.

You may have noticed that your ability to persevere happens naturally as you leverage the three fundamental powers of success (belief, clarity and passion) and (re)commit to your goal.

How to persevere more than anybody else

Imagine how much more you would accomplish if you could persevere ten times more than you currently do. Perseverance is a skill, and it can be learned. In addition to leveraging belief, clarity and passion, you can also use various tools and exercises to help you persevere.

In **Part IV** of this book, we'll discuss in great detail what you can do to skyrocket your ability to persevere. For now, let's have a look at what I called the *Bullet-Proof Timeframe*. This part is an extract from my book, *The One Goal: Master the Art of Goal Setting, Win Your Inner Battles and Achieve Exceptional Results.*

In, *The One Goal*, I discuss how to win your inner battles and develop an exceptional mindset to achieve your wildest goals and dreams in great detail.

The Bullet-Proof Timeframe

The *Bullet-Proof Timeframe* reminds you that you *do* have time. It also encourages you to keep working on your goal until you reach a specific point. This specific point is generally a deadline set two to three years from now.

The *Bullet-Proof Timeframe* provides the following benefits:

- It forces you to select a goal that truly matters to you. Why would you care about some distant deadline two to three years from today if the goal is unimportant?
- It reminds you that you have time. As you step back and consider the big picture, you're able to maintain a long-term perspective. This, of course, enables you to persevere.
- It helps you avoid "Shiny Object Syndrome," and prevents you from jumping from one thing to the next because you feel you aren't getting results fast enough. This is a major trap many people fall into.
- It gives you the option of giving up. You can give yourself total permission to give up, but *only* once you've reached a specific deadline, and never before.

You may wonder how long the *Bullet-Proof Timeframe* should last. For a major goal, I recommend a two to three year timeline, which is long enough for you to see tangible results. Please note, it's very common for people to give up within a year, and this is precisely the mistake I want you to avoid.

The art of persevering smartly

While perseverance is extremely important, it is even more essential you learn to persevere the correct way, or you may end up wasting your time.

In her book, *Grit: Why Passion and Resilience are the Secrets to Success*, Angela Duckworth tells the story of the cartoonist, Bob Mankoff, whose cartoons were rejected over two thousand times by the *New Yorker* between 1974 and 1977. One of his cartoons was eventually accepted and he ended up becoming a contract cartoonist for the prestigious newspaper.

The interesting part of Mankoff's story is that he didn't just persevere randomly; he had a strategy. First, he studied old cartoons published by the newspaper to discover what they had in common. As he recalls, "*I went to the New York Public Library and I looked up all the cartoons back to 1925 that had ever been printed in the New Yorker.*" He realized they all had one thing in common—they made the reader think. He also noticed every cartoonist had their personal style. Believing he could do as well as the other cartoonists, he continued submitting cartoons until one of them finally was accepted.

Here are three key lessons we can learn from Bob Mankoff's story:

1. **Passion leads to perseverance.** Bob Mankoff thought of himself as a funny guy and was willing to do what it took to make a living from his passion.
2. **We must do our best to understand what works.** For business-related goals, what works is often what people want. Once you understand what your clients or customers want, you can offer them the right products or services. In Mankoff's case, it was what the *New Yorker* (and its readers) wanted. Perhaps he had to compromise a little, but I'm sure he didn't regret doing so (see also *The Law of Flexibility*).
3. **We must have a degree of faith in our eventual success.** This means we must believe that, with enough work and perseverance, we have a reasonable chance of achieving our

goals. In this case, Bob Mankoff believed that he could make people think while maintaining his own personal style.

The bottom line is that persevering mindlessly isn't enough to achieve the results you want. You must assess your chances of success long term based on your level of passion, your strengths and your talents, and you must also be willing to change your approach whenever necessary.

* * *

Action step

Implement a *Bullet-Proof Timeframe* for your goal using the **Action Guide**. Commit to not giving up until you reach your specific deadline (*Part III. Section XIII. The Law of Perseverance*).

21

THE LAW OF COURAGE

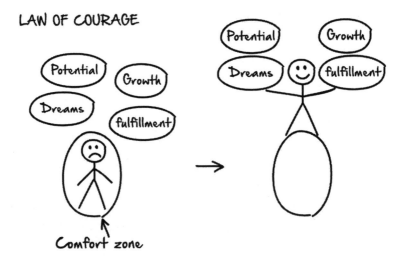

> Man cannot discover new oceans unless he has the courage to lose sight of the shore.
>
> — Andre Gide, novelist.

The Law of Courage states that the more often you can face your fear and move beyond your comfort zone, the more you'll achieve in life.

I believe one of the main purposes of life is to overcome our fear and to act more and more from a place of love. All the limitations we impose on ourselves are, for the most part, illusory. Our barriers are mostly mental ones.

Each of us holds a different set of beliefs, some are empowering, others are disempowering. These beliefs determine what we can and cannot do in this world. Some people are so afraid of public speaking they will do anything to avoid having to stand in front of a crowd. Some have so little confidence in themselves they believe they'll never amount to anything and others are terrified of trying anything new.

Have you ever done something you were scared of and felt wonderful afterward? Whenever you overcome limiting beliefs and fears, you often feel an immense sense of pride and joy. It's as though you rediscover your true self. For a brief moment, you see how much more you're capable of doing and feel wonderful as a result.

I believe our inner self wants to expand and rediscover its true nature. Inside us, there is a constant tension between our small self, who wants security and comfort, and our bigger self, who seeks to expand and experience more of what life has to offer.

How much more could you experience if you were able to move beyond your comfort zone and face your fears on a regular basis? How much better would you feel about yourself? And how much more of a positive impact could you have on the lives of other people?

In truth, no human being has ever been able to explore the whole immensity of their potential. We have almost infinite room to grow. We are the only species on earth that, through the power of imagination, can alter the course of its destiny. But to become more, we must develop courage. We must move beyond our comfort zone, even if this means starting something new and scary and facing our fears one at a time.

As we accept the need to feel discomfort, our comfort zone will naturally expand. What we believed was impossible yesterday will become perfectly normal today, and what we fear today will become easy to do tomorrow. When this happens, we will wonder why we've been so easily swayed by imaginary fears.

Such is the fate of human beings, or so it seems.

You have the courage within you to overcome all your limitations. Remember, courage is not the absence of fear. By definition, someone without fear can't be courageous. Courage is recognizing the fear, accepting it is part of the process and overcoming that fear with action. As you move inexorably toward your goals, your ability to face discomfort will not only determine the speed at which you will make progress, but also the likelihood you'll achieve your goal.

Developing courage

In his classic book, *The Magic of Thinking Big*, David J. Schwartz presents a simple formula to overcome fear which can be summed up in three words, "action cures fears."

As this concept suggests, immediate action destroys fear at its roots before it spreads and invades our minds.

Years ago, I went bungee jumping with a couple of friends. We were about to jump from a sixty-seven-meter-high bridge above a river and, when my turn came, I knew that I had to jump right away. If I had hesitated and looked down at the river, fear would have kicked in and I would probably never had jumped. So, when they told me to go, I jumped immediately.

The same happens in our daily life. When we hesitate, we give fear the opportunity to invade our minds. Immediate action is what prevents our minds from generating endless rationalizations and inflated stories that aren't grounded in reality.

A key point to understand is that our brain's primary function is to ensure our survival. This survival instinct tends to prevent us from doing anything new or scary and is our brain's way to avoid wasting energy and enhance our odds of survival. Our brains use rationalization and fear to prevent us from doing anything it perceives as a threat. Even in today's world, where most of us rarely face real physical threats to our survival, our mind interprets things like the risk of rejection and the exposure to new experiences as potential dangers, making us more and more risk averse.

Starting small

Moving out of your comfort zone doesn't mean doing something that scares you to death. You can gradually ease out of your comfort zone by taking small steps. For instance, I'm an introvert and I'm rather uncomfortable putting myself out there. This morning—as I'm writing this book—I was interviewed on a podcast. A few years ago, this sort of thing would have terrified me but, this time, I found it no big deal (though it was still a little uncomfortable). This is because I've already pushed myself beyond my comfort zone in the past by recording YouTube videos. The more videos I recorded, the more I grew used to the process. My next uncomfortable thing was doing Facebook Live. Again, the more experience I gained, the less scary it became. If I hadn't done these things before, being interviewed would have been far more uncomfortable.

The bottom line is, whatever your comfort zone is right now, you can dramatically expand it way beyond your imagination. In a few years from now, you could very well be doing things you would have thought out of the question today. This is a real possibility. Remember, the walls defining your comfort zone are purely created by your imagination.

Doing the impossible

What is the single most impossible thing for you to do? Is it making a speech in front of a large audience? Leading a team? Asking for a promotion? Cold calling a prospect?

Whatever it may be, let me tell you this: it is absolutely possible for you to overcome this fear!

So, what if you could do the impossible? What if you accomplish something today, this week or this month, you had always thought was impossible (for you)? How would it make you feel?

Doing something way beyond your current level of comfort can dramatically expand your comfort zone, and it can do so in a short period of time. Suddenly, you will realize how much more you're capable of achieving. You may even start thinking, "What else can I do?"

This will create a whole new dynamic in your life.

Getting support

Sometimes, finding the courage to take action on your own can be challenging and doing the impossible might be a little too overwhelming (for now).

Years after my bungee jumping experience, I went skydiving. This time it was different. I didn't have to make the jump alone. The expert I was tethered to did. Having someone to help me jump made things significantly easier. The point I'm making is, sometimes you need support to help you move beyond your comfort zone and unlock your potential.

Other people can help you grow by:

Being a role model. Comfort zones vary from one person to another. When you surround yourself with people whose comfort zone is larger than yours, you will start perceiving your fears and limitations differently. For instance, you'll be more likely to overcome your shyness if you share a house with outgoing people. This is because they are likely to put you in uncomfortable situations you normally avoid. Additionally, as you watch them interact with other people confidently, you'll start shifting your perspective into believing you can do the same thing. If you're willing to overcome your shyness, such an environment will help you tremendously.

Holding you accountable. It's easier to take actions and do things that scare you when someone such as a coach holds you accountable. Having an accountability partner can also be effective, providing both of you are fully committed and willing to call each other out (in a gentle and supportive way).

Encouraging you to take action. People can also offer encouragement. Support from family and friends can be extremely powerful. As we'll discuss in more depth in the section, *Leveraging the Power of Proximity*, your environment is key to your success.

* * *

Action step

What one thing have you wanted to do for a while but put off due to fear? Could you challenge yourself and do it this week? Write down one thing you could do to move beyond your comfort zone in your **Action Guide** (*Part III. Section XIV. The Law of Courage*).

22

THE LAW OF FLEXIBILITY

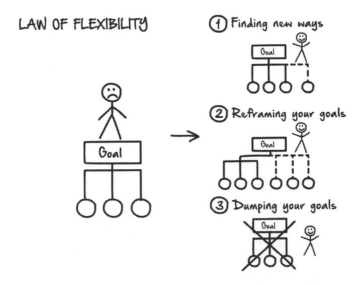

> For a flexible person, it is impossible not to reach his destination, because by using his ability to be flexible, he can easily define a nearer new destination!
>
> — MEHMET MURAT ILDAN, AUTHOR.

The Law of Flexibility states that the more you are willing to consider all the options available to achieve your goal, the more likely you are to succeed.

1. Finding additional ways to achieve your goal

We often have an idea of what our success should look like, but things don't always go as planned. Sometimes, what we thought would work doesn't and we feel stuck.

A goal is generally divided into milestones you need to pass before you can reach your final destination. However, not all these milestones are necessary. It is possible to find many alternative ways to reach your goals.

Let's take the example of someone who wants to become a writer. Perhaps that person identified "finding a publisher" as a key milestone to achieve their goals and can't seem to reach that milestone. Now, what if reaching that milestone isn't essential in the first place? What if that person could self-publish and make money that way? That's what some writers decide to do when they fail to land a publishing deal. Alternatively, what if that same individual doesn't want to get involved with book marketing, cover design, editing, et cetera? Perhaps they would be better off freelancing or ghostwriting.

Just because one door closes, doesn't mean you have to give up. Remember, if you're committed to your goal, you'll find a way to reach it, otherwise you'll find an excuse. Your greatest skill is your resourcefulness, so don't give up just because your original plan didn't work out as expected. Try an alternative approach. Be committed. Be fluid.

2. Reframing your goal

You may be narrowing your options unnecessarily by believing your current goal is the only one that can lead to your desired outcome. Don't get me wrong, I still believe one hundred percent in the power of perseverance and clarity. If you know exactly what you want, I encourage you to persevere along that path.

However, sometimes your goal might be only one of many manifestations of a bigger purpose. This is why I recommend you spend time identifying your overall purpose. You can then use this as a compass and set your goals with both determination *and* flexibility, knowing you're generally heading in the right direction.

As an example, my purpose is to inspire people to be the best person they can possibly be. Books are merely the medium I use to fulfill my mission, as it is aligned with my introverted personality as well as my talents and strengths. However, if I ever found myself facing a roadblock or if I chose to expand my reach, I might have to fulfill my purpose in a different way. For example, I could do more coaching, hold seminars, create training courses or teach in some way. One thing I will *not* do, though, is give up.

I would like you to think of ways you could reframe your goal to give yourself more flexibility.

To learn how to identify your life purpose and set the right goals, refer to my books *The Passion Manifesto: Escape the Rat Race, Uncover Your Passion, and Design a Career and Life You Love,* and *Goal Setting: The Ultimate Guide to Achieving Goals that Truly Excite You.*

3. Giving up on your goals

Another way to leverage *The Law of Flexibility*, is to give up on your goals. While I recommend you persevere, sometimes it is actually important to allow yourself to give up.

The truth is, you evolve over time. Goals you were originally excited about may not excite you anymore. If so, you must not be afraid to drop them. However, before you give up on a specific goal, I encourage you to ask yourself the following question:

Do I want to give up because I'm scared, lack confidence or feel tired? Or is it because I genuinely don't want to pursue that goal anymore?

Finally, remember that a goal is here to make your life better. While it may be challenging, it should also be exciting and enjoyable most of the time. If not, it might be time for you to dump your goal and work toward a more meaningful one.

We'll talk about the importance of emotional flexibility at greater length in **PART IV. Building Emotional Resilience.**

* * *

Action step

How can you use *The Law of Flexibility* to increase your chances of achieving your long-term goals? Write your answers in the **Action Guide** (*Part III. Section XV. The Law of Flexibility*).

23

THE LAW OF PATIENCE

> Patience is bitter, but its fruit is sweet.
>
> — JEAN JACQUES ROUSSEAU, PHILOSOPHER, WRITER AND COMPOSER.

The Law of Patience states that you must trust the process and remain consistent until you see the fruits of your labor.

As you remain consistent over the long term, you will often reach a tipping point that skyrockets your results, sometimes almost overnight. This is where the myth of the so-called overnight success comes from. While many people think in linear terms, success is far from being linear. In most cases, it is exponential. For instance, it is possible for you to have a sudden breakthrough that dramatically shifts your mindset and generates astonishing results. But, much more likely, thanks to your consistent work, you may finally knock at the right door and find the person or opportunity needed to accelerate your success.

The following story by the motivational speaker, Les Brown, illustrates the power of patience extremely well:

"The Chinese Bamboo tree takes five years to grow, and when they go through a process of growing it, they have to water and fertilize the ground where it is every day, and it doesn't break through the ground until the fifth year, but once it breaks through the ground within five weeks it grows ninety feet tall. The question is: does it grow ninety feet in five weeks or five years. The answer is obvious."

There will always be a gap between the time you plant the seed (i.e., start taking action toward your goal), and the time you witness results. While, initially, you may make good progress, often things slow down at some point. Then, the ambitious goal you set at the beginning of your journey will seem like a pipe dream and you seem miles away from attaining it within the original timeframe. This is when many people give up. It is, however, a normal process most people go through during their journey. I advise you to bear this in mind and remain patient.

Since I started blogging and writing books back in 2014-2015, I've failed to achieve my goals again and again. I keep missing my financial goals, my blog traffic barely increased and my books weren't selling well. Many times I said to myself, "What's the point writing books and articles? Nobody is reading them anyway. Why even bother?"

Despite my repeated "failures," I kept focusing on the process—the work I do daily—rather than focusing on my mediocre results. I remained patient, kept writing books and learned as much as I could about self-publishing. I started analyzing what other writers in my field were doing, trying to pinpoint key activities that may lead to better results. In short, I focused my efforts on improving the process, because I realized it was the only thing I had control over. I trusted the process, believing that, eventually, I would achieve my goal. And you know what? I've noticed promising results in the last few months and expect further growth in the near future.

***

Action step

Remember a specific time when you gave up prematurely on a goal. Imagine how things could have been different if you had used *The Law of Patience* and note this in your **Action Guide** (*Part III. Section XVI. The Law of Patience*).

24

THE LAW OF LONG-TERM THINKING

> The only thing worse than being blind is having sight but no vision.
>
> — Helen Keller, author.

The Law of Long-Term Thinking states that as you develop the habits of long-term thinking, you will become far more successful in *all* areas of your life.

One of the best predictors of success is your ability to think long term. Highly successful people project themselves into the future *all the time*. They hold a compelling vision they can't wait to make happen and move toward their goals with enthusiasm, confidence and determination. They follow a clear, written plan to reach their vision.

In his book *Goals!* the success expert, Brian Tracy, wrote:

"Dr. Edward Banfield of Harvard University concluded, after more than fifty years of research, that "long-time perspective" was the most important determinant of financial and personal success in life. Banfield defined long-time perspective as the "ability to think several years into the future while making decisions in the present."

"Average" people, on the other hand, seldom think in the long term. They're more concerned with receiving their paycheck at the end of the month or getting the latest technological gadget than they are about planning for their future. These people are unable to delay instant gratification and make sacrifices in the short term in order to gain everything they want in the long term. Sadly, over the course of their lives, they will have spent more time making grocery lists than they did on writing plans for the future.

What about you? How often do you project yourself one year into the future? Five years into the future? Twenty years into the future?

Your ability to think long term is an excellent indicator of your potential future level of success. If most of the things you do every day aren't activities you'll reap benefits from in the long term— whether it is investing your money, pursuing a worthy cause or taking care of your health—I seriously encourage you to rethink what you do.

Let me say it again. One of the main reasons people fail to achieve their goals is because they don't focus enough on the long term. You *must* develop the habit of continuous long-term thinking.

If you constantly think three or five years down the road and act every day in accordance with your long-term plan, you cannot fail to achieve significantly better results than you would while concentrating on the short term. This is inevitable.

The main characteristics of a long-term thinker

Do you often think of your ideal future? Do you take the necessary actions every day to make it a reality? Below are a few characteristics exhibited by people who think long-term:

- **They have a clear vision for their future:** They understand the power of clarity and know what they want their life to look like in five years, ten years or even longer.
- **They have a clear written long-term plan:** Successful people don't just fantasize about a hypothetical future, they are crystal-clear in what they want, and then they create a specific plan of action to make the vision a reality. They're practical dreamers.
- **They take their goals very seriously:** They don't just set goals and forget about them. They review their goals on a regular basis, often daily.
- **They're future-oriented:** They think of their future all the time and are continuously excited about their vision. They spend very little time thinking of the past except to learn from their failures.

So, how well do you fare on each of the above points?

Remember, successful people have a long-term vision they consistently move toward. They wake up knowing what they have to do that day and keep heading in the direction they've chosen.

Unsuccessful people, on the other hand, let external circumstances decide what their future is going to be.

Are you using each day to build your future?

What you do every day is either moving you closer to your ideal future or away from it. To design the life you want, you must spend a majority of your time working on tasks aligned with your long-term vision.

A key question I encourage you to ask yourself is, "If I keep doing what I'm doing today or this week, will I achieve my long-term vision?"

For instance:

- Is what you're working on today aligned with your vision?
- Does what you're eating today reflect the vision you have for your long-term health?
- Is the way you're managing your money today contributing to your future finance the way you like?

It sounds obvious, but if what you do every day isn't aligned with your vision, you will probably never achieve it.

The importance of having a compelling vision

Your ability to think long term is directly linked to your vision. One reason successful people constantly project themselves into the future is that their vision is huge, and they know it will require years of hard work before coming to fruition. What allows them to stay focused on their long-term vision is their level of clarity regarding what they want (the power of clarity) and the compelling nature of their vision (the power of passion).

Similarly, the clearer and more compelling your vision is, the easier it will be for you to focus on the long term.

Also, note that a big and compelling vision requires you demand more of yourself. Bestselling author, Brendon Burchard, has identified raising your standard as a key component of success. For instance, studies have shown that students perform above the norm when teachers expect more from them. This is known as the "Pygmalion Effect" and demonstrates that teachers' expectations influence their students' performance. The results of an experiment lead by Rosenthal and Jacobsen at an elementary school showed that students who were believed to display "unusual potential for intellectual growth" ended up scoring significantly higher when tested eight months later. The only issue is that they were selected randomly, not because of an unusual potential as teachers had been made to believe.

Similarly, if you set a compelling vision and decide you *must* raise your standards to perform at the highest level you possibly can, over the long term you'll improve significantly more than you otherwise would, perhaps even beyond your imagination.

The key is to believe you can improve regardless of your external circumstances. This is what Carol Dweck describes in her book, *Mindset*, as adopting a "growth mindset," as opposed to having a "fixed mindset," which means, holding the belief you can't improve.

Think long term and imagine yourself becoming one of the best in your industry within the next decade or two. Make it your responsibility to excel at whatever you do, whether it is to serve more people more effectively or to take better care of your family or community. Remember, someone with no compelling vision will seldom—if ever—excel at what they are doing.

We all know people who have been playing the same sports for decades as a hobby. Now, have any of them become world-class players? Of course, not. They wouldn't even do that with as many hours of practice as professional players. Why? Because their intent wasn't to become the best they can. Their intent was purely to play for enjoyment.

Unless you commit to raising your standards, you'll never uncover what you're capable of becoming. I encourage you to think bigger, be bolder and continuously seek clarity regarding what you want out of life.

If you're interested in raising your standards and becoming your best self, I encourage you to refer to my book, *Upgrade Yourself: Simple Strategies to Transform Your Mindset, Improve Your Habits and Change Your Life*.

Is your vision big enough?

Are you pursuing a compelling vision that keeps you awake at night and makes you jump out of your bed every morning?

One way to assess the size of your vision is to look at what you focus on. Are you merely focused on yourself, or are you thinking about what you can do for others? What do you say when you talk about your vision and what questions do you ask others? Do you ask vague and insipid questions, or do you ask powerful questions that reflect your ambitious vision? For instance, if you want to be a coach and serve people, which of the following questions would you ask a coach:

- How can I become a coach?
- How can I become one of the best coaches in the world?

Look at the type of questions you ask yourself and others. What do they say about the size of your vision?

Are your problems big enough?

The size of your vision also determines the size of your challenges. Do you think someone whose mission is to change the world focuses on petty things? Small people usually have small problems, while big people have big problems. If you keep worrying about minor issues that won't matter tomorrow or next week, it shows that your thinking is too small. As the size of your vision grows and your perspective on life changes, most of your small problems will vanish. You will stop paying them attention because you'll be thinking at a different, more significant level.

Your ability to act with the big picture in mind is critical. You need to set a long-term vision that excites you and use this excitement to raise your standards. Remember, the difference between high achievers and "average" performers is often that the former set a clear compelling vision for their lives and commit to making it happen at all costs.

* * *

Action step

Answer the following questions using the **Action Guide** (*Part III. Section XVII. The Law of Long-Term Thinking*):

- Will what you're doing today, or this week, allow you to achieve your long-term goals?
- What are you thinking about throughout your day? Make a list of some of the recurrent thoughts you entertain every day. Are they aligned with your long-term vision?
- What questions are you asking yourself and others? Are they empowering you or are they limiting your chances of achieving your goals?

In the next section, we'll discuss how to build emotional resilience in greater detail.

PART IV
BUILDING EMOTIONAL RESILIENCE

25

THE IMPORTANCE OF EMOTIONAL STABILITY

> Success consists of going from failure to failure without loss of enthusiasm
>
> — Winston Churchill

Life is made of ups and downs. One day you feel amazing and ready to conquer the world, the next day you feel terrible, wondering what you're doing with your life. To achieve your goals, you must be able to stick to the process for long enough, regardless of external circumstances. You must learn to trust the process, knowing that if you keep doing what you have to do every day, you will eventually obtain the results you want. You must remain consistent over time even when everything around you seems to fall apart. In many cases, this is what separates successful and unsuccessful people.

To remain stable, you must learn to control your emotions. People enslaved by their emotions will seldom find the discipline needed to do the things they know they should be doing. They will fall prey to negative emotions, giving up their goals prematurely.

On the other hand, if you can win the inner game and manage your emotions better, you will be able to achieve almost anything you want. Most of the laws and principles in this book will help you take control of your mind which, in turn, will help you achieve your long-term goals.

Remember, you are your own worst enemy. More than anybody else, *you* are the one standing in your own way and sabotaging your efforts. Learn to control your thought processes and emotions, and you will be more likely to achieve your long-term goals.

* * *

Action step

Rate yourself on a scale of 1 to 10 (1 being false, 10 being true) on the following points in your **Action Guide** (*Part IV. Section I. The Importance of Emotional Stability*):

1. I prepare myself for the worst and have contingency plans for my goals.
2. When I commit to something, I do it regardless of the way I feel.
3. I learn from each of my failures, and I am rarely affected by them.
4. I never beat myself up when things don't go as planned.
5. I'm self-compassionate and seldom blame myself or feel as though I'm a failure.
6. I cultivate gratitude every day.
7. My environment empowers me to be my best self.

Preparing for the worst

Who do you think is the most likely to succeed? The person who thought everything would be easy and the journey was going to be a breath of fresh air? Or the one who realized there would be tons of obstacles along the way and mentally prepared themselves for that?

When you set goals, it is essential you prepare yourself effectively. Your ability to imagine the worst and prepare for it will dramatically enhance your chances of success. It will also help you manage difficult times even more effectively.

You *must* paint a picture that is as close as possible to reality. In fact, I encourage you to paint an even gloomier picture. By envisioning the worst, you'll be far better equipped to deal with future setbacks and be much more likely to achieve your long-term goals.

For instance, when I started my online business, I envisioned the worst-case scenarios:

- My blog being hacked leading to the loss of all my articles.
- My Amazon KDP account being stolen resulting in the loss of my books.
- Not making any money for several years.

I intentionally forced myself to imagine the worst, which served me well. In June of 2017, my six-year-old computer broke down and I lost all the data on it, including two books I had finished writing. Thanks to the mental preparation I had completed beforehand, this event didn't affect me much, and I was able to rewrite those two books from scratch. One of my friends who is also a writer told me he would have committed suicide if the same thing had happened to him. Hopefully he was joking, but it does demonstrate the power of mental preparation.

A 4-step process to prepare yourself mentally

To strengthen your mental resilience, I invite you to follow the process below:

1. Write down the worst-case scenarios.

What would be the absolute worst nightmare? Just imagine the worst and write anything that comes to mind.

2. Visualize yourself experiencing these scenarios.

If the worst-case scenarios were to happen, how would you feel? What kind of thoughts would cross your mind? Visualize yourself experiencing them as vividly as possible.

3. Write down what you would do to overcome these challenges.

For each scenario, write down briefly what you would, or could, do to overcome these challenges.

4. Ask yourself what you're willing to endure before giving up.

What would make you give up on your goal? Deciding when to give up will help you persevere. As long as the conditions aren't met, you simply *have* to keep going.

* * *

Action step

Go through the 4-step process using the **Action Guide** (*Part IV. Section I. The Importance of Emotional Stability*).

26

OVERRULING YOUR FEELINGS

 I think self-discipline is something, it's like a muscle. The more you exercise it, the stronger it gets.

— DANIEL GOLDSTEIN

You are *not* your emotions. Sadly, most people act and react based on their emotions, failing to grasp this simple truth. They never realize they can overrule their emotions and take control of their destiny.

One effective way to start taking control of your emotions is through total commitment. Once you know what you want and commit to it, your emotions take second place, thereby losing some of their power. Commitment forces you to overcome negative emotions, such as fear, and to eliminate all your excuses so you can move toward your goal with much more conviction and determination.

In his book, *6 Months to 6 Figures*, Peter Voogd introduces a key concept he calls, "The Decision Train." With it, he argues that most people's way of making decisions is as follows:

Feelings > Actions > Decisions.

Here is how it works: people feel a certain way and, as a result, take a certain type of action, which translates into their final decision.

For instance, if they don't feel like working, they procrastinate, if they don't want to go to the gym, they skip it, and if they have no desire to wake up early, they sleep in.

On the other hand, the five percent, as Peter Voogd calls them, rely on the following decision train:

Decisions > Actions > Feelings

That is, regardless of how they feel, they make a decision first, then they follow through by taking the appropriate action and, as a result, they feel great about themselves.

For instance, they decide to write a book this year, complete it and feel wonderful as a result. Or they commit to exercise three times a week consistently and feel proud of it.

Do you see how overruling your feelings can allow you to build more self-discipline while stabilizing the chaotic process that success can often be?

I rely on this type of commitment to help me accomplish all my challenging goals. When I told my father my goal to write eight books this year, he asked me how I could come up with so many book ideas, but this is largely irrelevant to me. Why? Because I decide my goal first, then I find a way to achieve it. In short, I utilize the following process:

- **Decisions:** I decide what I will do and commit to it (writing eight books this year).
- **Actions:** I take actions (creating a writing schedule and sticking to it).
- **Feelings:** I feel good as a result (build more confidence and discipline as a result of achieving my goals).

To tell you the truth, I don't know what my next book will be about.

I'll think about it while finishing this one. My point is, I don't rely on luck or inspiration to reach my goals. Instead, I set a goal, commit to it and then find a way to achieve it. Then, I follow the most effective process I know of until I achieve my goal (see also *The Law of Effective Action*).

Please note, the goals I commit to are process goals—goals I have control over—not result goals over which I have only limited control. For instance, writing eight books is a process goal as it is almost entirely within my control. However, selling 10,000 copies of my books isn't. I have only partial control over this (although there are a lot of things I can do to promote and sell more books).

Remember, emotions fluctuate. You can overcome emotional rollercoasters by realizing you are not your emotions and by committing to well-defined processes and process goals. Your ability to overrule your feelings will allow you to achieve far better results than is otherwise the case.

* * *

Action step

Write down the following on a piece of paper or print out the corresponding page in your **Action Guide** and put it on your desktop where you can see it (*Part IV. Section II. Overruling Your Feelings*):

Decisions > Actions > Feelings

27

REFRAMING

> 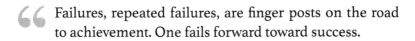 Failures, repeated failures, are finger posts on the road to achievement. One fails forward toward success.
>
> — C.S. Lewis, British novelist

Another way to achieve better control of your emotions is to shift your perspective and reframe the way you perceive negative events, thereby giving them a more empowering meaning. To learn more, you can refer to my book, *Crush Your Limits*.

We all react to events based on our experiences and our lifelong social conditioning. This is the main reason why you can put two people in the exact same situation and one will be happy while the other will be miserable. The happiest and most successful people use reframing to give a much more empowering meaning to life events.

Rethinking failures

For most people, failure is something to be avoided. And sadly, school does a bad job of teaching children how to deal with failures.

In truth, what constitutes a failure is largely subjective. You can change the way you perceive failures by shifting your perspective on them.

The way you experience life is shaped by the way you relate to various concepts such as success, happiness, money and work. Your life can be negatively impacted if you happen to hold limiting beliefs or incorrect assumptions regarding any of these concepts. For example:

- If you think success is an event rather than a process, you'll likely fail to achieve your long-term goals.
- If you believe money is the root of all evil, you might struggle financially for the rest of your life, because who wants to admit to yearning for an evil?
- If you believe happiness is having a bigger house and a nicer car, you may end up living a rather unhappy life.

What you believe about key concepts has tremendous consequences.

Failure is also a concept. It can mean different things to different people. In fact, to achieve your goals you'll have to try many things and many of these won't work. This is how the process we call success works. Now, whether you choose to see these events as failures or not is subjective.

To reframe failures and deal with them more constructively, it is essential you give them a more empowering meaning. After all, everything is a matter of perspective. Here are some of the things that may affect your perspective on failures:

- **Biology:** fear of rejection is a big threat. In the past, being rejected from a tribe could severely reduce the chance of survival. As a result, nowadays we tend to avoid situations that could lead to public humiliation or criticism. This often limits our willingness to try new things lest we look bad.
- **Social conditioning:** social conditioning plays a large part in

the way you perceive failure. When you were a kid, you may have been ridiculed when you failed to do something, or you may have witnessed other people being made fun of. Over time, you've learned to associate failure with pain.

- **Expectations:** for failure to exist there must be boundaries between what constitutes a failure and what doesn't. These boundaries result from your expectations. For instance, imagine you set a goal of losing twenty pounds by the end of the year and make it clear that you will settle for nothing less than that. In that case, if you end up losing only five pounds, you may see it as a total failure. From an objective point of view, however, it could also be interpreted as a positive result —you actually lost five pounds.
- **Lack of understanding:** the more you see so-called failures as part of the process that leads to the achievement of your goals, the less they will be perceived in a negative light. Failure and success are part of the same process, not separate from it.
- **Level of identification with failures:** failing to achieve something doesn't make you a failure. You merely tried something that didn't work. In fact, no amount of failure can fundamentally change the essence of who or what you are. Failures become less painful as you learn to separate your actions and behaviors from your identity. If something didn't work as planned, don't see yourself as a failure. Instead, reflect on your actions and behaviors and ask for feedback. Then, start again, but this time, make changes. As Einstein once said (and I paraphrase slightly), the definition of lunacy is repeating the same thing and expecting different results.
- **Timeframe:** your relationship with failure is greatly affected by the way you position an event in the big picture of your life. Put simply, a failure is less significant when seen as part of a long-term vision. For instance, if you give yourself three years to lose thirty pounds, losing "only" six pounds this year is not something you'll perceive as a failure, because you still have two more years to reach your desired weight. Similarly,

if you estimate it will take you five years to create a business, failing the first year will have less of a negative impact than if you give yourself only two years. The more long term you can think, the less short term "failures" matter.

Changing the meaning

Two people can experience the same event and interpret it in two radically different ways. The farmer may celebrate the onset of rain while the picnickers may curse it. It all depends on your perception of the event.

The way you interpret an event leads you to have certain thoughts, which creates emotions that drive you to take a particular action. Thus, if you want to change the way you respond to an event, you must start by changing the way you interpret it.

For instance, if every time something doesn't work you say to yourself, "I'm a failure," you'll experience negative emotions such as feelings of inadequacy, which may lead you to stop working on your goal. On the other hand, if you perceive failures as opportunities to learn, you'll be in a much more positive emotional state. Rather than ruminating on the event, you will be able to learn from it, so you can achieve better results next time.

Here is a great question to help you reframe a potentially negative situation, "What's great about it?"

This question always allows you to shift your perspective and focus on the positive side of things. If you can't think of anything, then ask yourself, "What *could* be great about it?" If you had to find something positive about an event that happens to you, what would it be?

For instance, let's say you got fired from your job. Obviously, this is a stressful event. But what could be great about it? Try it out yourself. Imagine you've just been laid off from your current job. What's great about it? How can you reframe that event so it empowers you to move forward?

What did you come up with?

Perhaps it gives you an opportunity to do something you've always wanted to try, but never dared to. Or it may give you a chance to move to another industry you've always been interested in. It could also provide you with more time to work on creating a small business.

The ability to reframe what happens is a powerful way to give meaning to seemingly meaningless or unfair events. In his classic book, *Man's Search for Meaning*, psychologist, Viktor E. Frankl, relates his experience in a concentration camp during the Second World War. He considers meaning to be one of the main reasons he was able to survive in such a cruel environment. Below is a great example of the reframing he used with one of his clients:

"Once, an elderly general practitioner consulted me because of his severe depression. He could not overcome the loss of his wife who had died two years ago and whom he had loved above all else. Now, how could I help him? What should I tell him? Well, I refrained from telling him anything but instead confronted him with the question, "What would have happened, Doctor, if you had died first, and your wife would have had to survive you?" "Oh," he said, "for her this would have been terrible; how she would have suffered!" Whereupon I replied, "You see, Doctor, such a suffering has been spared her, and it was you who have spared her this suffering—to be sure, at the price that now you have to survive and mourn her." He said no word but shook my hand and calmly left my office. In some way, suffering ceases to be suffering at the moment it finds a meaning, such as the meaning of a sacrifice."

Whether you face somewhat inconsequential setbacks or incredibly challenging times, learn to reframe the situation and to give it an empowering meaning that will allow you to keep going. If you look hard enough, you can find a positive meaning in everything. It's not what happens that determines the major part of our life, it's the meaning we create out of what happens and the action we take as a result of our interpretation.

* * *

Action step

Think of one major failure you had in your life. Now, come up with as many empowering meanings as you can and write them down using your **Action Guide**. What's great about the event? What did/could you learn from it? (*Part IV. Section III. Reframing*).

28

OVERCOMING CHALLENGING TIMES

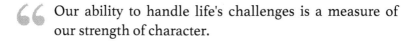 Our ability to handle life's challenges is a measure of our strength of character.

— LES BROWN, MOTIVATIONAL SPEAKER

One of the biggest problems people face is managing themselves during challenging times. You may be motivated to work on your goals when everything goes well, but you can easily become miserable when things don't go as planned.

What you do when facing setbacks or experience negative emotions is fundamental to your success. In this section, I will underline common pitfalls that may prevent you from achieving your long-term goals. By learning how to avoid these pitfalls, you'll be able to manage your emotions more effectively and persevere for longer.

1. Avoid the "I already screwed up" excuse

Many people are excited at the beginning of the journey. They joined the local gym or started a new promising diet, feeling more motivated than ever. However, after a few weeks, they become disheartened and fall off track. Perhaps their diet was going well but on a stressful day, they binge ate. Now they beat themselves up, blaming their lack of self-discipline. Then, they think, "I already failed, so I can eat anything I want. Screw the diet."

This type of black and white approach to goal setting can lead many people to sabotage their efforts. It comes from the belief that, if we are not consistent one hundred percent of the time, we are failing. Success, however, is a process and, as such, isn't black and white. It is far more nuanced and includes both successes *and* so-called failures.

A great analogy is the stock market. If you studied the fluctuations of the stock market over the past hundred years, you'll notice a general upward trend. Now, is it always going up? Of course not. There are ups and downs and sometimes even big crashes. But temporary downward trends don't prevent the stock market from increasing over the long term.

The same principle applies in your life. Binge eating one day doesn't prevent you from achieving your long-term weight-loss goal. Neither is skipping the gym for a week an invitation to screw up the past three months you spent working out! Avoid interpreting temporary setbacks as a means to beat yourself up. Instead, give yourself some slack and remember, success is a process and, therefore, takes time. As one of my friends once told me, life is a marathon, not a sprint, and self-compassion, not self-criticism, is the fuel you need to keep going long term and finish the race.

Thus, be extra careful whenever you notice you're falling off track. It doesn't mean you're a "failure" and is certainly not an invitation to blame yourself and give up. Remember, your ability to manage your feelings will determine for a large part whether you'll achieve your goals in the long term. It's easy to feel motivated when things go well. The real test is what you do when they aren't.

Realize success is a long-term, and often chaotic, process that includes multiple "failures" along the way. Keep focusing on the long term and cut yourself some slack when things don't work out exactly as planned. This will greatly increase your odds of achieving your goals.

2. Adopt an "I'll beat myself up later" mindset

The worst time to make a decision is when we're in a negative emotional state. Yet, this is when most people make poor decisions, such as giving up. The temptation to beat ourselves up can be high and, for some reason, we often enjoy playing the victim and derive a perverse pleasure when we inflict mental pain upon ourselves.

To avoid such situations, I encourage you to adopt an "I'll beat myself up later" mindset. In other words, whenever you feel down, avoid judging yourself and avoid making any decision that could have a negative impact in the long term. For instance, the worst time to give up on your goals would be when you feel discouraged or depressed. Always wait until you're in a positive mental state before making any important decision. Meanwhile, be self-compassionate, accept that disappointment is part of the process and hang in there. You'll have plenty of time to beat yourself up later when you feel better. But for now, give yourself a healthy dose of compassion.

3. Perform damage control during tough times

Remember, failures and disappointments are both part of the success process, not separate from it. The question is not whether you'll have challenging times, but how you'll deal with them. Rather than trying to avoid negative emotions, actively work to limit their impact and shorten their duration. If you can accept they are part of the process, you'll be far more likely to succeed long term.

4. Overcome recurrent negative thought patterns

We all buy into a specific story we call "our life." This story is made up of recurrent thought patterns. For instance, you probably have a few negative thought patterns that lead you to feel sad or depressed from time to time. It could be the, "I'm not good enough," "I'm worried about money," or "I'm not disciplined enough," pattern. If you recall, the 80/20 rule states that twenty percent of your actions leads to eighty percent of your results. It also works for your emotions. Twenty percent of your negative thought patterns can create eighty percent of your suffering. Your job is to identify what these specific thought patterns are and act to alleviate them.

Once you've identified the negative twenty percent, you want to look at the thought process behind them. What kind of thoughts are leading you to experience these negative emotions? Try to be as specific as possible.

After having identified these thoughts, ask yourself, "What underlying beliefs lead me to have these thoughts in the first place?"

Then, challenge each of these beliefs.

Finally, come up with new empowering thoughts you can focus on whenever your negative thoughts kick in. By doing so consistently, you will start weakening your negative thought patterns and create new empowering ones.

For example, one negative thought I often have is the fear of not making it as a full-time author. This manifests whenever things don't work out the way I want them to. It could be when I'm launching a new book and sales don't hit the stratosphere, when my overall sales drop or just when such negative thoughts occur randomly during the day.

While I always do my best to ignore these thoughts whenever they arise, sometimes they do trigger negative emotions. When it happens, I focus on positive thoughts that give me the confidence I will succeed as a writer. For instance:

- I think of all the successful authors in my genre. Especially, self-published authors. Sometimes, I even write down their names.

- I remind myself thousands of authors are successful, and I'm as capable as any of them.
- I remember I still have plenty of time and show a great deal of self-compassion. I also remind myself of my *Bullet-Proof Timeframe*, knowing all I have to do for now is to write. I can worry about the outcome later.
- I tell myself I can always improve my writing since I've only been an author for a few years.
- I reread all my book reviews and comments from people who told me I'm "on the right path" and should "keep inspiring the world."

You might want to think of this process as "closing a sale." When you try to sell a product or service to someone, they often come up with objections. Now, image if you knew each of these objections by heart. Wouldn't it be easier to close the sale? Similarly, if you have dozens of counter-arguments you can use when your negative thought patterns kick in, you'll find it easier to overcome these patterns and limit the negative impact they have on your life.

Note that the new empowering thoughts you use as counter-arguments can turn into deeper beliefs if you create a habit of focusing on them each day. This could be by repeating affirmations for instance (for more on this see *The Law of Conditioning*).

* * *

Action step

Go through the process below using the **Action Guide** (*Part IV. Section IV. Overcoming Challenging Times*):

- Remember a time you gave up on one of your goals. Visualize yourself encountering a similar situation in the future. Now, see yourself acting with self-compassion.
- Whenever you experience negative emotions, give yourself

some slack and wait until you feel better before making any important decisions.
- Identify recurrent negative patterns.
- Write down a few negative thought patterns that lead you to experience negative emotions.
- Go one step further now and identify the specific thoughts and images that go through your mind.
- Ask yourself, "What would I need to believe in order to experience these thoughts?"
- Come up with new empowering thoughts (counter-arguments) and use them when your negative thought pattern kicks in.
- Turn these new empowering thoughts into powerful beliefs through daily conditioning.

29

CULTIVATING SELF-COMPASSION

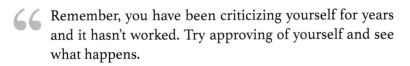 Remember, you have been criticizing yourself for years and it hasn't worked. Try approving of yourself and see what happens.

— LOUISE L. HAY, MOTIVATIONAL AUTHOR AND FOUNDER OF HAY HOUSE

Self-compassion beats self-criticism

For some reason, we like to blame ourselves whenever we fail to live up to our own high expectations. Even when we have every reason to be happy, our mind seems to be seeking ways to move away from that state of happiness. This is because our brain is not designed to make us happy but to ensure our survival. In addition, we often allow ourselves to be happy only up to a certain point before reverting to our natural happiness "set-point." To overcome these natural tendencies, it is important we choose to focus on the positive side of things.

Self-compassion is an effective way to deal with self-criticism and prevent unnecessary suffering. It can help you persevere during challenging times and reduce self-sabotaging behaviors. While you may believe you need to be hard on yourself to avoid slacking off, research has shown that self-criticism is, in fact, a subpar strategy in the long run. In, *The Willpower Instinct,* psychologist, Kelly McGonigal, wrote the following regarding self-criticism:

"If you think that the key to greater willpower is being harder on yourself, you are not alone. But you are wrong. Study after study shows that self-criticism is consistently associated with less motivation and worse self-control. It is also one of the single biggest predictors of depression, which drains both, "I will" power and "I want" power. In contrast, self-compassion—being supportive and kind to yourself, especially in the face of stress and failure—is associated with higher motivation and better self-control.

Here is a truth: self-compassion is more powerful than self-criticism. Thus, don't be afraid to be self-compassionate. It will serve you well long term.

Remember, self-compassion is an important component of the *Self-Empowerment Triangle* we discussed earlier. The more self-compassion you develop, the better you'll perform (and feel) in the long term.

Why sucking at most of the things you do is fine

We often have a specific image of how we should be and beat ourselves up when we fail to meet that standard. We also tend to compare ourselves with others, which can easily create feelings of inadequacy, even though these comparisons are unfair almost all the time.

There are many things you can't do well. And that's how it should be. This is why people specialize in different things. Thus, whether you're terrible at cooking, driving, writing or singing, it isn't an issue. Neither is having no sense of humor, zero public speaking skills or little charisma a problem in itself.

In truth, you can absolutely design a great life all the while doing a poor job at most of what you do. And what's the point in blaming yourself for things you cannot do anyway?

Often, the reason you're not good at something is merely that you lack the experience. If that's the case and if you wish to become better, the simple answer is to gain more experience.

Also, bear in mind you don't need to improve at everything you do. Sometimes, accepting your weaknesses and focusing on your strengths is a much better strategy. Being exceptional at a couple of things can often be enough to build a great career and a great life, not to mention it can also be far more enjoyable. The last thing you want is to spend your life doing things you're incompetent at. It will not only be exhausting, but it will also do a disservice to people who could benefit from your actual talents and strengths.

In short, when it comes to things you do poorly, you can do one of the following things:

- Accept completely your incompetence and be fine with it.
- Create a plan of action to become better (if you wish to).
- Ask someone else to do it for you.

Whatever option you choose is fine. There is no need to blame yourself or compare yourself to others because you can't do X, Y or Z. You just have to do one of the three points mentioned above and move on.

Avoiding the "I'm not good enough" trap

Even high achievers feel as though they aren't good enough and constantly try to prove themselves to the word. When they fail to live up to their expectations, they beat themselves up.

Wanting to become better isn't necessarily about trying to be good enough, though. It is about loving the process and feeling good about yourself as you become better each day. It doesn't come from a place of lacking, but from a place of curiosity and a desire to contribute more.

You can achieve great things while enjoying the journey. Seeking continuous growth while acknowledging your progress—as opposed to never feeling good enough—is possible. To do so, you must adopt the regular habit of celebrating your small wins. Unless you take the time to pat yourself on the back and savor your successes, you run the risk of feeling insecure and chronically dissatisfied.

To enjoy the journey, you need to realize this simple truth: you can always improve. You don't have to live in the future, hoping one day you'll make it. You don't need to suffer because you're not there yet. Where you are now in terms of skills and abilities is *exactly* where you're supposed to be. That's what we call "reality."

The first step is to acknowledge this undeniable truth and accept it completely. Doesn't it make you feel lighter to recognize you don't need to be there (yet), but can be happy here right now? The second step is to understand you can always grow and learn. The third step is to remind yourself you have time. You have years to improve and master whatever skills you want to master. The fourth and final step is to realize that becoming better over time is inevitable. If you follow the process in this book, you *will* become better. It *is* inevitable.

So, if you've told yourself, "I'm not good enough," replace this belief with, "I'm not as good as I want to be *yet,* but I'm good enough *for now.*"

The words "yet" and "for now" may seem insignificant, but they make all the difference in the world. "Yet" makes you realize you can always improve and eventually you will. "For now" indicates you're exactly where you're supposed to be and invites you to acknowledge everything you're doing well *at the moment.*

* * *

Action step

Complete the corresponding exercises in the **Action Guide** (*Part IV. Section V. Cultivating Self-Compassion*).

30

PRACTICING GRATITUDE

> Just to give a glimpse into its benefits, gratitude increases self-esteem, enhances willpower, strengthens relationships, deepens spirituality, boost creativity, and improves athletic and academic performance.
>
> — Dr Robert A Emmons, author of "The Little Book of Gratitude"

Gratitude is one of the most powerful forces on earth. Your ability to be grateful for all the things you already have will make you happier and help you become more resilient during difficult times.

Most people have a myriad of reasons to feel grateful, but few really are. Instead of counting their blessings, they obsess over trivial things, and thereby make their lives miserable. Whereas they could bring their attention to what goes well, they choose to focus on what they lack, constantly looking for faults in themselves and in others. As the business philosopher, Jim Rohn, said, *"The poor pessimist leads an ugly life ... He looks through the window and doesn't see the sunset, he sees the specks on the window!"*

Life may not be easy, but is there any reason to make it harder by focusing on the negative?

In truth, we've never had access to so many services in all of human history. Having food, shelter and a few trusted friends alone should already be enough to live a good life. Yet most of us take these things for granted, seeking happiness in acquiring more things, such as a bigger house, a nicer car or fancier vacations. While those are fine, why look for more if we aren't satisfied with what we already have? It is important to note that a poor person who cultivates the daily habit of gratitude will, over time, be happier than most rich people ever will.

How to develop gratitude

Have you ever felt sad or depressed, while nothing in the external world actually changed? This could be because of what you focus on.

For the most part, your ability to feel grateful results from what you choose to focus on in your daily life. If you focus on all your problems, you can quickly become depressed. On the other hand, if you look for wonderful things to be grateful for, you'll experience a deeper sense of gratitude.

To make my day more manageable when I was an unhappy employee, I would spend fifteen to thirty minutes every morning performing gratitude exercises.

Now, you might wonder how you can cultivate a deeper sense of gratitude, and I can tell you, the answer is simple: by practicing. Make it a habit to practice gratitude every morning. This way, you'll set yourself up for a great day. Below is a roundup of what I like to do when I wake:

- I close my eyes, think of someone, thank them and remember one or two things they have done for me. For instance, it could be advice they gave me or a lesson they taught me. I repeat the process with the next person who

comes to mind. You don't need to choose anyone in particular. Just let your mind wander. To elicit deeper feelings of gratitude, I like to listen to beautiful songs while doing this exercise. Consider doing this exercise for at least a couple of minutes each day.
- I read through my gratitude journal. This journal contains nice comments, compliments and book reviews I received. In my mind, I go through some of the entries and thank people for their support.

While this is what I personally do, many other ways are possible. For instance, you could:

- Write down things you're grateful for.
- Look at an object, think of all the people involved in its creation and fully appreciate how lucky you are to have such a thing.
- Ask yourself what you're grateful for and answer that question out loud. Try to come up with as many things as you can.
- Remember all the things that went well today before going to bed.

The wonderful thing about these exercises is that they give you a sense of control over your life. You can choose to do these exercises daily and look for the good, instead of letting your mind and external circumstances dictate your emotional state.

Practicing gratitude will make you happier and will strengthen your emotional resilience. This, in turn, will help you stay consistent over the long term, preventing you from giving up on your goals prematurely.

Remember, your capacity to deal with negative emotions will help you achieve your long-term goals. This is one of the fundamental components of success. Therefore, learn to see the glass as half full, and don't forget, there are always things to be grateful for.

What will you do every day to experience more gratitude and make your life even more precious?

* * *

Action step

Select one gratitude exercise from the **Action Guide** and stick to it for the next two weeks (*Part IV. Section VI. Practicing Gratitude*).

31

LEVERAGING THE POWER OF PROXIMITY

> 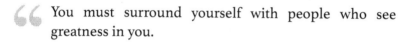 You must surround yourself with people who see greatness in you.
>
> — BO EASON, FORMAL AMERICAN FOOTBALL PLAYER AND SPEAKER

Imagine if all your friends were highly successful. Do you think you would achieve better results?

What if you were around healthy, fit people? Would that help you lose weight?

You are largely the product of your environment. Your subconscious continuously absorbs vast amounts of information without your awareness. To design the life you really want, you must optimize your physical and social environment. It is far easier to be successful when you are surrounded by people who uplift you and expect the best from you, than when you are in a toxic environment surrounded by people trying to sabotage your efforts.

How to design an empowering environment

To optimize your environment and increase your chance of success you must do one or more of the following:

1. Improve the quality of your daily input (i.e., the information you consume).
2. Surround yourself with people who lift you up.
3. Design an empowering physical environment.

1. Improve the quality of your daily input

The information you consume every day greatly impacts your psychology. Listening to the news can make you fearful and create needless stress and worry. Equally, consuming motivational and educational resources can motivate you to become a better version of yourself.

I encourage you to begin and end your day on a positive note. This will help because your subconscious mind is more receptive in the morning after waking and at night before falling asleep, thus enabling you to reprogram your mind more effectively.

Below are some of the things you can do in the morning, in the evening or both:

Exercising: exercising has been shown to improve your mood. Some studies even show it can be as effective as anti-depressants. Take care, though—heavy exercise in the evening can negatively affect your sleep.

Consuming inspiration materials: creating a daily habit of reading inspirational books or watching motivational videos will help you create a more positive mindset.

Practicing gratitude: spending time every day to express gratitude is an effective way to enhance your well-being (see also *Practicing Gratitude*).

Meditating: meditation is a great way to calm your mind and reduce negative emotions. It also teaches you to observe your thoughts and take them less seriously.

Asking empowering questions: asking yourself empowering questions is a great way to shift your focus toward the positive things happening in your life. Here are some fantastic questions to ask yourself at the end of each day:

- What are the three things I'm proud of today? (This is a great way to build your self-esteem and train your mind to focus on small wins).
- What are the three things I did well today? (Same effect as above. There may be some potential overlap in your answers).
- What am I grateful for today?
- What could I have done *even* better today? Note, the importance of using "even." You want to acknowledge yourself for what you did and think of how you could have done an even better job. You don't ever want to beat yourself up.

A few tips on the above:

- Make sure you give specific answers.
- Force yourself to come up with answers even if they seem insignificant. Things you are proud of could be little things such as waking on time, not beating yourself up too much or eating fruit.
- At the end of each week, try to remember the answers you've made during the week. It will help you rewire your brain even further.

This exercise doesn't have to take more than a couple of minutes each day, but it can be very effective when practiced consistently for an extended period. First, commit to doing it for two weeks and see the results you achieve.

2. Surround yourself with people who lift you up

People you hang out with most of the time will greatly determine your future. Needless to say, negative people with bad habits, poor self-discipline and little self-awareness will drag you down.

In fact, as we have seen, negativity usually wins over positivity. One negative person in a group of five positive people tends to have a greater negative influence on the whole group than a positive person will have in the reverse situation. This is why it is so important you surround yourself with positive people who encourage you to raise your standards.

Realize that your environment beats your willpower, because you're immersed in your environment 24/7, while your willpower requires a conscious effort and will inevitably diminish over time.

Continuously try to surround yourself with successful people who have already achieved the goals you seek to achieve. They will challenge you to raise your standards and, over time, you will naturally copy their mindset and adopt similar beliefs.

3. Design a physical environment to empower you

Your physical environment also has a massive influence and tends to be more powerful than your willpower. A good example is the way your physical environment affects your diet.

I've noticed the power of my environment on my diet when, in a rare moment of weakness, I caught myself eating nuts that were on my desk. As I put them in my mouth, I suddenly realized how mechanical the act was.

This is why you won't find any sweets or sugary drinks in my home or office (I have a sweet tooth). If I want to eat something sweet, I'll have to go out and buy it. By the way, as I'm editing this book, my internet modem is hidden in a drawer in another room. This way, I can stay focused on my work.

Here is another example of how your physical environment can affect your behavior:

Imagine your fridge is full of cans of your favorite drink. Every time you open your fridge, you have to exert willpower to refrain from grabbing one. You may also see your family members grabbing one, perhaps they'll even leave a bottle on the kitchen table.

In this example, it's as if your environment were screaming at you, "Go for it. Have that drink." At the end of the day, when you feel tired and have depleted your willpower, you won't be able to resist grabbing one can from the fridge. And it's no wonder!

When it comes to the principle of proximity, the rule of thumb is:

- Make it as difficult as possible to indulge in behaviors or activities you want to avoid.
- Conversely, make it as easy as possible to adopt desirable behaviors or activities.

Below are a few examples of what you can do to design a more empowering environment that supports your goals:

- **Remove all distractions from your workspace:** get rid of your smartphones and any documents or items on your desktop except for the ones you absolutely need. The added benefit of this method is that it primes your mind by telling you, "Now I'm working".
- **Sort out files on your computer and make sure you can access all the files you need immediately.**
- **Eliminate all unhealthy food from your home and replace it with healthy foods:** for instance, you could have a basket of fruit available in several strategic places.
- **Prepare your running gear the day before:** this will make it as easy as possible to go for a run whenever you want to.

To sum up, to leverage the *Power of Proximity*, you must make sure the things you need to improve your life are:

1. Around you
2. Close to you
3. As easy as possible to access, and/or
4. Automatized (through daily rituals).

***

Action step

Write down the things you will do to create a more empowering environment using the **Action Guide** (*Part IV. Section VII. Leveraging the Power of Proximity*).

PART V
WORKING WITH OTHERS

32

ADDING VALUE TO PEOPLE'S LIVES

> In our interviews, we found that high performers give an extraordinary amount of thought to questions of service: how to add value, inspire those around them and make a difference. Their attention in this area could best be described as a search for relevance, differentiation and excellence.
>
> — Brendon Burchard, High Performance Habits.

The million-dollar question

Have you ever experienced a sense of joy after donating money to charity? Have you ever felt valued after using your knowledge to help others?

While we tend to focus on our selfish needs, helping others can be far more powerful and beneficial in the longer term. Not to mention that it makes us feel good about ourselves.

In fact, experiments have shown that spending money on others tends to make us happier than spending it on ourselves. Thus, as much as we like to think of humans as selfish, this is not necessarily the case. In fact, if anything, helping others seems to be wired in our brain as a way to ensure the survival of the community. Yet, ironically, we tend to shy away from doing so, focusing instead on our own needs.

Here is the million-dollar question that I encourage you to keep asking for the rest of your life: "How can I help you?"

Constantly focusing on ways to help others, whether it is your family members, your friends, your colleagues or complete strangers, is one of the most powerful habits you can develop. I've found that if you're willing to go the extra mile to support others, they will almost automatically return the compliment in the future. Giving is one of the most effective ways to develop meaningful relationships in your personal and professional life.

Put yourself in other people's shoes

Understanding what people want and helping them get it, is one of the best things you can do to ensure your own long-term success. Practice seeing things from other people's perspectives. Discover their aspirations. Then, help them achieve their goals. If you can do this, they will likely go above and beyond to help you get what *you* want. Or, as the famous motivational speaker, Zig Ziglar, once said, *"You can have everything in life you want, if you will help other people get what they want."*

To identify other people's needs, you must understand the following:

- **Their career goals:** what do they want from their career? Do they want to grow their business? Earn a promotion?
- **Their issues:** what key issues are they facing in their lives right now?
- **Their vision:** what is their ultimate vision? Understanding other people's vision is critical. Once you know what they want to accomplish, it becomes easier to help them in a meaningful way.

- **Their values:** knowing their values will help you better understand the decisions they make. The more values you have in common, the easier it will be to build a meaningful relationship.
- **Their hobbies:** what do they enjoy during their spare time? Knowing their hobbies can help you identify some commonalities. You may even be able to help teach them something or share with them valuable resources.

Realize that most of the things you'll achieve in life, you'll need the help of other people. Thus, your ability to serve others and add value to their lives, whether they are clients, family members, friends or colleagues, will determine for the most part how successful you will be in all areas of your life.

How are you helping your spouse, your family, your friends or your colleagues achieve their goals? Do you even know what their goals are in the first place?

Focus on building long-term relationships

Most people mainly focus on the short term. They often hold a specific idea of how they want the other person to help. For instance, they may connect with them right before a new project hoping to receive their help. Or, to put it differently, they tend to prioritize the short term rather than seeing how the relationship could evolve long term.

However, it is far more effective to think of people you want to connect with as future friends you plan to hang out with for years. With such a mindset, you're coming from a place of helpfulness. Instead of trying to get something from them, simply connect with them, help them whenever you can and allow the relationship to evolve naturally from there.

After all, when you try to make new friends, you don't start by asking them for help or try to sell them something right away, do you? No. You learn more about them, look for common interests and see how you can create a win-win relationship, that is, a relationship you both want to be part of.

Learn to see others for what they could be

When you look at people, do you see their potential or their shortcomings? Do you encourage them to become more, or do you treat them as if they were doomed to stay forever where they are?

Successful people often make you feel you can accomplish far more than you believe possible. Small people, on the other hand, keep reminding you that your dreams are impossible, and you have little or no potential.

To help others more effectively you must see them for what they could be. Empowering them to grow will not only increase the odds they achieve *their* goals but also the odds *you* will achieve *yours*. This is because the more positive impact you have on other people, the more they will be willing to support you. Additionally, the more you can help others succeed, the more resources—influence, money, knowledge—they may have to support you in the future.

So, learn to believe in others. Refuse to see them as less than they can be. By doing so, you'll encourage them to improve their standards and achieve better results. In return, they will thank you by helping you.

Five tips to effective networking

Here's how you can use the information mentioned above to network more effectively:

1. **Listen attentively:** when networking, most people try to sell their products and services to someone they don't even know. Don't do that. Instead, learn to listen and show interest in what the other person is doing. Listen more than you talk and ask questions. A good rule of thumb is to avoid mentioning what you do before being asked. As Dale Carnegie wrote in his classic book, *How to Win Friends and*

Influence People, "You can make more friends in two months by becoming interested in other people than you can in two years by trying to get other people interested in you."

2. **Help others:** constantly seek to help people. Do so before asking for anything. If you know someone helpful you could introduce them to, let them know. If you have ideas that could help grow their business, tell them. The more you provide value to others, the more likely they are to help you in the future. In his book, *Influence*, Robert Cialdini identifies "reciprocity" as one of the rules we can all use to influence others. Use it to your advantage by genuinely seeking to help others first.

3. **Aim to build long-term relationships:** approach any relationships with the desire to make a new friend for life, which entails being genuinely interested in the other person rather than pushing your own agenda down their throats.

4. **Look for commonalities:** as you communicate with someone you'd like to network with, whether in person or via email, look for things you have in common. Do you have similar values or areas of interest? Do you share common goals or hobbies? Obviously, the more you have in common, the easier it is to create rapport.

5. **Focus on creating win-win relationships:** avoid trying to take from people. Instead, constantly seek to create a win-win relationship. To do so, make sure you understand what the other person is looking for and what their long-term vision is. If you can help them, whether by introducing them to someone, sharing your knowledge or offering something of value to their clients, they'll be keen to work with you.

* * *

Action step

Complete the corresponding exercise in the **Action Guide** (*Part V. Section I. Adding Value to People's Lives*).

33

DEVELOPING AN ASKING MENTALITY

 To be successful, you have to ask, ask, ask, ask, ask!

— JACK CANFIELD, SUCCESS COACH AND BEST-SELLING AUTHOR

Have you ever asked your boss for a pay rise? Did you ask that person you like out on a date? Have you reached out to the guy who has the career you want? If not, why not?

I often see people limiting themselves by failing to ask, and I'm certainly guilty of that, too. We seem to talk ourselves out of asking for what we want for fear of rejection, or disturbing people, or because of pride or simply because we believe it is not okay to ask for what we want.

The problem is, if you don't ask the answer will never be yes. There are over seven billion people on this planet and you're rarely more than one click away from most of them. Among them, millions have the resources you need to achieve your goal, whether it is money, time or important connections. Why not ask for their help?

There is a myth we can do things on our own without any help from others. This is reflected in the common expression "self-made millionaire." However, in truth, most of the things we accomplish, we do so with either the direct or indirect help of others. Self-made millionaires are nothing without their customers, the knowledge they acquired in books written by others or the technologies they use in their business. And what about the support they received from family and friends?

We are all interconnected, and the idea we can do things on our own is an illusion. It only appears that way because we generally fail to acknowledge how much we benefit from the work of others. For instance, without Amazon, you wouldn't be able to read this book. But, in turn, Amazon couldn't operate without its tens of thousands of employees, and all of this is made possible thanks to the internet.

The bottom line is, you cannot do things just on your own. It is not only okay, but it is *necessary* you ask other people for help. Learn to ask for help and you'll dramatically enhance your chances of success.

Remember, people are often more than willing to help you. As we discussed earlier, human beings are hardwired to help each other. We tend to feel good and valued when we're offered the chance to help other people. So why not let other people help you?

I want you to develop an asking mentality and create a habit of asking others for help whenever necessary. As success coach, Jack Canfield, wrote in his book, *The Success Principles*, "Learn to become an askhole". His popular book, *Chicken Soup for The Soul*, was rejected by 144 publishers before being published. Jack Canfield is definitely a big *askhole*. The worst that can happen when you ask is that people will say "no," but by failing to ask, you say "no" to your dreams.

Imagine how your life could change if you were to ask the world for what you want. What would you ask for and from whom? Would you ask for a pay increase? Would you try to get someone to mentor you? Would you ask the special person you fancy out on a date?

If you want to know how to develop an asking mentality in greater detail, refer to my book, *The Passion Manifesto: Escape the Rat Race, Uncover Your Passion and Design a Career and Life You Love.*

* * *

Action step

Answer the following question in your **Action Guide** (*Part V. Section II. Developing an Asking Mentality*):

What is one thing you could ask for but, so far, haven't dared to?

PART VI
BONUS

34

FIVE CORE BELIEFS TO ACHIEVE SUCCESS

We have covered the *Seventeen Laws of Success* and discussed the importance of developing emotional resilience. We've also seen the habits you can develop to receive people's support. Now, let's look at some core beliefs to help you build confidence so you can achieve your goals. These are core beliefs that I've been relying on myself over the past few years.

If you want to discover even more core beliefs that will help you change your life, I encourage you to check out my book, *Crush Your Limits*. In it, you'll learn how to replace disempowering beliefs with new empowering ones that will impact your life in a positive way.

Belief #1—If one, then one million

This is one of the core beliefs running through the back of my mind. Below are some examples:

- If I can sell one book to one person, then I can sell one million books to one million people. It is just a matter of finding a way to reach them.

- If I can make one dollar online, then I can repeat the process and make $100, $1,000, $10,000, et cetera.
- If I can find one client, I can find many more.

Can you see how powerful this belief is? Instead of doubting myself, as many people do, I merely seek to make my first sale or find my first client. Then, I know ninety percent of the work is done. From this point onward, I know I will be able to repeat the process. I just have to persevere and make necessary adjustments along the way.

Belief #2—If others can, I can

This is another simple, yet incredibly powerful belief I hold. I always assume that if other people can, then I can (and I will).

- If others are making money online, I can.
- If others are making a living as self-published authors, I can.
- If others are retiring early, I can.
- If others are having it all, I can.

The truth is that what other people can do, in most cases you can also do. This belief can boost your confidence and bring more certainty in your ability to reach your goal. For me, as soon as I see thousands of people around the world succeed at something, I know I can and will achieve the same goal, if:

- I apply the processes in this book, and
- I'm passionate enough about what I'm doing.

In short, I always assume that what others can do, I can, too. It may take tons of work and require more time than for other people but, eventually, I will achieve similar results.

What if you adopted the belief that what others can do, you can, too? How much more certainty and confidence would it give you? What different actions would you take, starting today?

Belief #3—I can get better

That's the whole point of this book, but let's repeat it: you *can* get better. In fact, as you practice the exercises in this book, getting better is inevitable. Keep practicing and learn from all your failures and you *will* improve.

I used to beat myself up for not being good enough, but then I realized something very powerful. Whatever I do right now is exactly what I'm supposed to. This is reality. *I'm good enough for now* and I can and will get better if I keep practicing.

In short, I shifted my focus from short- to long-term thinking. I gave myself some slack and reminded myself that I have time. The realization that I'm exactly where I'm supposed to be right now allowed me to relax more and stop beating myself up.

I now believe I can get better in each area of my life. I can overcome any major obstacle along the way, and so can you. After all, if other people can, I can. How? By practicing consistently, remaining patient and by managing challenging times effectively.

Belief #4—Others will give up, therefore, I will succeed

Many people will give up after encountering major setbacks. Few will have the perseverance to "fail" again and again and keep going until they achieve the results they want. Most of my competitors aren't really my competitors, because I know they will give up at some point, while I will keep going and improving until I achieve my goal. Understand that your ability to stay focused on the process despite all the inevitable ups and downs will contribute significantly to your long-term success (see also *The Law of Perseverance*).

Belief #5—Success is inevitable

Success is inevitable. That's a mantra I've been repeating to myself every day. I chose to believe success is inevitable because, after reading countless self-help books, I realized that, what determines our level of success is, for the most part, our belief in ourselves and in our visions.

In truth, I wasn't always confident in my ability to achieve my goals. Like most people, I doubted myself. However, as I kept progressing toward my goals, I developed more confidence in myself and in my vision. I did so by adopting new empowering beliefs like the ones in this section.

While I repeatedly failed to reach my targets, I still achieved many goals. I also adopted a morning ritual I stuck to every day for over six months. This discipline boosted my self-confidence. By shooting YouTube videos, doing Facebook Live and joining the public speaking group, Toastmasters, I expanded my comfort zone further building confidence.

By developing more confidence, you will be able to achieve most of your goals. And once you believe success is inevitable, giving up becomes irrelevant. You stop caring what people say you can and cannot do. Instead of worrying about the "how," you focus on the "why" behind your goals, trusting you are resourceful enough to solve any problem. Temporary "failures" become learning experiences you can use to reach your long-term goals. You come to realize that as long as you keep going, the game is still on. Life is a marathon, not a sprint. You have years to become better.

CONCLUSION

Thank you for purchasing this book and staying with me until the end. By doing so, you've already shown your commitment to transform your life. I applaud you for that.

You now understand at a much deeper level how success works. I encourage you to refer to this book as many times as necessary until you've become living proof of each of the concepts discussed in it. Remember, nothing changes until you do. Go deeper with everything you do and never forget that you can always become better. Keep improving until you become a master. If you can do this every day while remaining focused on your long-term vision, you'll be well on your way to designing and living a great life.

Also, understand that so-called failures are part of the process. Success is inevitable, but so is the occasional failure. On your journey toward your goals, you are likely to fail many times. Often, you will doubt yourself and will feel like giving up, but when this happens, keep focusing on the process and do what you have to do every single day. The ability to remain consistent regardless of external situations will allow you to achieve your goals in the long term.

Finally, if you believe this book can benefit people around you, make sure to tell them about it.

If you have any questions or want to share your story with me, you can contact me at any time at thibaut.meurisse@gmail.com. I love hearing from my readers.

All the best with your future goals.

Thibaut Meurisse,

Founder of Whatispersonaldevelopment.org

What do you think?

I'd be very grateful if you'd post a short review on Amazon. Your support really does make a difference.

Thanks again!

Thibaut

ABOUT THE AUTHOR

THIBAUT MEURISSE

Thibaut Meurisse is a personal development blogger, author, and founder of whatispersonaldevelopment.org.

He has been featured on major personal development websites such as Lifehack, Goalcast, TinyBuddha, Addicted2Success, MotivationGrid or PickTheBrain.

Obsessed with self-improvement and fascinated by the power of the brain, his personal mission is to help people realize their full potential and reach higher levels of fulfillment and consciousness.

In love with foreign languages, he is French, writes in English, and lived in Japan for almost ten years.

Learn more about Thibaut at:

amazon.com/author/thibautmeurisse
whatispersonaldevelopment.org
thibaut.meurisse@gmail.com

Master Your Life With The Mastery Series

If you're interested in further improving your life, you can check the **"Mastery Series"** at the URL below:

mybook.to/mastery_series

MASTER YOUR EMOTIONS (PREVIEW)

> The mind in its own place, and in itself can make a heaven of Hell, a hell of Heaven.
>
> — JOHN MILTON, POET.

We all experience a wild range of emotions throughout our lives. I had to admit, while writing this book, I experienced highs and lows myself. At first, I was filled with excitement and thrilled at the idea of providing people with a guide to help them understand their emotions. I imagined how readers' lives would improve as they learned to control their emotions. My motivation was high and I couldn't help but imagine how great the book would be.

Or so I thought.

After the initial excitement, the time came to sit down to write the actual book, and that's when the excitement wore off pretty quickly. Ideas that looked great in my mind suddenly felt dull. My writing seemed boring, and I felt as though I had nothing substantive or valuable to contribute.

Sitting at my desk and writing became more challenging each day. I started losing confidence. Who was I to write a book about emotions if I couldn't even master my own emotions? How ironic! I considered giving up. There are already plenty of books on the topic, so why add one more?

At the same time, I realized this book was a perfect opportunity to work on my own emotional issues. And who doesn't suffer from negative emotions from time to time? We all have highs and lows, don't we? The key is what we *do* with our lows. Are we using our emotions to grow? Are we learning something from them? Or are we beating ourselves up over them?

So, let's talk about *your* emotions now. Let me start by asking you this:

How do you feel right now?

Knowing how you feel is the first step toward taking control of your emotions. You may have spent so much time internalizing you've lost touch with your emotions. Perhaps you answered as follows: "I feel this book could be useful," or "I really feel I could learn something from this book." However, none of these answers reflect how you feel. You don't 'feel like this,' or 'feel like that,' you simply 'feel.' You don't 'feel like' this book could be useful, you 'think' this book could be useful, and that generates an emotion which makes you 'feel' excited about reading it. Feelings manifest as physical sensations in your body, not as an idea in your mind. Perhaps, the reason the word 'feel' is so often overused or misused is because we don't want to talk about our emotions. So, how do you feel now?

Why is it important to talk about emotions?

How you feel determines the quality of your life. Your emotions can make your life miserable or truly magical. That's why they are among the most important things to focus on. Your emotions color all your experiences. When you feel good, everything seems, feels, or tastes better. You also think better thoughts. Your energy levels are higher and possibilities seem limitless. Conversely, when you feel depressed, everything seems dull. You have little energy and you become unmotivated. You feel stuck in a place (mentally and physically) you don't want to be, and the future looks gloomy.

Your emotions can also act as a powerful guide. They can tell you something is wrong and allow you to make changes in your life. As such, they may be among the most powerful personal growth tools you have.

Sadly, neither your teachers nor your parents taught you how emotions work or how to control them. I find it ironic that just about anything comes with a how-to manual, while your mind doesn't. You've never received an instruction manual to teach you how your mind works and how to use it to better manage your emotions, have you? I haven't. In fact, until now, I doubt one even existed.

What you'll learn in this book

This book is the how-to manual your parents should have given you at birth. It's the instruction manual you should have received at school. In it, I'll share everything you need to know about emotions so you can overcome your fears and limitations and become the type of person you really want to be.

You'll learn what emotions are, how they are formed, and how you can use them for your personal growth. You'll also learn how to deal with negative emotions and condition your mind to create more positive emotions.

It is my sincere hope and expectation that, by the end of this book, you will have a clear understanding of what emotions are and will have all the tools you need to start taking control of them.

More specifically, this book will help you:

- Understand what emotions are and how they impact your life
- Identify negative emotions that control your life and learn to overcome them
- Change your story to take better control over your life and create a more compelling future, and
- Reprogram your mind to experience more positive emotions.

Here is a more detailed summary of what you'll learn in this book:

In **Part I**, we'll discuss what emotions are. You'll learn why you are wired to focus on negativity and what you can do to counter this effect. You'll also discover how your beliefs impinge upon your emotions. Finally, you'll learn how negative emotions work and why they are so tricky.

In **Part II**, we'll go over the things that directly impact your emotions. You'll understand the roles your body, your thoughts, your words, or your sleep, play in your life and how you can use them to change your emotions.

In **Part III**, you'll learn how emotions are formed. You'll also learn how to condition your mind to experience more positive emotions.

And finally, in **Part IV**, we'll discuss how to use your emotions as a tool for personal growth. You'll learn why you experience emotions such as fear or depression and how they work. You'll then discover how to use them to grow.

To start mastering your emotions today go to:

mybook.to/Master_Emotions

I. What emotions are

Have you ever wondered what emotions are and what purpose they serve?

In this section, we'll discuss how your survival mechanism affects your emotions. Then, we'll explain what the 'ego' is and how it impacts your emotions. Finally, we'll discover the mechanism behind emotions and learn why negative emotions can be so hard to deal with.

1. How your survival mechanism affects your emotions

Why people have a bias towards negativity

Your brain is designed for survival, which explains why you're able to read this book at this very moment. When you think about it, the probability of you being born was extremely low. For this miracle to happen, all the generations before you had to survive long enough to procreate. In their quest for survival and procreation, they must have faced death hundreds or perhaps thousands of times.

Fortunately, unlike your ancestors, you're (probably) not facing death every day. In fact, in many parts of the world, life has never been safer. Yet, your survival mechanism hasn't changed much. Your brain still scans your environment looking for potential threats.

In many ways, some parts of your brain have become obsolete. While you may not be seconds away from being eaten by a predator, your brain still gives significantly more weight to negative events than to positive ones.

Fear of rejection is one example of a bias toward negativity. In the past, being rejected from your tribe would reduce your chances of survival significantly. Therefore, you learned to look for any sign of rejection, and this became hardwired in your brain.

Nowadays, being rejected often carries little or no consequence to your long-term survival. You could be hated by the entire world and still have a job, a roof and plenty of food on the table, yet, your brain is still programmed to perceive rejection as a threat to your survival.

This is why rejection can be so painful. While you know most rejections are no big deal, you nevertheless feel the emotional pain. If you listen to your mind, you may even create a whole drama around it. You may believe you aren't worthy of love and dwell on a rejection for days or weeks. Worse still, you may become depressed as a result of this rejection.

In fact, one single criticism can often outweigh hundreds of positive ones. That's why, an author with fifty 5-star reviews, is likely to feel terrible when they receive a single 1-star review. While the author understands the 1-star review isn't a threat to her survival, her authorial brain doesn't. It likely interprets the negative review as a threat to her ego which triggers an emotional reaction.

The fear of rejection can also lead you to over-dramatize events. If your boss criticized you at work, your brain may see the event as a threat and you now think, "What if I'm fired? What if I can't find a job quickly enough and my wife leaves me? What about my kids? What if I can't see them again?" While you are fortunate to have such an effective survival mechanism, it is also your responsibility to separate real threats from imaginary ones. If you don't, you'll experience unnecessary pain and worry that will negatively impact the quality of your life. To overcome this bias towards negativity, you must reprogram your mind. One of a human being's greatest powers is our ability to use our thoughts to shape our reality and interpret events in a more empowering way. This book will teach you how to do this.

Why your brain's job isn't to make you happy

Your brain's primary job is not to make you happy, but to ensure your survival. Thus, if you want to be happy, you must take control of your emotions rather than hoping you'll be happy because it's your natural state. In the following section, we'll discuss what happiness is and how it works.

How dopamine can mess with your happiness

Dopamine is a neurotransmitter which, among other functions, plays a major role in rewarding certain behaviors. When dopamine is released into specific areas of your brain—the pleasure centers—you get a high. This is what happens during exercise, when you gamble, have sex, or eat great food.

One of the roles of dopamine is to ensure you look for food so you don't die of starvation, and you search for a mate so you can reproduce. Without dopamine, our species would likely be extinct by now. It's a pretty good thing, right?

Well, yes and no. In today's world, this reward system is, in many cases, obsolete. While in the past, dopamine was linked to our survival instinct, The release of dopamine can now be generated artificially. A great example of this effect is social media, which uses psychology to suck as much time as possible out of your life. Have you noticed all these notifications that pop up constantly? They're used to trigger a release of dopamine so you stay connected, and the longer you stay connected, the more money the services make. Watching pornography or gambling also leads to a release a dopamine which can make these activities highly addictive.

Fortunately, we don't need to act each time our brain releases dopamine. For instance, we don't need to constantly check our Facebook newsfeeds just because it gives us a pleasurable shot of dopamine.

Today's society is selling a version of happiness that can make us *un*happy. We've become addicted to dopamine largely because of marketers who have found effective ways to exploit our brains. We receive multiple shots of dopamine throughout the day and we love it. But is that the same thing as happiness?

Worse than that, dopamine can create real addictions with severe consequences on our health. Research conducted at Tulane University showed that, when given permission to self-stimulate their pleasure center, participants did it an average of forty times per minute. They chose the stimulation of their pleasure center over food, even refusing to eat when hungry!

Korean, Lee Seung Seop is an extreme case of this syndrome. In 2005, Mr Seop died after playing a video game for fifty-eight hours straight with very little food or water, and no sleep. The subsequent investigation concluded the cause of death was heart failure induced by exhaustion and dehydration. He was only twenty-eight years old.

To take control of your emotions, it is essential you understand the role dopamine plays and how it affects your happiness. Are you addicted to your phone? Are you glued to your TV? Or maybe you spend too much time playing video games. Most of us are addicted to something. For some people it's obvious, but for others, it's more subtle. For instance, you could be addicted to thinking. To better control your emotions, it is important to shed the light on your addictions as they can rob you of your happiness.

The 'one day I will' myth

Do you believe that one day you will achieve your dream and finally be happy? This is unlikely to happen. You may (and I hope you will) achieve your dream, but you won't live 'happily ever after.' This is just another trick your mind plays on you.

Your mind quickly acclimates to new situations, which is probably the result of evolution and our need to adapt continually in order to survive and reproduce. This is also probably why the new car or house you want will only make you happy for a while. Once the initial excitement wears off, you'll move on to crave the next exciting thing. This phenomenon is known as 'hedonic adaptation.'

How hedonic adaptation works

Let me share an interesting study that will likely change the way you see happiness. This study, which was conducted on lottery winners and paraplegics, was extremely eye-opening for me. Conducted in 1978, the investigation evaluated how winning the lottery or becoming a paraplegic influence happiness:

The study found that one year after the event, both groups were just as happy as they were beforehand. Yes, just as happy (or unhappy). You can find more about it by watching Dan Gilbert's Ted Talk, The Surprising Science of Happiness.

Perhaps you believe that you'll be happy once you've 'made it.' But, as the above study on happiness shows, this is simply not true. No matter what happens to you, you'll revert back to your predetermined level of happiness once you've adapted to the new event. This is how your mind works.

Does that mean you can't be happier than you are right now? No. What it means is that, in the long run, external events have very little impact upon your level of happiness.

In fact, according to Sonja Lyubomirsky, author of *The How of Happiness*, fifty percent of our happiness is determined by genetics, forty percent by internal factors, and only ten percent by external factors. These external factors include such things as whether we're single or married, rich or poor, and similar social influences.

This suggests, only ten percent of your happiness is linked to external factors, which is probably way less than you thought. The bottom line is this: Your attitude towards life influences your happiness, not what happens to you.

By now, you understand how your survival mechanism impacts

negatively your emotions and prevent you from experiencing more joy and happiness in your life. In the next segment/section we'll learn about the ego.

To read more visit my author page at:

amazon.com/author/thibautmeurisse

OTHER BOOKS BY THE AUTHORS:

Goal Setting: The Ultimate Guide to Achieving Life-Changing Goals (Free Workbook Included)

Habits That Stick: The Ultimate Guide to Building Habits That Stick Once and For All (Free Workbook Included)

Master Your Destiny: A Practical Guide to Rewrite Your Story and Become the Person You Want to Be

Master Your Emotions: A Practical Guide to Overcome Negativity and Better Manage Your Feelings (Free Workbook Included)

Master Your Focus: A Practical Guide to Stop Chasing the Next Thing and Focus on What Matters Until It's Done (Free Workbook Included)

Master Your Motivation: A Practical Guide to Unstick Yourself, Build Momentum and Sustain Long-Term Motivation (Free Workbook Included)

Productivity Beast: An Unconventional Guide to Getting Things Done (Free Workbook Included)

The Greatness Manifesto: Overcome Your Fear and Go After What You Really Want

The One Goal: Master the Art of Goal Setting, Win Your Inner Battles, and Achieve Exceptional Results (Free Workbook Included)

The Thriving Introvert: Embrace the Gift of Introversion and Live the Life You Were Meant to Live (Free Workbook Included)

The Ultimate Goal Setting Planner: Become an Unstoppable Goal Achiever in 90 Days or Less

Upgrade Yourself: Simple Strategies to Transform Your Mindset, Improve Your Habits and Change Your Life

Wake Up Call: How To Take Control Of Your Morning And Transform Your Life (Free Workbook Included)

Made in the USA
Columbia, SC
26 May 2024

36215921R00228